BJ
1401
R5
1975

Rice, Philip Blair.

On the knowledge of
good and evil

DATE			

On the Knowledge of Good and Evil

On the
Knowledge
of
Good
and Evil

Philip Blair Rice

GREENWOOD PRESS, PUBLISHERS
WESTPORT, CONNECTICUT

Library of Congress Cataloging in Publication Data

Rice, Philip Blair.
    On the knowledge of good and evil.

    Reprint of the ed. published by Random House,
New York.
    Includes index.
    1. Good and evil.   2. Ethics. I. Title.
[BJ1401.R5 1975]   170   75-8968
ISBN 0-8371-8124-0

Originally published in 1955 by Random House, New York

Reprinted with the permission of Random House, Inc.

Reprinted in 1975 by Greenwood Press,
a division of Williamhouse-Regency Inc.

Library of Congress Catalog Card Number 75-8968

ISBN 0-8371-8124-0

Printed in the United States of America

TO K. C. R.

Acknowledgments

I am indebted to Henry D. Aiken, Virgil C. Aldrich, John Crowe Ransom and Robert Penn Warren for reading all or part of the manuscript, and for giving valuable criticisms, some of which I have been unable to take account of fully in the revision. I am also much indebted to their writings and conversation, and likewise especially to C. I. Lewis and Charles Morris, to my students at Kenyon College and to my seminar and colleagues at Cornell University in the spring semester of 1952. I wish to express my gratitude to David McDowell of Random House for editorial guidance, and to Monyeene Elliott for typing the manuscript.

The present version of the book represents part of the work done with the aid of a Bollingen Fellowship in 1952–53; it grew out of work on related topics which was begun a number of years earlier on a John Simon Guggenheim Memorial Fellowship and has found publication hitherto only in the form of articles.

Portions of the book which have appeared in *The Philosophical Review* are reprinted by permission of its editors.

P. B. R.

Gambier, Ohio
August 30, 1955

CONTENTS

On the Knowledge of Good and Evil

INTRODUCTION: *Forbidden Fruit*

And the Lord God commanded the man, saying, Of every tree of the garden thou mayest freely eat:

But of the tree of the knowledge of good and evil, thou shalt not eat of it: for in the day that thou eatest thereof thou shalt surely die. . . .

And the serpent said unto the woman, Ye shall not surely die:

For God doth know that in the day ye eat thereof, then your eyes shall be opened, and ye shall be as gods, knowing good and evil.

And when the woman saw that the tree was good for food, and that it was pleasant to the eyes, and a tree to be desired to make one wise, she took of the fruit thereof, and did eat, and gave also unto her husband with her; and he did eat.

And the eyes of them both were opened, and they knew that they were naked; and they sewed fig leaves together, and made themselves aprons. . . .

And the Lord God said, Behold, the man is become as one of us, to know good and evil: and now, lest he put forth his hand, and take also of the tree of life, and eat, and live for ever:

Therefore the Lord God sent him forth from the garden of Eden, to till the ground from whence he was taken.

So he drove out the man; and he placed at the east of the garden of Eden Cherubims, and a flaming sword which turned every way, to keep the way of the tree of life.

We can only speculate as to what anxieties gave rise to this gorgeous and menacing story, which still has the power to move us. Its rich symbolism permits interpreters of each age to read into it their own preoccupations and to try out on it their special tools of explanation. For dealing with such stories, our own time has its elaborate schemes drawn from anthropology, depth psychology and the new literary discipline of myth criticism. What we have here is obviously something that is, in the language of the Jungians, "archetypal." In fact, it is an archetype of archetypes. The story's fecundity for religion and for the study of sexual mores, and even as a witness to perennial human political aspirations, is a matter into which we need not enter here.

Our concern is the peculiar pertinence of the Biblical story to philosophers, even to the logic-ridden professional analysts of the mid-20th Century. For we are still disputing about the knowledge of good and evil, and we manifest toward the topic an ambivalence—to use another key interpretative term of our day—that is not identical with the duality of opposed feelings shown in the myth itself but is nonetheless closely related to it. The ambivalence of the story consists in the simultaneous desire for knowledge of good and evil and fear of it. "Ye shall be as gods": and yet the fruit of the tree is death—if not literal death, the spiritual non-being of toil, exile and sin. Knowledge of the good, so runs this strange paradox, brings in its train privation of the good.

It is not hard to defend the justice of the paradox as a partial insight. The devastating irony may in part reflect the concern of priestcraft for its vested interests by setting up a "no trespassing" sign around the preserves of revealed wisdom. But we can also see in it—as traditional theology has done—a metaphysical parable of the grandeur and misery of freedom, in which knowledge is an indispensable element; and we can even read into it the disillusionment of the tired sage or moral philosopher who feels that he has missed many of the bounties of life by his prolonged and none too success- ful pursuit of wisdom in the abstract.

When we make out such a case for the story, its upshot may still seem to us cynical. The great Hellenic thinkers would never have agreed to the conclusion. Even if knowledge is not virtue, knowledge is divine, and the Idea of Good is at the apex of divinity; man with his limitations could only glimpse this summit, but even the remote view of which he is capable seemed to them the ultimate glory of his existence. Aristotle is less fervent than Plato on the subject, but he does not doubt that the rough knowledge which alone is attainable on moral questions can be beneficial to practice.

Contemporary philosophy would feel toward the story a dif- ferent ambivalence and find in it an even grimmer irony. The fact that philosophers for twenty-four centuries have striven for knowledge of the good without achieving anything re- sembling agreement, or even making demonstrable progress, has given rise to a new kind of doubt. The myth did not ques- tion the possibility of knowledge of good and evil, but merely its beneficence to man. Subsequent philosophy tended to limit itself to the irony that such knowledge was even harder to get than the Greeks thought. But in our time an honest and able group of thinkers have come to the conclusion that we cannot properly speak of "knowledge" of good and evil at all. The judgments in which our pretended knowledge of good and evil is advanced, such judgments as "This is good" and "That is wrong," are not, when we examine them closely, attempts to convey knowledge at all, but rather to do something else: to express an emotion, to command an action, or to facilitate the performance of a common task. The fruit of the tree is forbidden, not because the apple is poisonous but because it is an empty rind.

The contemporary view that, in the strict sense of knowledge, there can be no knowledge of good and evil, does not spring from any general skepticism. The very thinkers who urge this thesis are mostly men who have devoted the greater part of their professional lives to analyzing the language and methods of science, about whose fitness to achieve knowledge they have no misgivings. Nor—some of their more abusive critics to the contrary—are they special pleaders for some variety of irrationalism, totalitarian or otherwise, who offer this view with secretly subversive intent.

According to those who hold such a position, the general question of skepticism is irrelevant to the issue. Since ethical judgments, when properly understood, do not even claim to assert a truth but profess to do something else, the frustration to which a skeptical attitude leads need not be felt. This position carries with it a shock, but it is the shock of readjustment of our habits of language, rather than one which would come from the final bankruptcy of aspirations to knowledge. When we learn what ethical judgments really *mean*, so this position holds, we see that the question of their truth or falsity does not arise. And we are able to get on with the business of living, to participate in goods and avoid evils, more satisfactorily when we have realized that the fruit of the tree is hollow than we would if we continued to regard it as the source of exhilarating but illusory delights.

Such is, put briefly and crudely, the challenge that moral philosophy is having to meet at the moment. The position has grown out of some genuine insights into the language and methods of ethics, whether the correct conclusions have been drawn from them or not. And if we can come to terms with these insights, it may be that we shall find ourselves on firmer ground than that on which moral philosophy has rested hitherto, and that we shall be able to reconstruct our knowledge of good and evil in such a way as to avoid the quicksands that have undermined, in rapid succession, the imposing structures of moral theory built by the great philosophers of the past.

The non-cognitivist position, as this repudiation of the possibility of ethical knowledge is called, has acquired lively supporters in the past two decades, but is far from having gained possession of the field. During the earlier part of the 20th Century, the principal dispute in Britain and America was between two schools or tendencies, both of which accepted without question the classical view that knowledge of good and evil is possible and is the goal of moral philosophy. These two wings of the cognitivist position, both of which are still flourishing, are called Empiricism or Naturalism, on the one hand, and Intuitionism or Non-naturalism on the other. Their disagreement is over the method by which ethical knowledge can be achieved. The empiricists hold that value judgments, although they may differ in important ways from the propositions of the factual sciences with respect to their aims and their subject matter, nevertheless, like these sciences, make their ultimate appeal to observation and experience. The intuitionists, while allowing a certain scope to empirical methods in ethics, believe that these must be supplemented, at certain crucial points, by an appeal to *a priori* intuitions. Such intuitions are necessary to grasp the basic property which makes things "good" or "right," and also to establish certain normative principles which cannot be treated, like the laws of the factual sciences, as generalizations from experience.

Among the leading exponents of ethical empiricism in our century have been George Santayana, R. B. Perry, and John Dewey, all Americans; the chief spokesmen for intuitionism have been such British philosophers as G. E. Moore, C. D. Broad, A. C. Ewing and W. D. Ross.

Both groups hold the common assumption that, in the broadest sense of the term "science," there can be a science of the good and the right. Neither would deny that there is an art of morality or of rewarding living, nor even that such non-scientific enterprises as poetry and religion are pertinent to the good life, but they hold that ethical theory is itself a science—though perhaps a special kind of science called a normative science—and that the art of living can guide itself by judgments that have a claim to the title of knowledge. The naturalists are the most explicit defenders of scientific method in ethics, yet their most valiant adversary, Moore, paraphrasing Kant, prefaced his *Principia Ethica* (1903) by saying: "I have endeavoured to write 'Prolegomena to any future Ethics that can possibly pretend to be scientific.'"

The split between the empiricists and the intuitionists was primarily over the question to which of the two main groups of sciences ethics more nearly conformed. The empiricists wished to assimilate it to the *a posteriori* or factual sciences, the intuitionists held that in certain respects it more closely resembled the *a priori* sciences, including pure mathematics and —according to some of them—metaphysics, which rest their fundamental principles not on experience but on some kind of *a priori* intuition. Both empiricists and intuitionists agreed that there could be a "science" of ethics or value theory in the broad sense in which the word is a translation of the Greek *epistēmē* or the Latin *scientia;* that is to say, that value judgments and the principles which underlie them are forms of knowledge or cognition. In recent discussions, consequently, both groups are classified under the common heading of *cognitivists.*

In the past quarter century, this common assumption has been challenged by diverse thinkers who are grouped together as *non-cognitivists* in ethics. They hold that moral and other valuational judgments should be interpreted primarily as attempts, not to convey knowledge, but to do something else. The non-cognitivists in turn may be conveniently divided into two groups, according to how they conceive this function of the normative judgment which goes beyond the imparting of knowledge. These groups are referred to as the Emotivists and the Philosophers of Ordinary Language.

Emotivism got its name from the distinction between cognitive and emotive meaning first brought to the attention of a considerable public by C. K. Ogden and I. A. Richards in *The Meaning of Meaning* (1925). When we say that some object is good or some act is right, just as when we say that a poem is beautiful, the distinctive force of this statement is not, like that of an ordinary statement, to assert some property of the thing or act referred to, but to express or evoke an emotional attitude toward it. An ethical or aesthetic judgment, consequently, is not so much like a scientific (or descriptive) statement as it is like an exclamation or a command. The principal advocates of such a view have been Rudolf Carnap, Hans Reichenbach and A. J. Ayer. C. L. Stevenson has advanced a modified form of this position.

The adherents to Philosophy of Ordinary Language, also called the "Good Reasons" method, agree with the emotivists in rejecting the view that value judgments are primarily attempts to convey knowledge, but deny that their meaning is adequately conveyed by treating them as exclamations or commands. Their meaning is oversimplified if it is treated as simply "expressive" or "imperative," or a combination of the two, but is often better characterized as "performative" or "commendatory" or "gerundive" or "ascriptive." The important and characteristic functions of a term like "good" or "right" may be to facilitate the performance of a task, or to recommend an action, or to ascribe to something or someone a function or an obligation. The members of this group represent a "tendency" rather than anything resembling a school, but they are all more or less influenced by two Cambridge philosophers, Ludwig Wittgenstein and (in some respects) G. E. Moore himself. Most of the spokesmen for Philosophy of Ordinary Language in ethics so far, however, have been Oxonians. Those to be discussed in this book are Stephen Toulmin, R. M. Hare, Stuart Hampshire, Margaret Macdonald, J. L. Austin and H. L. A. Hart.

Following the lead of Wittgenstein, the members of this group are distrustful of elaborate theoretical constructions, with the accompanying baggage of technical terminology, and consequently are skeptical of the possibility of defining ethical terms or achieving any systematic set of principles in the field similar to the principles of a recognized science. They are impressed by the power of ordinary non-technical language, when skilfully used, to deal with the topics in question, and they are above all concerned that we should avoid mutilating the richness and complexity of ethical thinking by forcing it to conform to rigid artificial terminologies such as those employed in the sciences and in most traditional philosophies. For this reason, the group have been referred to as "Informalists." In one respect, however, Philosophy of Ordinary Language is closer to the cognitivists than to the emotivists: it treats ethical judgments as resting on "reasons" of a cognitive sort, even though the primary or distinctive function of the judgment is not to impart knowledge.

For expository purposes, then, the line-up of the principal contestants in recent ethical theory can be charted as follows:

Cognitivists	*Non-Cognitivists*
Empiricists or Naturalists	Emotivists or Logical Positivists
Intuitionists or Non-naturalists	Informalists or Philosophers of Ordinary Language

Any such scheme is of course a simplification, and more precise ways of characterizing these positions will be offered in the following chapters, but the classification may be useful to bring some sort of preliminary order into a field where there is a bewildering complexity of cross-currents of doctrine.

The dispute between the cognitivists and non-cognitivists has centered around the question whether goodness or rightness is a *property* (or characteristic) of objects, experiences and acts. The empiricists say that goodness consists in such a characteristic as pleasantness or capacity to arouse desire; the intuitionists identify it with a "non-natural" property of a special kind known by intuition. If there are such properties, so the cognitivists hold, then the judgment that something is good or right amounts to an assertion that the thing in question has the property. Such a judgment is, then, either true or false. When true, it legitimately claims to give us knowledge, and its truth rests on the same methods of validation, direct or indirect, that are used in testing other knowledge. The basic value-property, according to the empiricists, is a natural and empirically observable one; the intuitionists hold that it is a very peculiar sort of characteristic called a "non-natural" quality or relation, detected by a special organ or function of the mind quite different from our ordinary perceptual equipment. But in either case an uncertainty as to whether something is good is decided by finding that it does or does not have the property in question.

The non-cognitivists answer the question "Is goodness (etc.) a property?" in the negative. Although it may be necessary to take account of a great many properties in trying to solve an ethical problem, the value judgment, when carefully analyzed, turns out to be a radically different kind of expression from a statement that something has a specified characteristic. Its distinctive function is not to give us knowledge of the constitution of the thing about which the judgment is made, but to arouse or alter our attitudes toward it, or to prompt a certain performance with respect to it. Consequently the criteria by which we accept or reject the ethical judgment are not the ordinary criteria of truth or falsity.

Recent controversy has been complicated by a second major question, which cuts across the line-up of tendencies in a different fashion. The question has focused upon a great puzzle called the Naturalistic Fallacy. This so-called fallacy was given its name by G. E. Moore, who offered its exposure as his crushing argument against ethical empiricism. Although he stated it in several different ways, the formulation which we shall take as central declared the fallacy to consist in the identification of an ethical property such as intrinsic goodness with any "natural" or empirically observable property whatsoever. When goodness is identified with pleasantness, or capacity to evoke or to satisfy interest, etc., then we get into a hopelessly insoluble regress sometimes called the "open question," which this book will refer to as the Mountain Range Effect. If the naturalist equates intrinsic goodness with the property of, say, pleasantness, then he can always be asked, "Yes, but is this a *good* pleasure?" And if we can give a meaning to "goodness" in this question, then the simple identification of goodness with pleasure breaks down. The naturalist is forced to bring other properties into his analysis of goodness, and whatever other properties he may invoke are themselves, when scrutinized, seen to lie open to a similar question. The regress can be terminated, according to Moore, only by recognizing that goodness in its characteristically ethical sense refers to a "non-natural" property grasped by a kind of *a priori* intuition, which gives us the meaning of goodness once and for all so that no regress ensues.

The non-cognitivists accepted the force of Moore's argument against naturalism, but turned it also against his own positive position. Being unable to find any such non-natural properties as Moore and his fellow intuitionists thought they detected, they held the fallacy in question to consist in the identification of goodness with any property whatsoever, whether natural or non-natural. The Naturalistic Fallacy, then, for them becomes in effect the Cognitivist Fallacy. When a normative judgment is treated as a claim to knowledge of any kind of property, its distinctive force is lost. For the judgment that some object is good, or some act is our duty, is not an assertion about the nature of that object or that act, but an expression or evocation of some other kind of attitude toward it besides the cognitive attitude. What Moore mistook for a non-natural property is actually, according to both the emotivists and the informalists, an obscure awareness of the non-cognitive force of ethical terms—such as their motivational power—which is at the center of their "meaning."

The dispute as to whether goodness is a property has turned up many penetrating insights into the problem. But the position advanced in this book holds that the fundamental assumption which has made the dispute so protracted and so apparently hopeless of solution is, quite simply, the assumption that the question, "Is goodness a characteristic," can be answered "Yes" or "No." It proposes that the answer is a "Yes, but—," or the view that goodness refers to a property functioning in a peculiar manner. Or, still more precisely, it suggests that the question itself must be restated, so that we should ask, not whether goodness is a property, but whether the judgment, "This is good," is or presupposes *both* an assertion that this has a certain distinctive property *and* an assumption that the expression performs a certain distinctive function not comprised in such a judgment as "This is red" or "This is an asteroid." And this double-barreled question, it will be argued, should be answered "Yes." But this answer is only the first step in the solution of the problem. A complete answer should tell us, in the case of each of the needed normative terms, what property is being asserted, and what function the judgment performs. It should tell us, furthermore, what is the relation between the property and the function, how this relation is established and how any theory specifying it can be justified. Such a complete answer would be a complete ethical theory. Here we shall do what we can to sketch its outlines. Any attempt, in the present state of the subject, to fill in the details of an ethical theory would be unconvincing if it by-passed or skimped these two bothersome questions, namely, the question whether ethical terms refer to properties, and the question whether some kind of fallacy—whether naturalistic or cognitivist—is committed when normative judgments are treated as consisting in assertion of properties.

The following four chapters will examine each of the schools in turn. They will begin with ethical naturalism, partly because it has been the dominant ethical position in this country until recently, and partly because the other schools all take off from an assault upon it and its supposed fallacies. Chapters 2, 3 and 4 will show how the anti-naturalist reaction developed through the concern, first of the intuitionists with the Naturalistic Fallacy, and second of the emotivists and informalists with the Cognitivist Fallacy; and will attempt to exhibit some of the positive contributions made by these analyses. A great deal of hard and careful thinking has gone into each of the contemporary movements, and an advance from the present stalemate must be sought through a critical and selective synthesis of what is sound in each of these approaches rather than in further partisan elaboration and defense of any one of them, or in any radical and wholly new departure.

Chapter 5-8 will offer a systematic theory of the meaning of normative terms, and of the judgments which employ them. They will try not only to trace both the cognitive and the non-cognitive factors in normative meanings, but also to analyze in detail the relations between the two kinds of factors. Our basic thesis is that the language of ethics from the beginning has had two main functions: first, to guide conduct, or to prescribe our actions and the properties which they take into account; and second, to do this with the aid of such knowledge, or reflective awareness of the natural and human world, as can be found pertinent.

In Chapters 9–10, the concern will be with the problem of justification, which is distinguishable but not separable from the problem of meaning. This is the question how judgments of goodness or badness, rightness or wrongness—granting the meanings of these terms we shall have suggested—can be supported. Can such judgments be derived, deductively or inductively, from normative principles which furnish ethics with a respectable body of theory; and, if so, how can we justify these principles themselves? Is a rational justification of them possible, or must we rely on some kind of non-rational ground of adherence to them? Are there "limits of justification," whether rational or non-rational, so that ultimately our moral world is left hanging in a void? Can our ethical principles ultimately be founded on the structure of human nature, "the way we are built," or are they knocked into us through our encounters with an alien physical, human and social world, so that they rest on pragmatic grounds?

The subsequent chapters will outline a theory of intrinsic and extrinsic goodness, of aesthetic judgment and of moral obligation, by way of applying and testing the doctrine of justification proposed. The concluding chapter, "Naturalism and the Tragic Sense," will deal with the ever-imminent possibilities of tragedy in the ethical domain as it is here conceived, and also indicate what scope practical reason has in a moral life circumscribed and assaulted by irrational forces.

The controversies which this book tries to resolve have in some respects constituted an uncommonly rich and fruitful period in ethical thinking, and in other ways an arid one. Never before has there been such dogged and intensive analysis, by so many keen minds, of the problems which have occupied the scene. One enters the controversy with a sense of exhilaration: here are fundamental and momentous issues being fought out by honest thinkers struggling heroically to become clear about them. If we are concerned with understanding the good for man, we can ignore these battles only to our loss.

Yet in the present stage of the discussion the exhilaration often gives way to disillusionment and weariness. The opposing philosophical camps seem to be deadlocked in a kind of trench warfare which permits only dubious tactical advances won by overwhelmingly intricate technical machinery. Not only the man in the street and the boy in the classroom but the professional philosopher himself who seeks knowledge of good and evil is tempted, and justifiably, to turn away from this blighted no man's land to seek gardens where the tree bears visible fruit. The poets, novelists and historians can give us presentations of good and evil, even if they are tantalizingly oblique and somewhat casual. There are also the dense jungles of religious writings, the vehemence of prophets and the visions of saints, where flowers and weeds grow rankly. Theology has lately acquired a new lease of vigor. In fact, during the past decade or two the writings of Paul Tillich and Reinhold Niebuhr on human existence and destiny have evoked from thoughtful and groping people the same kind of sense of relevance that was accorded to William James, John Dewey, George Santayana and Alfred North Whitehead earlier in the century, and that, since then, has notably been withheld from the works of professional philosophers.

The pre-eminent qualification of philosophers to give us knowledge of good and evil has been challenged, not only from the side of the arts and religion, but also from that of the sciences of man. In psychology, for example, though the confusion over principles and methods and the disagreement over conclusions appear at least as far from solution as in philosophy itself, nevertheless a philosophical theory would be more firmly based if it could profit, more than most recent ethical writing has succeeded in doing, from the sifted results of empirical work in such fields as psychology of motivation, learning theory and personality studies, and if it could come into more fruitful and selective contact with the proliferating social sciences.

The existing posture of the intellectual situation being what it is, the philosopher can have little hope of arrogating to himself sole or even prime authority to speak on the topic of good and evil. In pursuing the problems in which philosophical ethics has lately embroiled itself, the moral philosopher must to a great extent appear to be simply an academic specialist, or one-sided man, among others. But this limitation is in some degree mitigated if he acknowledges frankly his shortcomings, draws on other sources of insight where he can find them, and engages in ethical theory with a view to that more rewarding day when he can practice it in closer conjunction with the actual making of ethical judgments. For philosophy is what it aspires to; and in this field its aspiration has ranged from the construction of a theory of ethical language to the effecting of a perennial transvaluation of values. Just now we seem far removed from being able to share in Plato's dream of the philosopher-king, or the proud conception of Nietzsche:

The real philosophers are commanders and law-givers; they say: "Thus *shall* it be!" They determine first the Whither and Why of mankind, and thereby dispose of the previous work of all philosophical laborers, and all subjugators of the past—they grasp at the future with a creative hand, and all that is and was becomes for them thereby a means, an instrument and a hammer. Their "knowing" is *creating*, their creating is a law-giving. . . . (*Beyond Good and Evil.*)

And indeed today the philosopher can conceive himself only as a collaborator in the envisioning of the good life and not as its self-sufficient legislator. If this book has any worth, it is as an attempt to contribute to the preparatory labor, as it tries to add in some measure to understanding; but set against our visions of a habitable dwelling for the human spirit it must be taken as humble spade work, and judged accordingly.

1

The Method of Experience

1. Values and Facts

One of the classic statements of the fundamental principles of empiricism, or the method of experience, is Aristotle's comment on his *Ethics* in the concluding Book:

Such arguments then carry some degree of conviction; but it is by the practical experience of life and conduct that the truth is really tested, since it is there that the final decision lies. We must therefore examine the conclusions we have advanced by bringing them to the test of the facts of life. If they are in harmony with the facts, we may accept them; if found to disagree, we must deem them mere theories.

Modern writers, however, have conceived the method of experience differently in several significant respects. They took their impetus, furthermore, from new hopes for intellectual advance stimulated by Newtonian science:

. . . As the science of man is the only solid foundation for the other sciences, so, the only solid foundation we can give to this science itself must be laid on experience and observation. It is no astonishing reflection to consider, that the application of experimental philosophy to moral subjects should come after that to natural, at the distance of above a whole century; since we find in fact, that there was about the same interval between the origins of these sciences. . . .

So wrote David Hume in the introduction to his *Treatise of Human Nature* (1738), subtitled "an attempt to introduce the experimental method of reasoning into moral subjects." Hume did not claim to be either the Bacon or the Newton of ethical empiricism but he credited a number of his predecessors with the initiation of this attempt to put the science of man on a new footing. More than two centuries have passed since Hume made his bold proclamation, and we are far from having achieved anything resembling agreement on the "ultimate Principles" to which Hume thought the new method would lead. He foresaw certain difficulties:

Moral philosophy has, indeed, this peculiar disadvantage, which is not found in natural, that in collecting its experiments, it cannot make them purposely, with premeditation, after such a manner as to satisfy itself concerning every particular difficulty which may arise.

Nevertheless, he would have been astonished and dismayed to find that in our own century, after an even more spectacular development in the other empirical sciences than he could have foreseen, the very applicability of empiricism to ethics has been stoutly questioned by many of the most acute writers on the subject.

Men like Hume and Bentham were possessed by the conviction that the everyday way of dealing with moral questions was vitiated by lethargy, prejudice and unexamined custom. By way of contrast, they saw that the application of empirical method in the physical sciences had enabled these to make rapid and enormous headway, and they proposed that we try to see what the application of critical procedures based on experience and observation could do to help us out of the pitiable messes that they believed men commonly made in questions of conduct, not only in matters of personal morals but in such fields as law and politics. Empirical method itself was conceived in rather rudimentary fashion in the 18th Century, and in fact it was only in the later 19th and the 20th Centuries that an empirical logic was developed in detail. Consequently there was an "if" embedded in the speculations of these earlier writers; namely, that if an empirical method were developed and extended to moral questions, it would be found to be as helpful here as in the physical domain. Although Bentham's sources seem to have been largely Continental rather than British, forty years after Hume's treatise the thirty-year-old Bentham echoed his language, in a manuscript dated 1778:

The present work, as well as any other work of mine that has been or will be published, on the subject of legislation or any other branch of moral science, is an attempt to extend the experimental [or, as we should now say, the empirical] method of reasoning from the physical branch to the moral. What Bacon was to the physical world, Helvetius was to the moral. The moral world has therefore had its Bacon, but its Newton is yet to come. (Quoted by C. W. Everett, *The Education of Jeremy Bentham*, 1931.)

One of the central assumptions in both Hume and Bentham was that men talk a great deal of nonsense on moral subjects, and that only if their ethical terms are given a meaning by reference to entities and properties that are discoverable in experience, can we deal with moral issues effectively. Bentham wrote, in the *Introduction to Principles of Morals and Legislation:*

Of an action that is conformable to the principle of utility, one may always say either that it is one that ought to be done, or at least that it is one that ought not to be done. . . . When thus interpreted the words *ought* and *right* and *wrong*, and others of that stamp, have a meaning; when otherwise, they have none.

We shall see that the utilitarians, for example, doubted that such a basic principle as the principle of utility could in the strict sense be proved, as a scientific law or hypothesis could be proved or verified. Their fundamental thesis rather was, that only by the assumption of this principle—an assumption that, so they believed, we all made in practice anyhow—could moral discourse be made intelligible. Without such a principle as that of utility for the specification of the meaning of ethical terms, and for a guiding rule of conduct, the way would be left open for the vagueness and the impostures that were embedded in legal and political theory, as well as in that "asceticism" with which Bentham found both the personal and the social morality of his day deeply infected.

If morality, like physical science, must ultimately appeal to experience, it is nevertheless to a different kind of experience in the two cases that the appeal must be addressed, according to Hume and Bentham. Whereas the physical sciences sought rigorously to exclude the subjective domain of feelings from admissible evidence, ethical judgments could be rendered intelligible and testable only in terms which contained a reference to feeling. For Hume, whereas reason determines the means, sentiment determines the ends of conduct. Bentham was even more explicit. He could not find any clear and operable meaning in moral concepts unless they could be analyzed in terms of pleasure and pain, either directly or by way of their consequences: "The only method by which any instruction can be conveyed is the reference to happiness and pain, the principle of utility." It followed that for Bentham the

term conscience, for example, could mean only the "Will . . .
as being acted on by pain or pleasure expected from causes
that are invisible."

From such crudities, subsequent empirical writers have tried
to develop a theory more adequate to the complexities of
moral experience, without sacrificing the basic assumptions
of the school. Some subsequent empiricists, such as R. B. Perry
and Dewey, believed that this acknowledgment of the evidential value of pleasure and pain, observed by "introspection," rendered the attempt of the utilitarians to establish an
empirical ethics self-defeating; and under the influence of
some form of behaviorism they have tried to restate ethics in
terms of drives, needs, lacks and so on, which omit this suspect
subjective reference to feeling and ground valuational propositions in externally or objectively observable activities. Hence
the major split which we shall treat in contemporary empiricism between the "affective" version of the theory and the
"conative" version, treating values in terms of feeling and
striving respectively.

Empirical ethics in the 19th and 20th Centuries has had to
adjust itself to refinements that have been made in conceptions
of empirical method itself. There has been, for example, a
fundamental shift from the assumption of Locke, Berkeley and
Hume that all admissible ideas are derived from experience,
to a methodology which looks to experience not so much for
the source of our meaningful ideas as for their clarification
and verification. Our ideas may originate in a variety of ways,
but according to 20th Century empiricism the verification of
all ideas except those of pure logic and pure mathematics rests
upon a prospective reference to experience, upon the capacity
of propositions to provide predictions which will be borne out
by experience. More recently, even some of those who profess
themselves to be empiricists have often acknowledged certain
"limits" of empiricism. Although all true propositions, in both

the scientific and the valuational domains, must ultimately be tested or verified by experience, many empiricists hold that the ultimate principles or presuppositions of empirical knowledge are not themselves "verified" by experience, but are justified in some other way; they may hold that such principles rest in part on unlearned or congenital tendencies of the organism or the mind—so that we may have the basis here for a naturalistic restatement of what is tenable in the notion of the *a priori*.

So far we have followed the common practice of speaking of empiricism *or* naturalism, as though the two terms were identical. It is useful, however, to conceive empiricism as primarily a doctrine of method, whereas naturalism has often meant something different. Although many who call themselves naturalists—notably most of the contributors to the symposium, *Naturalism and the Human Spirit* (1944), edited by Y. H. Krikorian—identify naturalism with commitment to scientific or empirical method, to use naturalism in this way is to impoverish our philosophical vocabulary. For the term naturalism, at least as frequently, has been applied not to a doctrine of method but to a metaphysical or an ontological doctrine. Democritus and Spinoza, for example, although they were far from being empiricists in methodology, are usually called naturalists in ontology. Naturalism so conceived, then, is primarily a theory of reality, and is opposed to supernaturalism, whereas empiricism is most commonly opposed to rationalism. In this sense, naturalism may be characterized as the view that nature is a self-contained system, operating according to immanent laws, without intrusions such as miracles from a supernatural realm outside of it; and a system in which the "higher" structures and qualities have developed from the "lower."

Naturalism in ethics, then, would be simply a theory which is consistent with such a doctrine of reality. As many of its proponents understand it, ethical naturalism does not necessarily imply any commitment to such notions, sometimes called naturalistic, as those which rest on the premise that whatever is natural is right, or theories which try to explain values by quasi-biological laws such as the will to power or survival of the fittest, which were supposed to have prevailed in a state of nature preceding the appearance of human society, or even of the human species. Contemporary naturalism holds, not that the characteristics of the human mind are identical with those of the non-human animals or of undeveloped humans, but that these characteristics have developed out of, or emerged from, more primitive vital functions.

Since Darwin naturalism, as a philosophy of mind, has been roughly identical with the acceptance of the evolutionary hypothesis as an explanation of mentality. The notion of development or emergence in a "non-reductive" naturalism conceives the properties of the human mind as in some respects novel or unique; it holds that although they are temporally continuous with those of the ancestral lower forms of life, and share many characteristics with them, they are not to be described exhaustively in the terms that suffice for the treatment of animal behavior.

Like all ontological positions, naturalism has its mysteries, and these are two: existence and emergence. These are mysteries in the sense that they cannot be "explained" or deduced from something better established, but must simply be accepted as brute facts, or as basic presuppositions without which no further knowledge is possible. Naturalism does not try to explain the fact that the world as a whole exists; it simply acknowledges:

> That anything should be—
> Place, time, earth, error—
> And a round eye in man to see;
> That was the terror.

(Mark Van Doren, *The Last Look and Other Poems*, 1937).

The emergence of novel properties in the course of the natural process is likewise not ultimately to be explained, but is to be accepted with natural piety as a manifest character of existence: we observe it to be going on all the time around us. The mysteries of naturalism, then, according to its proponents, have this advantage over the mysteries of supernatural systems: that they are not only mysteries but also facts; whereas the mysteries of supernaturalism refer to beings and events whose reality is highly doubtful.

Just as ethical empiricism holds that understanding of values rests on observation and experience, so ethical naturalism holds that moral and other values are "natural," that they come into existence through the operation of the world process and do not have to be accounted for by reference to a transcendent source. This basic assumption leaves room for a considerable variety of doctrines as to the nature of goodness and obligation. Contemporary naturalism takes the view that "nature is what nature does," and hence it should have no need to try to explain away the unique data of moral experience, as naturalists have often done. There is no reason why it should not conceive the ethical consciousness as a complex and distinctive development of human nature, generating some categories of its own, and to be understood in terms which cannot be derived from those of physics and biology. It does not have to commit the "genetic fallacy" by treating as illusory any valuational data which cannot be deduced from the principles which describe the behavior of more primitive organisms. Its commitment to the genetic method need go no farther than the intellectual requirement that it seeks to establish continuities between the higher and the lower, and to show that the evolution of moral data as they manifest themselves is a "real possibility" in the kind of universe that naturalism finds this one to be. If there is a point beyond which we cannot explain but must merely acknowledge, this is a point reached by all systems. This kind of naturalism, humble rather than arrogant, accepts like some other philosophies certain surds or "absurdities" in the nature of things. But the recognition that the cosmos is in some respects an absurdity does not license us to be absurd in our thinking about it.

Most of the writers with whom we shall be concerned in dealing with this school are both empiricists in methodology and naturalists in ontology. But neither of the two positions logically implies the other, nor in fact have all the philosophers who subscribed to the one also accepted the other. There are supernaturalists who profess to be empiricists in method, and conversely some naturalists rest their basic principles about reality on *a priori* intuitions or on "animal faith," rather than upon inductive inference from experience. Most adherents of the three contemporary schools which oppose "ethical natural-ism"—the intuitionists, emotivists and philosophers of ordinary language—are either naturalists in their general philosophy or else have taken no position on the doctrine of reality that is involved. The so-called non-naturalists themselves make their appeal to the *lumen naturale* and not to supernatural sources of ethical insight. In fact, for Moore, those supernaturalistic theories which identify duty with following the will of God (conceived as an existent fact) are examples of the "Natural-istic Fallacy."

It must be concluded that the labels which have stuck to the positions we are treating are unfortunate, and generate more confusion than they dispel. The term empiricism is some-what more appropriate for the ethical position in question than is the term naturalism. For the current dispute in ethics is primarily over method rather than over a theory of reality. But even the term ethical empiricism is misleading. For some of the opponents of this position—notably the logical positiv-ists, who tend to be emotivists in ethics—have expressed a preference for the label, logical empiricism, to describe their general philosophy. They oppose empiricism in ethics on the ground that ethical judgments are not verifiable and, hence, do not purport to give knowledge at all; rather than on the ground that empiricism is an inadequate doctrine of knowledge, to be replaced in this sphere by some other kind of knowledge.

The labels for the various schools, however, have become so firmly attached that more confusion would be caused than cured by an attempt to change them at this late date. Consequently, we shall continue to use them, with the proviso that in ethics the terms "empiricism" and "naturalism" should be understood as enclosed in quotation marks even when these are not used.

2. Goodness as Feeling

Empiricism or naturalism in ethics and value theory may be represented schematically as any position which holds that "This is good (right, etc.)" means, in whole or in large part,[1] "This has the V-property," where the V-property is some natural quality or relation, such as pleasantness or capacity to arouse or to satisfy desire, that can be observed or inferred from experience. Each normative term, such as "intrinsically valuable," "extrinsically valuable," "right," and so on, has its own V-property which is related to that of the others but is not identical with it.

The disputes among different versions of empiricism hinge

---

[1] The opponents of ethical empiricism have attributed to that position the view that the *whole* meaning of "This is good" is expressed by a specification of the V-property; most empiricists themselves, however, as we shall see, have taken this definition to express only the cognitive or descriptive element in its meaning.

on disagreements as to what the V-property is. Not all naturalists hold that the V-property is definable, and hence those who
do not cannot be charged with committing the Naturalistic
Fallacy, according to one of Moore's chief characterizations
of that alleged fallacy. C. I. Lewis, for example, does not *define* his basic concept of "intrinsic value" in any of the usual
senses of the term definition, though he characterizes it by
reference to natural and empirically observable properties;
and Dewey, a professed empiricist and naturalist, does not
define any of his concepts in value theory, any more than in
any other branch of his philosophy (though this practice is
perhaps more to the general bewilderment than the general
edification). Empiricists do, however, work on the assumption
that the meanings of their basic value concepts can be analyzed or identified with some precision, whether the analysis
or explication be offered formally as a definition or not; and
many of them spend a good deal of time in trying to give
definitions.

The basic split among empiricists, as I have suggested, is
between an affective theory and a conative type of theory.
The former holds that the basic value-property, usually called
intrinsic goodness, must be conceived in terms of *feelings*
such as pleasures, enjoyments, hedonic tones, etc. The conative theory, on the other hand, treats the basic property as
a function of such processes as desire, interest and goal-
seeking, all of which are modes of *striving*. It regards the
feeling-accompaniment of these processes as a by-product not
suited to occupy a central place in the analysis of normative
concepts.

The commonest classical form of an affective theory has
been, of course, hedonism, which received its fullest statement in the writings of the utilitarians. When hedonists
identified the basic value-property with pleasure, they did not
equate value or goodness in all its important meanings with

this notion. Much less did they (with some exceptions such as the view attributed to Eudoxus by Aristotle) hold that the *highest good* or *moral goodness* could be treated as synonymous with pleasure. Only in the sense of *intrinsic* goodness could "This is good" be held to mean the same thing as "This is pleasant." And something could be called intrinsically good only in so far as it was considered for its own sake, or without regard to its consequences.

Many hedonists have blithely assumed that we all know what pleasure is, and that, having once so defined the intrinsically good, no further analysis is needed. Thus Bentham: "Pain and pleasure at least are words which a man has no need, we may hope, to go to a lawyer to know the meaning of." For Bentham's purposes, indeed, the terms pleasure and pain were sufficiently clear to support his main point against the lawyers he was criticizing. Whatever the vagueness of these terms is revealed to be when a precise analysis of them is attempted, at least they communicated a common meaning more clearly than the legal "fictions" which Bentham was trying to explode. But in the detailed development of a hedonistic position, some of its advocates have tended to stress one kind of pleasure rather than another; and the opponents of hedonism have often given the word a bad odor, not altogether absent from common usage, by restricting it to the "lower" or "sensual" enjoyments. Despite the efforts of such hedonists as Mill in rebuttal to prevent limitations of this kind in the scope of the term, many affective theories have found the prevalent linguistic habits such a formidable obstacle that they prefer some other word, such as "enjoyment" or "satisfaction," to designate the basic V-property. But each of these terms has acquired a specific shading of its own, so that the value-property for an affective theory is most adequately characterized, not by any single synonym, but by a more elaborate statement such as that of C. I. Lewis. The intrinsically or immediately valuable, he writes, should not be conceived as a single quality, but as a "dimension-like mode" of qualities, whose range is indicated as follows:

If 'pleasure' or any other name is to serve as synonym for the immediately and intrinsically valuable, then it must be adequate to the wide variety of what is found directly good in life. It must cover the active and self-forgetting satisfactions as well as the passive and self-conscious ones; the sense of integrity in firmly fronting the 'unpleasant' as well as 'pleasure'; the gratification in having one's own way, and also the benediction which may come to the defeated in having finished the faith. It must cover innocent satisfactions as well as those of cultivation; that which is found in consistency and also that of perversity and caprice; the enjoyment of sheer good fortune, and that which adds itself to dogged achievement. All this in addition to the whole range of the sensuously pleasing and the emotionally gratifying. And the immediately disvaluable has its equal and corresponding variety. Such immediate goods and bads are ill compressed into any single term or pair of them. Attempted synonyms are likely to be misleading just in measure as they appear illuminating; because this sense of calling to mind what was not already clear, is all too likely to come from their aptly naming some one type only, and thus identifying the intended generic character with that of some included species. We do better to call upon our pervasive sense of this mode of all experience, and the multiplicity of its modalities, to correct any chosen name, than we should in depending on the name to conjure up the requisite inclusive sense of the possible goods of life. The variety of our adjectives of prizing is better taken as indicative than would be any one of them; which might well be too narrow. So far as words go, the commonest and widest ascription of all— merely 'good'—is probably best; although that term fails of precision by covering also all manner of extrinsic values, in addition to the directly found good which alone is here in question. (*Analysis of Knowledge and Valuation*, 1946, Ch. XIII.)

Lewis' most common shorthand designation, however, for the range of qualities so suggested is "enjoyment."

When the immediately valuable is characterized in this way, it follows of course that the term can be predicated only of experiences or conscious states of living beings. Pleasantness, enjoyment, etc., are not constituent qualities of the physical objects that give rise to them in experience but are related to them in a more indirect way. Thus the capacity to produce enjoyment in someone's experience is not called a "quality" of the object which has this capacity, but a causal or dispositional property—that is to say, a potentiality of producing an actualized property under certain conditions. It is not coffee but the taste of coffee that is intrinsically good; when we say that coffee is good, we are referring to its effect on us, actual or potential, and we should mean that the coffee is valued because it can produce this effect. Properly speaking, then, the coffee itself should, according to Lewis, be called *extrinsically* good. And Lewis in turn distinguishes between two different ways in which an object can be so. The two types of extrinsic value are "inherent" and "instrumental" goodness. If we are referring to the capacity of the coffee to produce upon presentation of it a taste that is good in itself, Lewis says that the coffee has *inherent* goodness (and the goodness of works of art, for example, falls within this class); if we mean that the coffee is worthy of being prized for its more indirect consequences, which themselves are good extrinsically, as when the coffee is valued because it helps us to work more efficiently, Lewis would say that it is good *instrumentally.* Such are the simplest ways in which something can be "good for" rather than "good in itself"; but there are so many different ways in which something can be good for something else that the notion of extrinsic goodness includes a nest of concepts.

For an affective theory, the "right" or the "morally good" must be located primarily among the more complicated species of extrinsic goodness, though a consideration of the intrinsic values of the right act or the morally good person need not be excluded. Thus when we are judging an act to be right · we are not referring, in the main, to the pleasantness of the act itself, but to the results of the act in enjoyment or suffering for those affected. But it is the *total* result, so far as it can be anticipated, that is in question, and hence the property of rightness must be stated in such a way as to provide a criterion for balancing and combining goods and evils. "Conduciveness to happiness" is the usual name for such a principle in traditional hedonism, and happiness is used as synonymous with the maximum of pleasure or, alternatively, with the maximum of pleasure and the minimum of pain, or the maximum balance of pleasure over pain. Some way of comparing goods, and setting them off against evils, is obviously needed in an affective theory, but the attempt of traditional hedonism to formulate this with precision has been none too successful. The principle must obviously be in some sense quantitative, so that we can say "This is better (*more* good) than that"; but the attempt of Bentham to break pleasures and pains down into numerical units which could be added and subtracted was so obviously artificial that subsequent affective theorists such as Lewis have abandoned it and instead have taken the property of moral goodness to consist in capacity to promote a "Gestalt of values" in which the elements are combined in a more organic sort of whole that is not susceptible of measurement but, when comparisons are made, must be assessed by a kind of "synthetic intuition," which is empirical rather than *a priori*.[2]

----

[2] In the last two sentences of his book, Lewis distinguishes questions of valuation, apparently including those as to "moral goodness," from ethical judgments about the right and the just, which he suggests must be treated by non-empirical methods.

A similar stumbling block to traditional hedonism has arisen over the attempt to balance the goods and ills of one person or group against the goods and ills of others. To what extent, for the sake of the maximum balance of goodness over badness, are we justified in inflicting evil on some of those affected for the sake of a greater good to others? This is the so-called problem of distribution, and in order to solve it Sidgwick, for example (in *The Methods of Ethics*) was forced to supplement what is otherwise a largely empirical version of hedonistic utilitarianism by appealing to certain *a priori* axioms of distribution, those of Justice and Benevolence, just as he had to invoke an *a priori* maxim of Prudence to deal with the balancing of goods and evils in the moral economy of the individual.

3. *Value as a Function of Striving*

The conative theorists have believed that feelings are too slippery to serve as the basic property for a "scientific" theory of value and that, when we focus our attention on such qualities as pleasantness and enjoyment, we are abstracting unduly from the total value fact. Some proponents of this type of theory, furthermore, under the influence of such laboratory methods as behaviorism, have held that a definition of value in terms of feeling does not give us a sufficiently "objective" foundation for a theory that professes to be scientific; so that we should seek a property that is not observed primarily through introspection but can be detected by external observation, and thus enables us to judge the values manifested in the behavior of other people besides ourselves and of animals. Consequently the basic term in the analysis of the good is taken to be one which includes the notion of striving toward an object or striving away from it—as R. B. Perry puts it in *General Theory of Value* (1926), "the primitive polarity of 'for' and 'against.'" "Desire," "interest," "appetency," "purpose," "preference," etc., are such terms. We can observe an amoeba or an earthworm moving toward or away from a stimulus, and such observations offer us the primitive fact of positive or negative value, which persists throughout the most developed human behavior, so that we can establish that continuity between lower and higher forms of valuing which naturalism seeks. Certain writers, such as Laird, have gone further and found the elementary duality of good and bad manifested even in the attraction of an electron for a proton and in the mutual repulsion of two electrons.

Although behaviorist tendencies in psychology have bolstered the appeal of a conative theory to certain circles in recent discussions, the position is a very old one. Hobbes advocated such a view, and a carefully qualified version of it is found in Spinoza alongside an affective theory. But even in the *Republic* the good at one level is characterized as "the object of desire," for as H. A. Prichard has argued, a naturalistic theory of value is to be found in Plato together with a non-naturalistic doctrine of moral goodness. Aristotle likewise, at the beginning of the *Nicomachean Ethics,* characterized the good in its most general sense as "that at which all things aim," though he later modified this to make the good the object of *rational* desire.

Recent versions of the conative theory have sought to define with precision a basic or "generic" sense of value—usually not to be identified with intrinsic value—which expresses what the various normative concepts have in common, and which will serve as a foundation for the more complex senses. Thus Perry, who has constructed the most detailed and the most influential version of a conative theory, defines value as "any object of any interest"; or more precisely, he equates "x is valuable" with "interest is taken in x." And interest, in turn, is characterized as "a motor impulse or disposition, a doing

36

or undoing, an activity which takes effect in the existence or non-existence of its object." Something is good, then, in the minimum sense, when some person or living thing strives to obtain it or to hold on to it; something is bad when an organism strives to avoid it or to get rid of it.

The more complex senses of value, according to Perry, are based upon various relationships to interest into which an object may enter. Let us take, for example, the notion not of mere goodness but of comparative goodness—of "better" or "more valuable." To say that something is better than something else may mean: (a) that the first is an object of more intense interest; or (b) when the interests are equally intense, that the first advances the interest further toward fulfillment; or (c) that the first object will foster the satisfaction of a greater number of interests than the second. When these criteria conflict, the only one that is fitted to take priority over the others is (c), which Perry calls the Criterion of Inclusiveness. So Perry is led to conceive the Highest Good, or Superlative Value, not as a Gestalt of feelings called happiness, but as that organization of possible objects which will satisfy all interests of the individual, or, in the case of the social ideal, of the community of individuals. This ideal is often referred to as that of Integration or Harmony of Interests; and morality consists in action guided by knowledge and directed toward the attainment of this *summum bonum*.

In the development of Perry's theory there is a shift, as he progresses from the simpler to the more complex normative concepts, away from the notion of the good as that which *arouses* interest to the notion of it as that which *fulfills* or *satisfies* interest. And indeed the mere fact of eliciting desire does not supply us with the kind of value property that empirical theories are seeking. For such theories are after *knowledge* of the good, and it is a common observation that what initially arouses or stimulates desire is not always that which upon ultimate reflection is judged to be good. Consequently, Perry's definition of generic value does not state the property which makes a thing good, or constitutes the good. His definition is rather a characterization of the act of valuing than of the property of goodness itself; it specifies not what *is* good, but merely what *seems* good, or is *responded to as though it were good*. In short, when the basic property is defined in Perry's terms, it does not allow for the essential distinction between what is correctly and what is mistakenly taken to be good.

Consequently, some other versions of the conative theory define "*x* is valuable" not as "*x* arouses interest" but as "*x* satisfies* interest." An example of such a theory, in terms of a more recent type of behaviorism, is C. L. Hull's "Value, Valuation and Natural Science Methodology" (*Philosophy of Science*, vol. 12, 1945), where the value of anything is equated with its capacity to terminate, or to reduce, a drive or a need. The difference between such a theory and Perry's centers mainly about the elementary or generic sense of value, since, as we have seen, the more complex senses of goodness for Perry himself are treated in terms of fulfillment or satisfaction of interest rather than its mere arousal.

Dewey criticizes both the affective theory and the other versions of the conative theory along pretty much the same lines. Neither the fact of being enjoyed nor the fact of arousing or satisfying desire by itself suffices to make something valuable. The dominant note in Dewey's discussion of valuation throughout his many treatments of the subject (see especially his *Quest for Certainty*, 1929, and "Theory of Valuation," *International Encyclopedia of Unified Science*, vol. 2, 1939), is his emphasis on the importance of reflective thinking and remedial action. Like other departments of his philosophy, Dewey's value theory is centered about his conception of the "problematic situation." When everything is going smoothly with us, there is no occasion for valuation; and, he assumes, where there is no explicit valuation, there is no value. Desire and striving, and with them thought, arise only when some "difficulty" or "trouble" upsets our equilibrium and creates a "need" or a "lack." We then cast about for ways of supplying the lack and of restoring equilibrium. The general end, consequently, is always abolition of need, or achievement of coordination among our various impulses and between them and the environment. The specific ends are the objects and activities that will further this result. These activities are therefore always means as well as ends: they are instrumentalities for restoring order. Normative or valuational expressions state relations between things as means and other things as consequences. They are empirical statements, because they are based upon previous experience of the capacity of a given kind of thing or activity to resolve a difficulty of the sort in question, and upon the present calculation or prediction of its capacity to do so, given knowledge of the existing situation.

Although some pain or discomfort sets off the valuational process, and although enjoyment will usually result if the situation is restored to smooth functioning, our explicit valuation is not concerned, as in affective theories, with calculating and comparing enjoyments and disenjoyments, but with the "objective" or "publicly observable" instrumentalities for abolishing the lack or difficulty. There is no suggestion that we can compare enjoyments and sufferings themselves, and choose among plans of life on the basis of the kind and degree of affectively toned experience that will result. In fact, Dewey rules out such comparison of feeling qualities by his tenet—fundamental to his variety of "social" behaviorism—that feelings as experienced by the individual are "private" and "ineffable," and therefore cannot aid us in the public verification that he believes is demanded by an empirical methodology. Feelings and other private states, he holds, can never serve as evidence for value judgments; the only evidence that is relevant is that which is derived from scientific observation of the fitness of objects and acts to promote "co-ordination" and restore harmony to the troubled situation. Capacity to do this constitutes for Dewey the value-property, which would serve as the basis for a definition if he offered one.

Until recently, ethical empiricists in America were occupied mainly with disputing among themselves as to the preferability of one of these sets of alternative value-properties over others, and with trying to characterize adequately the properties which they favored. The alignments within empiricism had been drawn pretty tightly, and the result appeared to be something like a stalemate. Within the past few years, however, empiricists have been forced to devote more and more of their attention to meeting powerful criticisms brought by the anti-empirical schools against the whole enterprise as they had conceived it. The intuitionists have urged that the basic value-property is not a natural and empirical characteristic like any of those the empiricists had been seeking. And the non-cognitivists have insisted that there is no stable ethical property of any kind to be looked for. Consequently, any attempt to choose among the different versions of empiricism would be superfluous unless some way were found of coming to terms with these criticisms.

2

The Method of Intuition

1. *Moore and the "Naturalistic Fallacy"*

It would not be a great exaggeration to say that recent ethical controversy in Britain and America has consisted in an effort to answer the questions put by G. E. Moore in *Principia Ethica* and, more particularly, those which center about his notion of the "Naturalistic Fallacy." Very few moral philosophers have accepted Moore's positive views, but even those who for some time shrugged them off have been forced increasingly to take account of his formulations of the problem. Moore's tenacious desire to be clear as to what question it is we are trying to answer, before we try to answer it, has brought the dispute to a focus, even though it may have caused us to restrict our attention to too narrow a range of possible answers, and thereby defeated its own purposes. For the meaning of questions is not as independent of the attempt to answer them as Moore's procedure suggests. The danger is particularly great when it leads us at the outset of the inquiry to limit severely the context within which the answer is to be sought. Moore is consequently to be held responsible for some of the inhibitions and limitations of recent ethical discussion—notably its tendency to focus exclusively on logical and linguistic questions—as well as for some of its keenest insights.

Moore's central question is "What is meant by the good?" and the main point he tries to make is that this question cannot be answered by identifying goodness with any properties of the kinds proposed by empiricism. In *Principia Ethica* he holds that the term "good" refers to a property, but not to a property that can be observed empirically, or can be described by psychology, physics or any other natural science. Moore labels as naturalistic any view which identifies goodness with such a property, and he charges naturalism with committing the "Naturalistic Fallacy."

Moore sometimes characterizes the "Naturalistic Fallacy" as the mistake of confusing the property of goodness with some other property. But, as so stated, this characterization is inept and is too general to express Moore's full intention. For the error is committed by any mistaken ethical philosophy, provided it holds that goodness is a property at all, and is therefore not peculiar to naturalism.

Moore also suggests at times that the "Naturalistic Fallacy" consists in holding that the good is *definable,* though he does not formally define the "Naturalistic Fallacy" in this way. Not all naturalists, however, hold this position. As we have seen, Lewis does not offer his analysis of the "intrinsically good" as a definition, and Dewey does not define any of his ethical terms. So the charge against naturalism makes sense only if we interpret Moore as intending to assert that naturalism identifies goodness with some property that, in Moore's view of definition, is *capable of being defined,* whether the natural-ist in question holds that it is definable or not. But here again, other philosophies besides naturalism hold this view; so that W. K. Frankena has proposed that if the view that good is definable is mistaken and if the mistake is properly to be called a fallacy—both of which assumptions are debatable—it should rather be referred to as the Definist Fallacy. ("The Naturalistic Fallacy," *Mind*, vol. 48, 1939.)

Moore's specific charge against naturalism, and the one on which our attention should be centered, is that naturalism errs by identifying goodness with a "natural" or empirically observable property, or by equating it with such a property in a definition. This is how Moore characterizes the Naturalistic Fallacy on pages 13 and 40 of *Principia Ethica*, and clarity would have been promoted if he had limited the term to this position alone. Let us, then, take Moore to mean by the Naturalistic Fallacy the procedure which identifies goodness with a natural property. This is the gravamen of his charge against naturalism.

Our two principal questions, accordingly, are what Moore means by a "natural" property, and why he holds that a view which identifies goodness with such a property is mistaken.

It is clear what Moore means denotatively or ostensively by a natural property. The examples he gives are: yellow, green, blue, loud, soft, round, square, sweet, bitter, productive of life, productive of pleasure, being willed or being desired or being felt. Only the last five of these, of course, have been advanced by ethical philosophers as candidates for value-properties.

Moore's general statement of what he means by a natural property is more puzzling. By "nature," he means "that which is the subject matter of the natural sciences and also of psychology." It is said to include all that has existed, does exist, or will exist in time. "Any object which exists, has existed, or will exist in time is a natural object." But, he continues, some properties of natural objects, including goodness, are not themselves natural properties. A natural property is one that can be "imagined as existing by itself in time." Such properties, for example, as yellow and pleasantness, are "rather parts of

which the object is made up than mere predicates of it." This
discussion in Chapter II is about all that Moore says on the
subject in *Principia Ethica,* and it has satisfied none of his followers themselves.

Moore's view of *why* it is wrong to identify goodness with
a natural property is treated somewhat more fully. A large
part of his criticism of naturalism is devoted to asserting that
goodness is a simple, unanalyzable quality like yellow, and
then to drawing the conclusion that if it is simple and unanalyzable, it cannot be identified with a relational property
like *conduciveness* to pleasure or *capacity* to arouse interest.
For these properties are complex, and being relational can be
analyzed into the relation (that is, a causal relation between
an object and an experience) and the terms which it relates.
But if we search carefully through *Principia Ethica,* we find
that Moore assumes that goodness is simple and unanalyzable
and nowhere argues the point. In fact, this thesis, though it
is not explicitly so characterized, seems to be one of those
"self-evident" propositions "which are incapable of proof or
disproof," and therefore seems to rest on an intuition.

Not all naturalists hold that goodness is a complex relational
property. Many hedonists, for example, would hold that pleasure or intrinsic goodness is a simple quality, like yellow. (Or,
more precisely, as with Lewis, that it is a spectrum or
"dimension-like mode" of such qualities; each particular manifestation of the general property is, however, held to be simple.) Furthermore, some non-naturalists, such as Ewing, deny
that goodness is a simple quality, and treat it as a relational
property. In fact Ewing argues, in exact opposition to Moore,
that naturalism errs precisely by treating goodness as a quality, and overlooking its relational character. Consequently, this
line of argument of Moore's is not an effective way of refuting
naturalism in general.

Likewise with Moore's attempted refutation of naturalism

on the ground that goodness is indefinable. Definition for him consists in exhibiting the parts or elements of which a complex thing or idea is composed. In consequence goodness, not being complex, cannot be defined. But neither can yellow, which is also a simple quality, though a natural one. Hence for Moore it must be the non-naturalness of goodness, rather than its simplicity, which is at the root of the naturalist's confusion.

We must conclude that so far as this main argument of Moore's goes, it boils down to this: If goodness is (a) simple, (b) indefinable, and (c) non-natural, and if the naturalist denies any one of these three theses, naturalism is mistaken. But (a) and (b) both would be agreed to by many naturalists and rejected by many non-naturalists, and in any case do not seem to be indispensable to the naturalist position. So Moore's criticism of naturalism along these lines simply reduces to (c), that goodness is non-natural.

If this were all that Moore had to say on the subject, we would be forced to conclude that his treatment of the Naturalistic Fallacy in *Principia Ethica* rested on a dogmatic assertion plus a misrepresentation of the position he is attacking, and hence that the fame of the book is undeserved. But before we draw this conclusion we should consider some of Moore's more detailed criticisms of naturalism.

Let us consider the following passage from Chapter I:

. . . Thus it is very easy to conclude that what seems to be a universal ethical principle is in fact an identical proposition; that if, for example, whatever is called 'good' seems to be pleasant, the proposition 'Pleasure is the good' does not assert a connection between two different notions, but involves only one, that of pleasure, which is easily recognised as a distinct entity. But whoever will attentively consider with himself what is actually before his mind when he asks the question 'Is pleasure (or whatever it may be) after all good?' can easily satisfy himself that he is not merely wondering whether pleasure is pleasant. And if he will try this experiment with each suggested definition in succession, he may become expert enough to recognise that in every case he has before his mind a unique object, with regard to the connection of which with any other object, a distinct question may be asked. Every one does in fact understand the question 'Is this good?' When he thinks of it, his state of mind is different from what it would be, were he asked 'Is this pleasant, or desired, or approved?' It has a distinct meaning for him, even though he may not recognise in what respect it is distinct. Whenever he thinks of 'intrinsic value,' or 'intrinsic worth,' or says that a thing 'ought to exist,' he has before his mind the unique object—the unique property of things—which I mean by 'good.' Everybody is constantly aware of this notion, although he may never become aware at all that it is different from other notions of which he is also aware. But, for correct ethical reasoning, it is extremely important that he should become aware of this fact; and, as soon as the nature of the problem is clearly understood, there should be little difficulty in advancing so far in analysis.

The point most worthy of our attention here is Moore's obstinate conviction that a word like "good" must mean *something different from*, or at least *something more than*, any such property as pleasantness. This is the basis of his famous criticism of J. S. Mill's supposed "proof" of hedonism on the ground that "the sole evidence it is possible to produce that anything is desirable, is that people do actually desire it." The fact that we desire happiness is evidence for the proposition that happiness is *capable* of being desired. But if "desirable" is used in the ethical sense, it means more than this: It means what *ought* to be desired or *deserves* to be desired. "Mill has, then, smuggled in, under cover of the word 'desirable,' the very notion about which he ought to be quite clear." And on similar grounds Moore approves of Sidgwick's criticism of Bentham's doctrine that "right" means "conducive to the general happiness."

When the empiricist—as his language so often suggests that

he is doing—simply identifies goodness with any such factual characteristic as pleasantness, or when he reduces a normative statement to a descriptive assertion, there arises, according to his critics, a particularly worrisome predicament which we may call the Mountain Range Effect in ethics. If the empiricist defines the intrinsically good as the pleasant, so it is asserted, we can always ask him, "Yes, but is this a *good* pleasure?" or "Is it good to seek pleasure?" If the empiricist says that "*x* is right" means that "*x* will harmonize the interests of all concerned" or "*x* will lead to the maximum of happiness" the rejoinder is: "But is it always *right* to seek harmony (or happiness)?"

Since such questions do not seem to be mere meaningless tautologies, the critic concludes that the empiricist in his definitions and analyses is begging the question, and that in attempting to explain the normative he is leaving out its essential characteristic. Whatever reply the empiricist makes to such questions, he must either characterize the normative further in descriptive terms—in which case a new normative question can be asked—or else he smuggles a normative term into his analysis without admitting it. Just as the mountain climber in trying to cross the Alps or the Rockies struggles to the top of a ridge only to see another and higher range looming before him, and conquers that only in order to be confronted by still another range, and so on indefinitely; likewise with the empiricist in trying to subdue normative expressions. Behind every factual meaning to which he claims to have reduced the meaning of a value term, there looms up a new value to be accounted for; after every resolution of the "ought" into an "is," the empiricist seems to be confronted by a new "ought," and so he appears to be enmeshed in a hopeless regress. The Alps rise ever higher and higher, and by this route, it is claimed, we can never pass over the watershed to descend to the flatland in possession of a workable theory which would enable us to dispense with further theoretical problems and get on with the practical business of living. The empiricist, if his critics are right, is condemned to an ever wilder debauch in the winter resort country of meta-ethics, and forced to befuddle himself with ever more heady stimulants, until finally he must collapse and be enveloped by the eternal snows.

The argument for the Mountain Range Effect does not establish, as Moore thinks it does, that goodness is unanalyzable or indefinable. It shows at most that empirical theories have offered the wrong analysis, or the wrong kind of analysis. It may still be possible to give a different kind of analysis that will avoid the regress that the naturalist gets himself into. Nor does the argument show that we must conceive goodness as some sort of non-natural quality. For its meaning may be explicable on naturalistic assumptions in some other way than by identifying its meaning simply with the value-property. But Moore's argument does put on the naturalist the responsibility of showing that his position can avoid the regress to which Moore has called attention, and ultimately, I believe, it requires him to give a radical restatement of his position.

What Moore is appealing to throughout these arguments is his *working sense* of how a term is used, and not merely how it is actually used—for there may be a great deal of variation in linguistic habits—but how it is correctly used. Nor is Moore merely appealing to introspection for this sense of usage. Although he asks his reader to "attentively consider with himself what is actually before his mind" when he asks such a question as, "Is pleasure good?" he goes on to recommend that in effect we consider also the implications ordinarily held to follow from the question, and to render our treatment of its meaning consistent with these implications. Moore speaks of meaning as a "unique object" that is "before the mind" and thereby slips into the assumption that it is a "unique property of things" which we can directly inspect just as we can inspect the property yellow by sense-perception.

Very few subsequent philosophers have thought they were able to detect any such simple non-empirical quality of goodness when they have looked carefully at what is before their minds. Therefore it would be easy to conclude that Moore is merely suffering from an hallucination. But, actually, Moore is doing his own case an injustice when he puts it in this way. It may be that he is justified in feeling dissatisfied with the type of naturalistic analysis in question, without having offered a plausible alternative to it. There may be "something more" to goodness than pleasure, and yet this additional element in the meaning may consist in something besides a non-natural quality that we can directly inspect. In order to deal with this matter, we need a more developed theory of meaning than Moore has attempted to supply in *Principia Ethica*.

Indeed Moore himself, in reply to critics many of whom are also of the non-naturalist persuasion, has subsequently acknowledged the inadequacy of the view of natural and non-natural qualities that he presented earlier. In his essay in *The Philosophy of G. E. Moore* (edited by P. A. Schilpp, 1942), C. D. Broad, who is in general sympathetic to Moore's approach, points out that "every property of a natural object answers to Moore's criterion of non-naturalness"—namely, that it cannot be conceived as existing in time *all by itself*. Such properties as brownness and roundness exist in time only as properties of such objects as pennies (even if we conceive these properties, as some philosophers do, to be eternal essences—so Broad might have argued—they do not exist in time but subsist in eternity), and yet Moore certainly counts these as natural characteristics. In commenting on this argument of Broad's, Moore in the same volume stated with his usual honesty that his earlier doctrine of natural or non-natural properties was "silly and preposterous," and confessed: "I did not give any tenable explanation of what I meant by saying that 'good' was not a natural property." Moore does not offer in detail a revised account of the point in question, but says that his account in *Philosophical Studies* (1922) "may possibly be true." He summarizes that account as follows: "an intrinsic property is 'natural' if and only if, in ascribing it to a natural object, you are *to some extent* 'describing' that object (when 'describe' is used in one particular sense): and that hence an intrinsic property, for example the sense of 'good' with which we are concerned, is not 'natural' if, in ascribing it to a natural object you are not (in the same sense of 'describe') describing that object *to any extent at all.*" But, he goes on, "It is certainly the case that this account is vague and not clear. To make it clear it would be necessary to specify the sense of 'describe' in question; and I am no more able to do that now than I was then." What this boils down to is that Moore inclines to, or at any rate does not reject, the view that a non-natural intrinsic property is non-descriptive, in some sense of non-descriptive yet to be determined. He goes on to say that it is also possible that Broad's account of the distinction between "natural" and "non-natural" reported below "may be true."

Intuitionists, however, have not been discouraged from trying to save the notion of non-natural properties by making this notion intelligible. Broad, for example, in the essay just quoted, offers an "epistemological description," as distinguished from a logical definition, of a "natural characteristic":

I propose to describe a 'natural characteristic' as any characteristic which either (a) we become aware of by *inspecting* our *sense-data* or *introspecting* our experiences, or (b) is *definable* wholly in *terms of characteristics of the former kind together with the notions of cause and substance.* . . . It would, for example, cover yellowness, both in the primary *non-dispositional* sense . . . 'Gold is yellow.' . . . and also psychological characteristics, whether non-dispositional or dispositional. We know, for example, what is meant by the fear-quality, the anger-quality, etc., through having felt afraid, angry, etc., and having introspected such experiences. And we know, for example, what is meant by timidity, irascibility, etc., because these dispositional properties are definable in terms of the fear-quality, the anger-quality, etc., together with the notions of cause and substance.

A characteristic would be non-natural if it could not be classified under either (a) or (b) above.

Broad himself does not proceed in this passage to assert that goodness is such a non-natural characteristic. He limits himself to pointing out that goodness, *if* it is a characteristic at all, whether simple or complex, must be a non-natural one, since it can not be apprehended by either inspection or introspection. But in this late essay he concludes that he is not sure that goodness is a characteristic of any kind, thus leaving the door open for a non-cognitivist position.

Other intuitionists have clung to the notion of a non-natural ethical property, known by intuition, even though the deliverances of their respective intuitions are highly variable from one non-naturalist to another. For Moore only intrinsic goodness is a non-natural property, and other ethical concepts are definable in terms of it, together with certain natural properties, and subject to empirical verification. Thus to say that I *ought* to do an act means for Moore that the effects of the act upon the universe will be better than those of any act that I could do instead.

Rightness or the "ought" is defined in such a way as to include the non-natural property of goodness, but it is apparently not itself a non-natural property, and although a moral judgment rests upon intuition of the goodness or badness of the ends which it contemplates, such a judgment itself is not decidable by intuition, since it is primarily an assertion about the connection of means with ends, and for Moore this can be discovered only through generalizations from experience.

2. *"Ought" as a Non-Natural Relation*

A. C. Ewing defines naturalism in ethics as the position which
"analyzes ethical concepts in terms of a natural science . . .
usually psychology. . . ." (*The Definition of Good,* 1947). He
summarizes his objections to naturalism as two. First, he believes that it implies the consequence that all ethical disputes
could be settled by collecting statistics as to what people in
fact desire or how they in fact feel. To Ewing, "this kind
of answer seems utterly irrelevant to this kind of question."
Ewing's second main objection to naturalism is based on
the Mountain Range Effect that we have already considered:
No matter what the alleged characteristic definition of good
is, "we can always see that it is quite sensible to ask whether
something which has the property put forward in the definition is or is not good, and that therefore the definition is
wrong. For, if it were right, to say that something which had
the defining property was good would be to utter a tautology,
and to question whether it was good would be to ask whether
what is good is good."

Ewing also accepts the first half of Broad's revised statement
of what a "natural property" is in general: it is a property that
is "apprehended by sense-perception or by introspection, as I
can discover by introspection whether I am angry or feel hot";
non-natural properties are properties that are not so apprehended. Non-naturalism is the view which holds that there is
at least one ethical property that is not completely analyzable
by reference to natural properties.

In his specific analysis of the uses of key ethical terms,
Ewing in essentials reverses Moore's view. The basic indefinable non-natural property is that referred to by "ought," in one
of its two principal senses, and "good" is definable in terms of
it. The basic ethical property "ought" is, furthermore, a relational property—*i.e.,* it consists in a relation between a subject

and an object, and not in a simple quality of an object as such. This view, Ewing thinks, will take care of the chief naturalistic objection to Moore's view, the inability of the naturalist to find any such simple quality as Moore has indicated. ". . . Naturalism is commonly supported by doubts as to whether we can really be aware of an indefinable quality, goodness, but it is impossible to doubt at any rate that we are aware of some relation signified by the term 'ought' and primarily different from any purely logical relation." The only "concrete more distinctly perceptible element" in the ethical data is, Ewing agrees with the naturalist, such a property as pleasantness or interest. But in analyzing ethical concepts, naturalists are said to ignore the relational element, thus falling into a common philosophical error, for "it is a well known historical fact that philosophers have been apt to overlook the importance of relations."

The principal ambiguity of the term "ought," Ewing says, consists in the two senses in which it refers to the relation of *fittingness* and the relation of *moral obligation*. It is the former of these senses which is basic to ethics; and moral obligation, like goodness, can be analyzed in terms of "fittingness" together with natural properties. Since fittingness is unanalyzable, its meaning can be indicated only by showing its relation to other ethical concepts. Thus "good" means "what *ought* to be the object of a pro attitude," in the sense of that which is a *fitting* object of a pro attitude. And a "pro attitude" in turn refers to such psychological elements as desire for and interest in an object. The ambiguities of "good," Ewing says, are derived from the variety of possible pro attitudes.

Now Ewing's principal point here—and it is the crux of his case against naturalism—is that no naturalistic analysis can account for the necessary or categorical character of the ethical judgment: that goodness and obligation are not apprehended

by empirical observation, such as sense-perception or introspection, "is surely shown by the fact that, when we see that
something is intrinsically good or some act morally obligatory,
we also see that it must be so—its factual properties being
what they are." No actual observation that people do act in
such and such a way can account for the peculiar kind of
compulsion which the ethical judgment exerts upon us.

3. *A Plurality of Non-natural Properties*

Before we ask how Ewing knows this compulsion, when it is
not apprehended by sense-perception or introspection—which
is the question how intuitionists conceive intuition—let us
indicate still another conception of non-natural properties,
W. D. Ross's. He holds a pluralistic view, according to which
the several meanings of goodness are distinct, and neither
goodness nor obligation is a function of the other. In *The Right
and the Good* (1930) he argues that "good" cannot be defined
in terms of "ought" or duty, because to say that something is
good is not to say, as Ewing would hold, that we have a duty
to desire it, but only that we have a *prima facie* duty to desire
it. Nor can duty be defined in terms of goodness as Moore
would have it, because it is not self-evident to Ross that we
always have an obligation to desire the greatest goodness.
The various ethical concepts are distinct from each other, and
separate intuitions must be invoked in the case of each of
them.

Ross's notion of a *prima facie* duty has acquired particular
importance in ethical theory, but as his views are subtle and
complicated, we can notice them at this point only to illustrate
the fact that the deliverances of the intuitionists' intuitions are
highly variable from one moral philosopher to another, and
thus to raise an initial difficulty about a theory which claims, if

54

not always to offer infallibility, at any rate to provide an avenue to greater certainty than is afforded by empirical theories.[1]

---

[1] Some intuitionists in the past have claimed that intuition is an infallible faculty, which always gives certainty. Contemporary intuitionists, however, tend to treat this matter in a more qualified fashion. Ewing writes: ". . . It may well be the case that all differences in people's judgments whether certain actions are right or wrong or certain things are good or bad are due to factors other than an irreducible difference in ethical intuition. But, even if they should not be, we must remember that ethical intuition, like our other capacities, is presumably a developing factor and therefore may be capable of error." This view is put by Ross as follows: "That an act, *qua* fulfilling a promise, or *qua* effecting a just distribution of good, or *qua* returning services rendered, or *qua* promoting the good of others, or *qua* promoting the virtue of insight of the agent, is *prima facie* right, is self-evident; not in the sense that it is evident from the beginning of our lives, or as soon as we attend to the proposition for the first time, but in the sense that when we have reached sufficient mental maturity and have given sufficient attention to the proposition it is evident without any need of proof, or of evidence beyond itself. It is self-evident just as a mathematical axiom, or the validity of a form of inference, is evident. The moral order expressed in these propositions is just as much part of the fundamental nature of the universe (and, we may add, of any possible universe in which there were moral agents at all) as is the spatial or numerical structure expressed in the axioms of geometry or arithmetic. In our confidence that these propositions are true there is involved the same trust in our reason that is involved in our confidence in mathematics; and we should not have justification for trusting it in the latter sphere and distrusting it in the former. In both cases we are dealing with propositions that cannot be proved, but that just as certainly need no proof." Ross's comparison of ethical propositions with mathematical axioms

4. *The Meaning of "Intuition"*

We may ask, then, What do the intuitionists mean by intuition? And this will be only a preliminary to a still more crucial question: What makes intuitionists think they have intuitions? The functions of intuition, according to Moore, are two. First, intuition seems to be a way of apprehending a *quality*, the non-natural quality of goodness. Second, it is a way of obtaining assurance of the truth of certain *propositions*. Propositions known by intuition are those for which "no relevant evidence whatever can be adduced: from no other truth, except themselves alone, can it be inferred that they are either true or false." And again, "when I call such propositions 'intuitions,' I seem to myself to assert that they are incapable of proof: I imply nothing whatever as to the manner or origin of our cognition of them." Now Moore's language here is that

---

connects intuition more explicitly with traditional rationalism than either Moore or Ewing has done, and raises all the difficulties that have led modern mathematicians to reject the view that axioms are self-evident truths. But what concerns us here is the apparent implication that if we do not share Ross's intuitions we are mentally and morally immature, a view that, of course, puts an end to the argument. Such a view is one that, when taken by parents and teachers, infuriates children or students without convincing them; if we were to engage in sociology of knowledge, we might add that it also suggests the time-honored upper class British doctrine of "good form" or "doing the right thing." A gentleman will know what these mean; a bounder will not, and with bounders there is no arguing. It is noteworthy that this variety of intuitionism has been particularly strong in Britain, and among an older generation of philosophers; also that a younger generation of moralists, who grew up in the new, more democratic England, are adopting a more casual doctrine more closely allied with emotivism.

of traditional rationalism, and suggests among others the first full statement of the theory of self-evident first principles given in Aristotle's *Posterior Analytics*. Moore, however, is careful not to commit himself here to any specific theory of knowledge, such as Aristotle's or Descartes', which does give an account of the "manner and origin" of cognitions. Consequently, we should note that Moore's bare characterization of intuition is not incompatible with the position held by certain empiricists with respect to the definitions or fundamental principles of ethics. For as we shall see, both Bentham and Mill—to mention only these—held that ethical principles were not capable of "proof" in the strict sense, but only in a Pickwickian sense; and yet they would hold that such propositions are true. Other philosophers, however, including the empiricists in question, would not have such a short way as Moore's in dealing with the question of truth when he writes:

When, therefore, I talk of Intuitionistic Hedonism, I must not be understood to imply that my denial that 'Pleasure is the only good' is *based* on my Intuition of its falsehood. My Intuition of its falsehood is indeed *my* reason for *holding* and declaring it untrue; it is indeed the only valid reason for so doing. But that is just because there is *no* logical reason for it; because there is no proper evidence or reason of its falsehood except itself alone. It is untrue, because it is untrue, and there is no other reason: but I *declare* it untrue, because its untruth is evident to me, and I hold that that is a sufficient reason for my assertion.

Nor would other philosophers, even intuitionists themselves, be readily satisfied by Moore's refusal to offer an account of the "manner or origin" of our cognition of such "unprovable principles."

Ewing, for example, says that ethical concepts known by intuition, though they are not derived from sense-experience, are nevertheless "given in experience in the wider sense of the

word." He treats intuition as an ultimate form of awareness of
meaning and truth, itself not analyzable but having an analogy
with visual perception: "We are in last resort forced to fall
back upon our consciousness that a proposed analysis does or
does not express what we mean . . . *I see* that propositions
about what is good . . . are propositions which cannot be
analysed adequately in psychological terms; *I see* . . ." etc.
But he makes it clear that it is not the physical eye that does
the seeing, but rather some mysterious organ which Strawson
refers to, in Aristotelian language, as the "eye of the mind."
(P. F. Strawson, review of Ewing's *The Definition of Good*, in
Mind, vol. 58, 1949.)

   To sum up: The intuitionist way of giving quietus to the
"open question" or the Mountain Range Effect is to conjure up
a non-natural quality or relation, known by *a priori* intuition,
to which ethical terms refer, and which gives the term its peculiar directive or normative force. Such intuitions tide the
non-naturalist over all the difficult passages in ethics. If we
have such an intuitive grasp of normative meanings, then we
can recognize the presence of normative properties when they
occur. Intuition is also invoked to deal with a problem which
has caused the intuitionists much concern: that of connecting
the non-natural property of goodness or rightness with certain
natural or empirically observable characteristics which contribute to the goodness or rightness of an object or an act. In
Broad's language, this is the problem of connecting the good
with the good-making, or, as Moore puts it, the ought with the
ought-implying. These connections, according to Broad and
Moore, are synthetic *a priori:* that is to say, they are synthetic
because they do not follow from an analysis of the meanings of
the terms in question, and they are *a priori* because they are
not derived from experience. Finally, intuition may be offered as a solution to the problem of justification or validation
of both particular normative judgments and general ethical

principles. Since the intuitionists in both cases reject the ordinary methods of empirical validation, they have recourse to special *a priori* ways of establishing such principles and judgments.

The intuitionist answers have not proved convincing to any of the other schools. Other philosophers have not been able to identify in objects or in their own fields of awareness anything recognizable as a non-natural property, nor are they able to achieve any *a priori* intuitions having the cogency claimed for them. Even more important, the type of rationalistic methodology and epistemology on which the intuitionist view rests has been widely discredited in other fields, such as mathematics, having more tenuous connection with matters of fact than ethics, and the persistence of such a methodology here is suspect.

Nevertheless many of the intuitionists' critical analyses are so acute that they cannot simply be shrugged off as resting on hallucinations. We may ask, then: What makes intuitionists think they have intuitions?

They have, I think, got hold of something, and this consists of a working grasp of the global meaning or total functioning of a normative term, so that when an empiricist defines the intrinsically good as pleasure or the right as conduciveness to the integration of interests, the intuitionist replies: "No, not that." The intuitionist is sensitive to the nuances of ordinary language; he is well trained in the use of his mother tongue, and his operative understanding of it enables him to tell when a term is given an inadequate analysis, even though he himself is not able to supply an adequate analysis in its place. Instead, he invokes an ineffable property which, like the God of the mystics, is characterized largely by negations such as "non-natural."

The irony in the development of this school is that, although intuitionism professes to be an "analytical" philosophy, in its methodological aspect it may be considered as an injunction to stop analysis at a specified point—that is to say, at the point where we come upon certain supposedly unanalyzable properties. In its metaphysical aspect, it is an injunction to seek properties of a radically different kind from those recognized in ordinary experience or capable of being given meaning in terms of it. The other schools of moral philosophy have not been willing to acquiesce in these injunctions, but have persisted in trying to push analysis further, and to carry it out in terms of properties less mysterious.

3
Emotivism

---

1. *Ethical Terms as Expressive or Evocative*

Before we succumb to such a desperate remedy as the intuitionists propose, we can try out another type of answer offered by the emotivists and, more subtly, by Philosophy of Ordinary Language. This is that such terms as "goodness" and "ought" do not designate properties at all—not any kind of property, whether a quality or a relation, whether natural or nonnatural; but do a different kind of thing.

The confusion, according to one version of emotivism, arises from a misleading grammatical form. When we say "This pie is good" or "That act is right," we seem to be making an assertion just as we are when we say "This pie is round" or "That act is deliberate." But actually such expressions, which appear to be asserting ethical predicates, do not, like the others, serve to give information at all but rather to vent an emotion or to evoke an attitude, etc.

This becomes clearer if we consider "ought" rather than "good" as our basic ethical term. For "ought" is not an adjective, but an auxiliary verb, and therefore seems to express a certain relation to action instead of designating a property.

Even here, however, grammar causes a certain confusion, because when we say "You ought to do this," we are still using
the grammatical form of an indicative or declaratory sentence,
or one which closely resembles such a sentence, since a common mode of speech is: "It is false that you ought to do this"—
and hence truth or falsity seems to be assigned to the original,
whereas it is grotesque to say "It is false that do this!" or "It is
false that hurrah for this!" Consequently, in order to be un-
ambiguous we should translate an alleged ethical proposition
into "Hurrah for this!" or "Do this!" where the real intent will
be clearer. For a sentence using "good" or "ought" really conveys no more information about the object than does such an
exclamation or imperative.

The early logical positivists who reasoned along these lines
adopted a sharp dichotomy between "cognitive" and "emotive"
meaning, and dumped all the functions of language besides assertions of fact into the emotive bin.

There was some uncertainty among the early emotivists, in
their rather scanty writings on ethics, as to just what relation
to emotion an ethical term bore. Thus in *Language, Truth and
Logic* (1936), A. J. Ayer conceived an ethical expression as primarily an ejaculation, or a venting of the emotion of a speaker.
The presence of an ethical word, such as "wrong," in a sentence, adds nothing to its factual content. "You acted wrongly
in stealing that money" means simply "You stole that money"
plus a tone of horror. Or, "Stealing money is wrong" is simply
equivalent to "Stealing money!!" where the double exclamation point expresses a special sort of moral disapproval. Ayer
did, however, say that an ethical judgment could be used to
arouse feeling in a hearer as well as to express the feelings of
the speaker.

It is this second type of function that was stressed by
R. Carnap, who wrote in *Philosophy and Logical Syntax* (1935)
that "Killing is evil" is equivalent to "Do not kill!" and that the

62

latter is a grammatically less misleading form of expression. It is emotive in the sense that it seeks to move, or to motivate, someone. Carnap's reason for this view was based on the assumption that all cognitive statements imply predictions about future occurrences, as "This is a circle" implies "If I look at this from a forty-five degree angle, it will appear elliptical." But, Carnap writes, "From the statement 'killing is evil' we cannot deduce any proposition about future experiences. Thus this statement is not verifiable and has no theoretical [cognitive] sense, and the same thing is true of all other value statements." It might be thought that such a consequence as "If a person kills anybody, he will have feelings of remorse" is deducible from the expression in question, but Carnap says that this proposition is deducible not from the ethical expression but only from psychological propositions about the character and emotional reactions of the person. These belong to the science of mores, and not to ethics proper, whose peculiar function consists in the issuing of commands.

2. Stevenson: Belief and Attitude

These simple versions of the emotivist position were given an elaborate development, and the position was modified in the process, by C. L. Stevenson, first in a series of articles, then in his book, *Ethics and Language* (1944). The modifications consisted chiefly in a subtler analysis of the non-cognitive functioning of ethical expressions and a recognition of a somewhat more extensive cognitive element in their meaning than Carnap and Ayer had provided for.

Stevenson's professed aim in the book is to find out how and to what extent ethical disputes can be settled. His main conclusion is that disagreements can be resolved by rational means in so far as they are based upon disagreements in *belief* but not in so far as they result from disagreements in *attitude*.

And as many disputes, including the most violent, rest upon a clash of attitudes, there are limits to the extent to which ethics, as a rational inquiry, can hope to adjudicate them. "Belief" is Stevenson's term for the cognitive element, and "attitude" for the non-cognitive.

At the very beginning, Stevenson links this position with what amounts to his own rendering of the Naturalistic Fallacy. Ethical terms, such as "good" or "desirable" in the normative sense, cannot be analyzed primarily as references to properties of the objects to which they refer, such as the property of being desired, because of the job they do: "Statements about what is desirable, unlike those about what is desired, serve not to describe attitudes, but to intensify or alter them." Thus Stevenson turns Moore's discussion of Mill's error against Moore's own position as well as Mill's. It makes no difference whether the property in question be conceived as natural or non-natural; therefore the mistake consists in treating an ethical judgment as the assertion of a property of any kind, and hence as a form of knowledge. So the Naturalistic Fallacy, for Stevenson, becomes in effect the Cognitivist Error. Where Moore went astray was by "intellectualizing . . . emotive meaning into an indefinable quality." "Wherever Moore would point to a 'Naturalistic Fallacy,' the present writer . . . would point to a persuasive definition." In one respect, however, Stevenson is closer to ethical naturalism than to intuitionism, for he holds that the descriptive element in the meaning of "good" is exhaustively definable in naturalistic terms. And even the non-cognitive elements are treated on naturalistic assumptions, though they are not conceived as properties of the thing or act referred to by the ethical judgment.

Stevenson makes two successive approximations to an analysis of the ethical judgment, which he refers to as his first and second models. By the first model, "This is good" means "I approve of this; do so as well!" The first clause contains both a descriptive and an emotive element. It expresses a feeling or an attitude, and it also describes that attitude—that is, characterizes it as one of approval rather than disapproval. The second clause, being an imperative, is predominantly emotive: it seeks to arouse an emotion or an attitude. The central "ethical" property—capacity to move the hearer—is conceived by Stevenson as a natural property, but a property in the first instance of the *verbal sign itself* (*e.g.,* "good" or "ought") and not a property of the thing or object signified by the ethical sentence. It is not a quality, such as redness or squareness, which can be significantly predicated of a single thing, but a relational property: one which holds between two or more things. "Good" therefore, when it is used effectively, functions by evoking a relation between the word itself and the person addressed, namely the relation of moving the hearer. But where a relation, R, relates two terms, x and y, it may be treated as a property either of x or of y. Consequently, the emotive meaning may be conceived conversely as a property of the person—namely, the capacity *to be moved* by the sign.[1]

Emotive meaning, furthermore, is most usefully conceived as a special kind of relational property called a *dispositional property.* This is presupposed in Stevenson's definition of the meaning as a "power." The mere fact that a word happens to move us on one occasion does not suffice to give it emotive meaning; the word must have a reliable *tendency* to move us on repeated occasions of its use. A dispositional property,

[1] Of course, if the relation in question is conceived as holding between three terms—the sign, the person and the object designated—it may be treated as constituting a relational property of the object also: its capacity, when represented, to move us. This mode of analyzing the situation, however, is not considered by the emotivists.

furthermore, is one which something manifests if certain conditions are fulfilled. Thus a rubber ball exhibits the property of
bouncing on a particular occasion when it is dropped; bouncing is a simple or non-dispositional property and as such can
be directly observed. On the other hand, when we say that the
ball is resilient, we mean that it bounces (and will or would
bounce) *if* dropped. A property is a first-order disposition
when only one condition needs to be fulfilled; a second-order
disposition when two conditions need to be fulfilled. Thus
when we say that a certain object is "magnetic"—a first-order
dispositional property—we mean that it will manifest the observable property of attracting a small piece of iron if placed
near the iron; when we say that it is "magnetizable"—a second-order disposition—we mean that it becomes magnetic *if*
an additional condition is fulfilled, that is, if an electric current
is passed through it in a specific way.

A term has first-order emotive meaning, when it will produce a *feeling* (for example, of pleasure), in the presence of
an object, emotive meaning of the second-order when it will
produce an *attitude* toward the object; namely a feeling which
carries with it a *disposition to action*—that is, when the feeling
has the power to move us toward the object. Both first- and
second-order emotive meaning, according to Stevenson, are
acquired by a process of social conditioning which gives words
their power to evoke feelings or attitudes. Emotive meaning,
like other dispositional properties, is not as such directly observed, but, we may assume, is inferred from repeated observations that the utterance of the word is followed by the
occurrence of a feeling or an attitude, together with the "explanation" of this by means of a law of conditioning. The law
of conditioning is stated in terms of cause and effect; hence
emotive meaning satisfies Broad's second criterion of a natural
property as one whose meaning can be analyzed into inspect-
ible or introspectible properties together with the notion of

cause. But the error of ethical naturalism, Stevenson says in effect, is to make the distinctive meaning of a normative term a property of the object rather than a property of the word or of the person using the word.

Stevenson has been criticized by Moore ("A Reply to My Critics," *The Philosophy of G. E. Moore*), on the ground that an ethical judgment does not assert the attitude of approval, but at most "implies" it in some sense of "imply." But Stevenson has, at least in part, anticipated this objection: "When a man says 'x is good' he is seldom called upon to prove that he now approves of x. He is called upon, rather, to adduce considerations which will make his attitude acceptable to his opponent, and to show that they are not directed to situations of whose nature he is ignorant." So that the cognitive element in the meaning is not adequately revealed in Stevenson's first model analysis: it is manifested rather in the *reasons* adduced to support the judgment that something is good. For we do adduce such reasons when challenged. And here arises the great problem which the non-cognitivist has to solve: "Although imperatives cannot be 'proved,' are there not reasons or arguments which may 'support' them?" Further: "One of the peculiarities of ethical argument lies in the inference from a factual reason to an ethical conclusion." But this transition is not, strictly speaking, to be called an inference at all. For Stevenson holds that the "reasons" work not by implying or verifying the judgment but by calling the attention of the hearer to aspects or consequences of the situation which will evoke the desired attitude. So that the "reasons" themselves, though they describe an element in the situation, operate simply by instigating an attitude and not, except in an auxiliary way, by bringing intellectual conviction. They do the latter only in so far as they enlist the belief of the hearer that the situation is actually as described; and this in turn is merely instrumental to the arousal of the attitude. The object is described, as in a radio advertisement, in order to make the listener's mouth water and dispose him to try the product.

It is, however, possible to bring the relevant factors described by the "reasons" into the analysis of the meaning of the ethical judgment itself. This is done by Stevenson in his second working model; where " 'This is good' has the meaning of 'This has qualities or relations x, y, z . . . , except that 'good' has as well a laudatory emotive meaning which permits it to express the speaker's approval, and tends to evoke the approval of the hearer." This model is not offered as a definition of "good," but as a "formal schema for a whole set of definitions." When the variables x, y, z are filled in by such expressions as "greatest happiness of the greater number" or "integration of interests," the result is what Stevenson calls a *persuasive definition.*

The second model makes explicit the descriptive element in the judgment, that is, the ideas different people may have as to what properties good things have in common. But, as Stevenson argues, it does not fundamentally alter the analysis he has previously given; indeed the examples he gives of persuasive definitions state a miscellaneous list of properties, at various levels of generality. For the x, y, z is chosen *ad hoc,* not with the purpose of getting at knowledge of good and evil, but for the purpose of persuading the person to whom the definition is proffered. No ethical definition is cognitively more valid than another. "To choose a definition is to plead a cause, so long as the word defined is strongly emotive"; and such a definition "is unlikely to represent detached, neutral analysis. It is less likely to *clarify* normative ethics [which for Stevenson is the process of effecting persuasion or achieving agreement] than to participate in it." The "good" definition is simply the one that effectively serves the cause, and if it does this, apparently, anything goes.

Now this aspect of the emotivist position has led to the

charge that its proponents are opening the doors to all sorts of irrationalism, even that they provide a justification for unprincipled rhetoricians with dictatorial ambitions who make "doublethink" their stock in trade. Such conclusions the emotivists, being contemplative persons with democratic and liberal sympathies, have repudiated with horror. But it still remains possible to ask whether they have squared their theories as so far propounded with their convictions.

One way emotivists have of replying to such accusations is that the emotivist analysis is only a "non-normative metanormative inquiry." That is to say, it does not propose an ethical theory for the guidance of people's conduct, but—as indeed Stevenson said of his first six chapters in the book—an analysis of the "nature and effectiveness of methods that are in fact used in daily life." In other words, he has given us not an ethics but a semantics of moral rhetoric.

But actually, in his first two paragraphs of the book, he makes much greater claims for it than that. Although he does not claim to furnish "any conclusions about what is right or wrong," he does profess as his first objective "to clarify the meanings of ethical terms," and as his second objective, "to characterize the general methods by which ethical judgments can be proved or supported." If he really does succeed in clarifying—in whole or in part—the meanings of such terms as "good" and "right," it would seem that this would have some normative effect: that we should be able to use them better after reading his book. And I believe that there is an indirect sense in which this is true. For even though his analysis is incomplete, it may be the case that he has contributed to a fuller analysis, provided he helps others—perhaps by way of provocation—to make it. And this I think he does. But in his statement of his second objective, there is the implication that he has not only exhibited some general methods by which ethical judgments can conceivably be in fact supported bv somebody, but *the* general methods—that is, the best ones to be found. And so, to this extent his book must be taken, even if unwittingly, as an attempt at a normative meta-normative inquiry, and not as a non-normative one.

To make the point clearer, we can put it in the following way. A normative meta-normative inquiry (or, in less formidable terms, an inquiry that seeks to determine the *proper* uses of ethical language) would hold that some conceptions of good and right are more adequate than others, and that some methods of supporting ethical judgments are better than others—and hence would recommend some rather than others for adoption. If Stevenson shows us the more adequate conceptions and the better methods, then his book is normative. If it does not profess to exhibit these, however, how can it claim to exhibit accurately even the *de facto* meanings of "good" and "right"?

In his reply to his critics, Stevenson wishes to show that he is not a skeptic or a nihilist, but that his theory, though itself non-normative, still leaves the way open for a normative meta-normative inquiry. Such a normative inquiry must propose certain ethical concepts and attitudes as, if not "true," at any rate more adequate or more correct than others. Now Stevenson, in denying that he has had such a concern, forces us to ask whether in his book he has been concerned to analyze (a) only adequate uses of normative expressions, or (b) only inadequate uses, or (c) both (a) and (b). We can, I think, rule out (b), for if this is all the book gives, it is a simple pathology of rhetoric—and pathology itself presupposes some conception of health. We are left then, with (c): that Stevenson conceives himself to have given us the adequate and inadequate forms of ethical expressions indiscriminately, or that he has given us the features common to both types. But in this case, it would seem that however well Stevenson has laid the groundwork, the main job in ethics is still to be done, for he certainly has not proposed any criterion for distinguishing the more adequate from the less adequate—unless indeed "more adequate" simply means "more moving." Nor can we be sure he has included the more adequate in his examination. Here again we have a rhetorical rather than an ethical criterion. Since I can see no way in which Stevenson could answer this objection, I am forced to conclude that he has not even given us an adequate semantics of the subject, for it still remains an open possibility that he has left out the correct or the adequate meanings of such terms as good. If this should prove to be the case, we shall be forced to give consideration to Plato's view in the *Phaedrus* that dialectic (that is, in ethics, a normative meta-normative inquiry) is the true rhetoric.

3. The Normative Assumptions of Emotivism

Nevertheless, I think we can discover in or behind Stevenson's book certain normative assumptions. And I am not referring merely to such obvious ones as that clarity is a good thing, for this is not an assumption distinctive of ethics. A writer's assumption as to what is good in a particular subject matter is rather to be found by asking what aspect of it he singles out for special attention. And in this case, the key term is "agreement." Stevenson is concerned with ethical agreement and disagreement and the methods by which he can maximize the former and minimize the latter. And he also deals especially with the methods by which disagreement in attitudes can be resolved by rational means—that is, by resolving disagreement in belief. There does, then, seem to be a general assumption that agreement in attitudes is an important constituent of the good life or good society, and that it is good to achieve this where possible by achieving agreement in belief—that is, what Dewey calls the method of "pooled intelligence." It would look, then, as though Stevenson might be predisposed

toward a theory like that of Dewey's or Perry's, which would
define, whether merely "persuasively" or otherwise, the *summum bonum* as a reflectively achieved harmony of interests or
integration of attitudes. But we cannot be sure that Stevenson
would favor such a position so long as he has given us no
other criteria for choosing among ethical principles than those
vested in his doctrine of persuasive definition.

There is, however, some corroboration of this interpretation
of Stevenson if we search hard enough for it. In Chapter II,
he writes that a supporting "reason" for an imperative "describes the situation which the imperative seeks to alter, or
the new situation which the imperative seeks to bring about;
and if these facts disclose that the new situation will satisfy a
preponderance of the hearer's desires [italics mine], he will
hesitate to obey no longer." It looks, then, as though for
Stevenson the effectiveness of an ethical expression depends
on its capacity to lead to satisfaction of desire, and that a
redirection of belief will produce a redirection of attitude
only when the hearer is persuaded, explicitly or implicitly,
that such satisfaction will result. If this is the case, then
Stevenson is assuming so far as the cognitive factor is concerned a conative theory, and one of the "satisfaction" variety.
He is assuming that the word "good" will have emotive effect
when, and only when, "x is good" means for the hearer "x has
the property of conduciveness to a preponderance of desires
for it," plus the emotive effect of the expression. And the
emotive effect in turn depends on the discovery that x actually possesses this property. If this is so, then only this
definition will be persuasive, and the substitution of alternative
values of the variables x, y, and z . . . will be ineffective. We
are, then, forced to reject the notion that "anything goes" in
the way of a persuasive definition, and that Stevenson's second
model is not really as tolerant a schema as he suggests. In
fact, whatever criterion Stevenson offers as the principle of

conditioning or motivation—whether it be that of satisfaction of desire or some other—will, on his own assumptions, fix the cognitive elements in the situation. (It will also, incidentally, in consequence, raise anew the problem of the Naturalistic Fallacy.) Or, as I shall put it later, Stevenson's principle of motivation will furnish us with some kind of an Identifying Property of goodness, whether an adequate one or not. Of course, it is possible for Stevenson to escape from the predicament by saying that there are no principles of motivation and learning and that "conditioning" is a purely haphazard and chaotic affair.

Still more fundamental criticisms of Stevenson's position have been directed against two assumptions which he nowhere establishes. First, his sharp distinction between attitude and belief is untenable. As we shall try to show later, any attitude above the most elementary impulsion is itself grounded in a belief, explicit or implicit, even though the knowledge involved is at the level of perceptual cognition; and the connection between them is not merely adventitious or haphazard. Second, even though we accept what seems to be Stevenson's principal normative assumption, that agreement is in general a good thing, and a major desideratum, it does not follow that agreement is the central element in the good or the right. The search for ethical knowledge often springs from the need to learn what should be done, when there is the most bewildering and irremediable variety of opinion about it.

4

Philosophy of Ordinary Language

The emphasis on non-cognitive meaning, initiated by the logical positivists, has been continued by a group of young British philosophers, whose writings on ethics have appeared for the most part since World War II and, despite their rather scanty volume to date, have offered a challenge to all the three schools we have considered so far. The chief influence, direct or indirect, on the group has been that of the late Ludwig Wittgenstein who, during his tenure of the chair of philosophy at Cambridge, broke radically with the earlier logical positivism of which he was one of the founders, though, indeed, signs of his divergence from the school were evident in the conclusions of *Tractatus Logico-Philosophicus* (1922). Moore's emphasis on the use of common sense and on the avoidance of technical terminology wherever possible, as well as some of his specific methods of analysis, has also been influential. But most of the ethical writing of the group so far has come from Oxford, where the influences of Gilbert Ryle and J. L. Austin have played a predominant part in giving a new turn to the restatement of philosophical problems, and the effect of such older Oxford moral philosophers as Ross and H. A. Prichard has not been negligible. In general, the Oxford group try to salvage much more from classical philosophers such as Aristotle and Kant than the Cambridge writers believe is possible.

The tendency represented by the writings of this group is referred to as Philosophy of Ordinary Language, or Informalism, though like all such labels these are in some respects misleading. The label was originally applied to the later position of Wittgenstein, presented as a "therapeutic" positivism, which professed to show that philosophy, with its elaborate artificial terminologies and efforts to be systematic, was a mistake arising from semantic confusion, and which offered techniques of linguistic analysis that would cure the philosophical neurosis and enable its sufferers to get on with less deluded pursuits, such as those of science, the arts and practical affairs. The semantic strategy of Wittgenstein's disciples, however, has changed somewhat: instead of offering a cure for philosophy, they now represent what they are doing as itself constituting philosophy, and a mode of practicing it which will not be subject to the errors with which the traditional philosophies are infected. This shift in strategy offers, among other advantages, that of enabling them to occupy chairs in philosophy without qualms of conscience.

The Oxford wing of the movement—with which we are here concerned—has found its leading spokesman in Ryle, who has recently insisted that philosophy should not be conceived as the attempt to justify ordinary linguistic usages, which are often confused and corrupt, but as the effort to study the uses of words in ordinary discourse ("Ordinary Language," *Philosophical Review*, vol. 62, 1953). *Usage* is a matter for factual study, to be left to the dictionary-makers, whereas the study of *use* is not a matter of linguistics but of "logic." The uses of such terms of ordinary discourse as "know" and "good" are not to be exhibited by creating ideal languages, or making artificial logical constructions to exhibit their meaning—an error common both to much of traditional philosophy and to the earlier logical positivism—but rather by looking more closely at how such terms function in the context of everyday situations in which they are employed, by seeing what kinds of jobs such terms can do when they are used effectively. There is also a tendency in Ryle, and in some of his associates, to seek to clarify linguistic usages on the assumptions of rather crude behavioristic and pragmatic principles resembling those current in the United States a generation ago but since repudiated in the development of these schools in this country.

Although the application of the techniques in question to ethics is even more fluid than to other philosophical problems, we may point to certain assumptions or tendencies shared by most members of the group: (1) A pluralistic view of language, which makes it impossible to fit ethical meanings into the dichotomy of "cognitive" and "emotive." (2) Attention to the kinds of "reasons" we give to back up ethical judgments, as a clue to the nature of the cognitive factors involved. (3) An approach to understanding the uses of a word by examining how we learn to use it. (4) Opposition to "definitions" of ethical terms, which propose an artificial substitute for its working meaning, and a tendency to substitute "models" for definitions. (5) Advocacy, by some but not all members of the group, of a special "logic" for ethics which would reveal that ethical reasoning follows different procedures from those of deductive and inductive logic. Several of these tendencies, incidentally, we have already encountered in Stevenson, who was trained at Cambridge and whose views the members of the group have carefully sifted.

1. *Linguistic Pluralism*

The subtlety and variety of the uses of language is such, according to this group, that they cannot all be classified as

76

either "cognitive" or "emotive," even when "emotive" is given such a broad scope as Stevenson assigns to it. Austin has devoted a good deal of attention to the analysis of such statements as "I promise," "I agree," and "I do," which although they are cast in the indicative mood, and are translated only with awkwardness into some other mood such as the imperative, nevertheless are not primarily attempts to convey information but rather are ways of engaging the speaker to undertake a performance. (See his "Other Minds," *Logic and Language*, 2nd Series, edited by A. G. N. Flew, 1953.)

In an article, "The Ascription of Responsibility and Rights" (*Logic and Language*, 1st Series, edited by Flew, 1951), H. L. A. Hart has argued that certain linguistic usages in law and ethics or in the overlapping zone between the two, such as "This is mine," or "This is yours," or "He did it," can best be characterized as ascriptive: they ascribe to someone a responsibility for a past action or an obligation to act in a certain way in future, rather than merely state a fact. Ethical judgments, according to the Philosophers of Ordinary Language, must be conceived as more closely related to expressions like these than to scientific statements or commands or ejaculations. While the writers of this group assign to the cognitive elements a more important role than does even a modified emotivism such as Stevenson's, nevertheless they hold that the distinctive function of a normative judgment is not to convey knowledge, but to do another kind of thing.

Hampshire says that "the distinguishing characteristic of practical judgments is that they have a prescriptive or quasi-imperative force as part of their meaning." What is prescribed, however, is not an attitude but "a course of action, or a way of life." For if we examine the *uses* of ethical judgments, we see that these all center about the problems of the moral agent, who is trying to decide what to do in a situation where he has to make a choice and then to act upon it. ("Fallacies in Moral Philosophy," *Mind*, vol. 59, 1948.)

According to Hare (*The Language of Morals*, 1952), ethical terms function in certain contexts as prescriptive or imperative. More commonly, however, this function is better described as "advisory" or "commendatory," since they are not issued with the bluntness or the arrogation of authority that is characteristic of a command.

For Toulmin (*The Place of Reason in Ethics*, 1950), the characteristic function of moral judgments is not, as with scientific judgments, to alter expectations, but to alter feelings and behavior, that is, to point out to us what is *to be done*. Consequently he characterizes them as "gerundive" rather than "imperative," etc. The good or the right is not the *desideratum*, nor even the *desiderabile*, but the *desiderandum*. The term "gerundive" is taken over from grammar, rather than from logic, and Toulmin nowhere gives us an extensive analysis of it, though he does say that the name is appropriate because ethical terms can all be analyzed as meaning "worthy of something-or-other." Whether our understanding is materially furthered, however, by taking the key term from such a loose science as grammar is questionable. Presumably Toulmin prefers it to, say, logic, because it remains closer to the ordinary workings of language and has not been developed in accordance with the needs of the exact sciences.

In "Ethics and the Ceremonial Uses of Language" (*Philosophical Analysis*, edited by Max Black, 1950), Margaret Macdonald urges that we should conceive ethical judgments neither after the pattern of scientific judgments, nor after that of commands or expressions of personal attitudes. They are to be analyzed rather by analogy with, or upon the "model" of, certain kinds of ceremonial utterances, such as those of religious ritual and legal procedures. They have, like them, "a public and impersonal character and carry authority," characteristics which are absent from mere expressions of personal attitudes. Although, like commands, ethical judgments are directed toward the accomplishment of certain actions, the fact that they are usually cast in indicative rather than imperative form is significant of the authoritative claim they make: the individual is not simply expressing his own will but speaking in the name of an impersonal authority which prescribes common ends or a common task. The characteristic function of normative judgments, then, is described as "performatory." But the analogy with ceremonial language is not thoroughgoing. The two kinds of expressions are distinguished as follows: "Moral judgments certainly commit their users to do or refrain from certain actions. They do not invariably, however, like ceremonial utterances, form part of the performance to which they oblige, for we do not always do as we ought."

2. Giving "Reasons"

Even though normative expressions are not, in their primary intention, cognitive, nevertheless when challenged they are commonly backed up by citing factual evidence. Consequently the cognitive element in moral statements is best exhibited by examining the kinds of "reasons" we give for ethical judgments. When my statement that I ought to contribute to a certain charity is challenged, I may defend myself by pointing to the fact that those who will benefit from my contribution are without food or clothing. This is a factual reason that, so it is asserted, does not logically imply or entail the "conclusion" I draw from it, but is nevertheless accepted as "relevant."

Usually the philosophers in question do not offer any very definite criteria of "relevance" or "irrelevance" but rest their case on our working sense of what is relevant or irrelevant in particular or exemplary cases. Sometimes, indeed, the question of relevance is itself held to be irrelevant. Thus some members of the school hold that it is beside the point to give "reasons" for such a statement as "I ought to keep my promise," since in making the promise I have already engaged myself, and the "ought" is contained in the very notion of a promise. Others hold that promises are "defeasible," and though I cannot meaningfully offer reasons for keeping a promise, I can offer relevant reasons, on certain occasions, for breaking one— as when major suffering would result from keeping a promise, of a sort that was not foreseen when the promise was made. In dealing with such matters, the procedures of Philosophy of Ordinary Language are in practice very close to intuitionism, even though the philosophers in question reject the explicit methodology offered by the intuitionists in support of their position. The result—for example, the final stand often taken, "I know that this reason is relevant (or irrelevant),"—may be offered in such a dogmatic way that the representative of this school is liable to the charge of being a *crypto-intuitionist.*

It is this reliance upon a bed-rock conviction of the "relevance" of certain kinds of reasons that constitutes informalism's divergence from emotivism on the issue of the cognitive factor in ethical reasoning. Whereas emotivism seems to suggest that any kind of reason that moves us is ethically relevant, this group tries to escape the vitiating relativism of the apparent consequence that "anything goes" by offering a direct and quasi-intuitive awareness that only certain kinds of reasons are appropriate and valid in ethics. Whether such a position can adequately answer the change of arbitrary dogmatism is a matter for detailed inquiry.

3. *The Genetic Approach*

Unlike the intuitionists and emotivists, Philosophy of Ordinary Language makes some employment of a genetic approach to clarifying the meaning of ethical terms. Wittgenstein offered rather elaborate techniques for exhibiting the meanings of certain terms through a study of how we learn to use these terms in everyday life. Procedures resembling these techniques are frequently offered by the Oxford moralists. Thus Hare rests his analyses of such words as "right" and "good" on imaginative experiments purporting to show how we teach a foreigner (or shall we say an extra-terrestrial?) to understand these in one easy lesson. We may call this procedure the Berlitz method in moral philosophy. Whatever its philosophical merits, it may prove stimulating to science fiction, and bear fruit in a future Galactic Era.

4. Definitions and "Models"

According to Wittgenstein (*Philosophical Investigations,* 1953), our concepts in aesthetics and ethics do not and cannot have the sharp edges that would permit them to be encompassed by a definition. The terms we use in these fields do not refer to a group of objects showing common properties, but rather to groups exhibiting "family resemblances" within each. In actual families there is no one common configuration of traits, combining for example complexion, shape of nose and temperament, but rather "a complicated network of similarities over-lapping and criss-crossing: sometimes overall similarities, sometimes similarities of detail." Language is not like a game where the rules are or can be established systematically once and for all, but like a game where we make up the rules as we go along—even at times like one where we change them as we go along. There can, then, Wittgenstein implies, be no universally satisfactory definition of "good" or "beautiful"; on the contrary, clarity and accuracy in talking about our subject matter require that we respect the "open texture" of language, and seek to trace the somewhat haphazard ramification of properties and relationships on which a study of the field embarks us.

Hampshire, in the essay previously cited, says that definitions have been the "will-o'-the-wisp" of ethical theory. The pursuit of them has rested on the assumption that a single formula, such as the greatest happiness principle, could be found from which it is possible to deduce in a simple way judgments about what is good and what is right. Although definitions, or verbal equivalents, have some use as "preliminary steps" toward answering moral questions, differences over the answers can be clarified only by asking under what conditions we make moral judgments and what kinds of reasons are regarded as sufficient to justify them. Instead of offering definitions to settle such matters, the moral philosopher should devote himself to giving "specimens" of reasons that would be accepted as pertinent, and "describing specimens of conduct to which they are applied. . . . An informative treatise on ethics—or on the ethics of a particular society or person— would contain an accumulation of examples selected to illustrate the kinds of decisions which are said to be right in various circumstances, and the reasons given and the arguments used in concluding that they are right." We thus seem to be urged to go back to Cephalus in the *Republic:* The meaning of such a concept as Justice is to be exhibited by a collection of statements about the kinds of conduct that are held to be just, such as speaking the truth and paying your debts.

When the writers of this group attempt to carry out such a program in detail—as in the only two book-length treatises that have come from the group so far, those by Toulmin and Hare—they find themselves compelled, in order to bring some sort of *rationale* into the subject, to offer for the clarification of the meaning of ethical terms, concepts or principles of a higher degree of generality than this program initially envisaged. Thus Toulmin equates the *meaning* of "right" with its non-cognitive force, which for him is "gerundive," a notion which he nowhere tries to put into the form of a definition. Yet when we go on to "analyze" the term right, Toulmin says that we give reasons of a factual or cognitive sort, and the admissible reasons either show that the act accords with the accepted customs and rules of a society, or, when these are disputed, with what amounts to an impoverished version of the ultilitarian principle. The utilitarian principle thus serves for Toulmin in practice, as Broad has shown in his review of the book (*Mind*, vol. 51, 1952), as a definition of the cognitive element in the term's meaning. It is curious that Toulmin should exclude the chief concept in the "analysis" of the term, and the one that most closely resembles a defining property, from its "meaning." For what does analysis analyze if not the meaning? The assumption seems to be that the non-cognitive factor alone is worthy to be dignified with the status of the meaning, and that the cognitive elements are no part of it. Such a restricted conception of meaning, however, is nowhere defended explicitly by Toulmin.

Hare, similarly, distinguishes between the "meaning" of a word and the "criteria for its application." In the case of what is called instrumental goodness, for example, the meaning of the notion cannot be stated by offering in a definition a property which is common to all instrumentally good things. The properties which make something instrumentally good vary hopelessly from one class of objects to another, for example, from hockey sticks to fire extinguishers. The understanding of the meaning of the term requires a working "understanding of what it is to choose," and if the person who is learning the word has this understanding, then it is possible to teach him in one easy lesson—for example, by a practical demonstration —what are the criteria for instrumental goodness in a particular class of objects: that is, how to use the stick or extinguisher effectively. The general meaning of the term intrinsic goodness, then, is exhausted in a grasp of the inducement that the term offers to choose this rather than that—that is, in its commendatory or prescriptive function—and among the objects that elicit this function no common property can be found which clinches the choice and is capable of serving as the defining property. Such, at any rate, is Hare's theoretical position. In practice, however, he does offer a distinction between two senses of the term instrumentally good: (1) "the common *property* . . . of being conducive to 'good' in the intrinsic sense," and (2) the property of "being conducive to the end it is used for" (a non-ethical or non-valuative sense of the term). Now these properties seem to be properties of the *kinds of object* in question, and not merely of the words "instrumentally good"; furthermore, it is noteworthy that they are precisely the properties which Lewis, a naturalist, offers to define and distinguish what he calls, respectively, "extrinsic goodness" and mere "utility." Has Hare perchance stumbled on definitions of the cognitive element without realizing it? The fact that instrumental goodness has the ambiguity pointed out is no obstacle to taking the characteristics in question as defining properties; for this analysis simply shows us that ordinary language here is a blunt instrument, and that for the sake of precision we need two concepts and two terms, which it seems *prima facie* at least that we can make a stab at defining, instead of the one vague and ambiguous notion embedded in everyday discourse.

Indeed, at the end of his inquiry, Hare offers a "model," admittedly artificial, to clarify the meaning of the term "ought," which "approaches" in meaning to that of the natural word, and which can serve as a partial though not a complete substitute for it. This model performs the prescriptive but not the descriptive function of the natural word. Yet the word, according to Hare, does have descriptive functions, although these are not of such a sort that they can be exhibited in any such model. He nevertheless holds that the model "defines" the prescriptive functions, even though it does not supply a "definitive analysis."

Hare, at any rate, means by a "model" something closer to what has traditionally been sought from a definition than do other members of the group. Miss Macdonald, for example, seems to mean by a model simply a form of expression which supplies a partial analogy to illuminate the use of the term in question, as we have seen in her discussion of ceremonial language as a means of exhibiting certain functions of ethical language.

Whether or not the informalists have succeeded in laying the ghost of ethical definitions once and for all, they have at least forced us to reopen the question and to rethink the matter from the ground up.

We shall not, perhaps, be able to tackle the question with any assurance until we have gone into the matter of the nature and function of definitions in general—which is one of the most confused and most scanted topics in contemporary philosophy.

5. A "Third Logic" for Ethics

If descriptive meaning can be assigned to basic terms, the logical inference made in normative reasoning, as will be shown, would be not perhaps simple but at any rate exempt from any formidable difficulties in principle. But the problem is an especially acute one for Philosophers of Ordinary Language. While they reject definitions, at the same time they are trying to rehabilitate the importance of "reasons" for ethical judgments, as against the emotivists and some of the intuitionists; and giving reasons would seem on the face of it to involve some reasoning.

For those who do hold that something like reasoning is legitimate in ethics, the great obstacle is the Naturalistic Fallacy, in the form in which it presents itself to this school. Our "reasons" are often in the form of descriptive statements. Yet our conclusions are normative judgments. If the reasons were related deductively to the conclusions, then we would be committing a formal fallacy by smuggling into the conclusion something that is not in the premises. Even if the relation is conceived as an inductive rather than a deductive one, there would be an analogous abuse of the logic of probability. Hence the Naturalistic Fallacy is usually stated by this group as *the error of inferring a normative conclusion from non-normative premises.*

In order to avoid this error, some of the Philosophers of Ordinary Language have appealed to a "third logic"—neither deductive nor inductive, but one that has been called "seductive"—which would skirt this fallacy. Just how the fallacy is to be avoided has nowhere been made clear, since none of its proponents has stated the forms of this third type of inference.[1] But in practice the Philosophers of Ordinary Language get over the hump by invoking the notion of "reasonableness," so that we "just see" or "just know" that a given reason supports the conclusion, even though the relation is not susceptible of being analyzed.

Not all members of the school, however, have recourse to this desperate remedy. Hare avoids it by proposing a shotgun

---

[1] Although they are not members of the informalist group, G. H. Von Wright, in "Deontic Logic" (*Mind,* vol. 60, 1951), and E. W. Hall, in *What Is Value?* (1952), have worked out distinctive syntactical forms which they hold to be suitable for ethical reasoning. However, Hall's syntactical scheme points at most to a "three-valued" logic, and Von Wright's calculus to a quasi-"modal" system —both variants of ordinary deductive procedures.

wedding between the descriptive and prescriptive elements in the meaning of normative judgments, so that their offspring are made logically legitimate.

Thus, if we introduce a prescriptive element into the premises, imperatives can be shown to follow the same forms, deductive or inductive, as indicative sentences. Hare offers as an analysis of the imperative syllogism:

> Use an axe or a saw!
> Do not use an axe!
> Therefore use a saw!

the following expansion of it:

> Use of an axe or saw by you shortly, please!
> No use of an axe by you shortly, please!
> Therefore use of a saw by you shortly, please!
> ("Imperative Sentences," *Mind,* vol. 58, 1949.)

The descriptive element follows the pattern of the ordinary disjunctive syllogism, and the imperative element ("please") does not affect the pattern, and gives rise to valid inference, provided it is included at the appropriate point in the process. Such a technique at least offers hope of dispelling the mysteries of the seductive logic; whether it can offer a marriage between the two parties that is made in heaven, or at least by the natural affinities of the parties concerned and not by the philosopher's shotgun, is a matter yet to be determined.

5

Have Naturalists Committed the Naturalistic Fallacy?

1. Moore's Criticisms of Mill

Let us summarize the various criticisms of naturalism which, as indicated in the preceding chapters, are now current under the label of the Naturalistic Fallacy. Since at this point we do not wish to prejudge the issue as to whether the alleged fallacies are really fallacious, let us call them simply the Naturalistic Theses. And, since it is still to be determined whether people who call themselves, or are called, naturalists, actually hold these theses, let us regard the label "Naturalistic Theses" itself as though it were enclosed in quotation marks. The characterization of naturalism by means of them, it should be noted, has been made by the critics of naturalism; the theses are not slogans devised and adopted by the naturalists themselves. We find, then, four theses or assumptions one or more of which are alleged to be held by naturalists and to be the source of their errors:

NT 1: That the meaning of a normative term can be *analyzed* without remainder into non-normative or factual characteristics.

NT 2: That an ethical term can be *defined* by means of non-normative or descriptive terms alone.

NT 3: That a normative judgment is a descriptive or factual *statement* rather than some other kind of expression such as an interjection or a command.

NT 4: That a normative judgment can be inferred, deductively or inductively, from non-normative premises alone.

Of these four, only *NT 4* can in the proper sense be called a fallacy, *i.e.,* a formal error in reasoning, though the others— which, if mistaken, would consist rather in the faulty practice of analysis or in incorrect doctrines as to the meaning of normative terms—might in the process of argumentation give rise to errors in inference.

All four ways of stating the issue agree in holding that the naturalistic error in its various forms springs from omitting something essential from the analysis of normative terms. According to the intuitionists, naturalism overlooks a non-natural quality or relation, largely ineffable but at least characterizable negatively as grasped in some other way than through the ordinary procedures of sense-perception or introspection. The two non-cognitivist schools, being unable to find such a non-natural property, agree that naturalism leaves something out, but propose that we take the element omitted to consist in the non-cognitive meaning or function of the term, whether that be labeled "emotive," "imperative," "prescriptive," "ascriptive," "performative," "commendatory," etc.

The emotivists and informalists, however, as we have seen, go much farther than this minimum criticism of the naturalists. They hold that the basic cognitivist fallacy, shared by the naturalists with the intuitionists, consists in treating a normative judgment as referring to a property at all. The non-cognitivists would answer the question, "Is value a property?" by a flat negative. And by this negative they mean to deny not only that goodness is a *mere* property, but even that it is a property *plus.* Reference to properties, they admit, is involved in the analysis and justification of normative judgments; but they believe that there is no one property that can be assigned as the stable core of the descriptive element in the term's meaning. For the emotivists, the descriptive element is hopelessly variable, and any uniformity in the meaning must be sought in the non-cognitive factor. According to those who use the "good reasons" approach, the reasons we offer in support of ethical judgments point to a variety of properties, some of which are relevant and some irrelevant, but there is no common and systematic structure exemplified by the properties referred to, so that we could hope to express the descriptive element in a coherent body of theory, as the cognitivists have assumed through their search for a set of comprehensive principles.

The basic naturalistic error, both for the intuitionists and for the non-cognitivists, thus consists in assuming that we have grasped a natural or descriptive property as constituting the meaning of the normative term, and then proceeding to infer that because something has this property it is therefore good or right. Where the naturalist does commit himself to NT 4, then, the fallacy in the inference is not a simple formal error in logic but goes back to a more radical error consisting in an inadequate assumption as to the meaning of normative terms.

Let us, accordingly, take a brief glance at the history of naturalistic theories in order to see if the leading naturalists have actually held any or all of the four theses imputed to them. We shall, I think, find grounds for holding that the critics of the empiricists have read them hastily and even with malice aforethought; and for doubting that they have actually committed the errors with which they are charged, at least in the simplified way in which they are accused of doing so. We expect British philosophers to acquire their opinions about

American philosophy by divination, but there seems to be less excuse for such cavalier treatment of a good Englishman like J. S. Mill.

It is necessary to start with the latter, since it was Moore's criticisms of him which touched off the whole controversy, and which are still cited by many as the decisive arguments against naturalism. Moore's most often quoted criticism was directed against NT 4, which is, as stated in recent controversy: "That a normative statement can be inferred, deductively or inductively, from non-normative premises alone." Moore charged that Mill's "proof" of the principle of utility rested on his using the term "desirable" in an ethical sense in his conclusion and in a non-ethical sense in his premise.[1] Mill's conclusion is that "happiness is desirable, and the only thing desirable, as an end." "Desirable" is here used in a normative sense, where its meaning is equivalent to, or inclusive of, "good." The reasoning by which Mill supports this conclusion is:

The only proof capable of being given that an object is visible is that people actually see it. The only proof that a sound is audible is that people hear it; and so of the other sources of our experience. In like manner, I apprehend, the sole evidence it is possible to produce that anything is desirable is that people do actually desire it.

The fallacy, according to Moore, consists in taking "desirable" in the premises to mean "able to be desired," just as "visible" means "able to be seen," whereas in the conclusion it means

----

[1] In the following discussion of Moore's criticisms of Mill, I am much indebted to E. W. Hall's "The 'Proof' of Utility in Bentham and Mill" (Ethics, vol. 60, 1949), though our interpretations disagree on a number of points. See also R. H. Popkin's "A Note on the 'Proof' of Utility in Mill" (Ethics, vol. 61, 1950).

what *ought* to be desired, or *deserves* to be desired. In the first case it is used in a descriptive sense, in the second in an ethical sense. We thus have, it appears, a clear case of NT 4 which amounts to the fallacy of shifting terms. And this in turn, Moore argues, goes back to Mill's error in holding NT 1 or NT 2, as shown by his statement "that to think of an object as desirable (unless for the sake of its consequences), and to think of it as pleasant, are one and the same thing"; or by his equating intrinsic good with pleasure and the supreme good with happiness—both of these being psychological concepts.

This famous passage of Mill's is elliptical and itself full of confusions. But when it is read in context, it cannot be held to be the simple and clear-cut example of the fallacy that it is taken to be. In interpreting it, we must above all ask what it is whose "proof" is in question. The critics fail to distinguish between the ways of establishing a particular value judgment, such as "This poem is good" or "This action is right," and a general normative principle such as the principle of utility itself. Mill is explicitly concerned here only with the latter, though the analogy which he uses when regarded out of context suggests that he is treating both kinds of normative expressions in the same way. When we look at Mill's position as a whole, it is clear that he never holds that a *normative judgment*—i.e., an assertion that an individual thing or kind of thing is good or right—can be inferred from a factual statement alone, such as a statement that something is desired or desirable. According to Mill, it can be inferred only from a factual minor premise *together with a major premise* which is at the level of a "principle" and can itself be "proved" only in a special sense of proof. For a moral judgment proper, the major premise is always the principle of utility; for a judgment of intrinsic value it is the hedonistic principle. The simplest scheme for establishing a normative judgment, consequently, would be of the following form:

> Whatever is pleasant (or desirable for its
> own sake) is good in itself.
> This is pleasant (etc.).
> Therefore, this is good in itself.

Or:

> Whatever leads to the greatest happiness is right.
> This action leads to the greatest happiness.
> Therefore this action is right.

The ethical term "good" or "right" is not "smuggled" into the conclusion as Moore charges; on the contrary, it is explicitly introduced through the ethical principle, which serves as the major premise. Mill does hold that a minor premise of a factual character is also required, and this he refers to as the "evidence" for the conclusion, but no inference is possible unless this evidence is taken in conjunction with the principle.

In the passage about the desirable, Mill is not directly concerned with how a particular ethical judgment is established, but, as the title of the chapter indicates, with "what sort of proof the principle of utility is susceptible." And here indeed he ultimately does, after a roundabout argument, base the acceptance of the principle in part on a question of psychological fact—*i.e.,* psychological hedonism or the supposed descriptive or explanatory law that we can never desire anything for its own sake but pleasure and the absence of pain. I believe that Mill's reasoning here was faulty. But his error, if error it was, did not consist, as Moore and his followers suggest, in naïvely overlooking a glaring ambiguity in the term "desirable," nor in a simple mistake in formal logic. Mill was struggling seriously if not very successfully with the most difficult problem in ethical theory: namely, the problem of how ethical principles are justified. He was quite explicitly aware that neither the principle of utility, nor any ultimate principle in any other field, is "capable of proof in the ordinary and popular meaning of the term." And if he finally rested his proof of the utilitarian principle, in his Pickwickian sense of proof, upon some kind of appeal to the facts of human nature, he did so with his eyes open and not by way of a simple lapse in logic. Mill at least has the merit, not shared by his more contemptuous critics, of basing the question of justification of principles on an examination of the wider context in human nature and society out of which they arise and within which they function, and not upon a simple appeal to self-evidence or common sense or ordinary usage.

Whatever Mill's shortcomings—and his discussion of these matters is certainly too brief and too unguarded to be satisfying in the light of questions that have subsequently been raised—he was actually less open to such criticisms than a number of other empiricists. He did not take first principles as simple empirical "hypotheses" to be verified forthrightly by the ordinary inductive procedures. When we get to first principles, we reach the limits of ordinary deductive-inductive "proof"—and Mill agreed with Moore explicitly on this point, even though he sought other means than intuition as a recourse in dealing with this problem.

Part of Mill's difficulty in giving an adequate statement of his position springs from the fact that, far from ignoring the non-cognitive factor, he explicitly recognizes it. One reason he gives why his first principle cannot be "proved" is that its peculiar function is to "propose an end" and not simply to make an assertion of fact. "Questions of ultimate ends are incapable of proof. . . ." The supreme ethical principle, then, is not an assertion that goodness and pleasure are *in fact* identical,[2] or that these words are in fact used synonymously,

---

[2] We can't even say that Mill proposes to *identify* them. In practice he usually treats the distinctive normative force of "good," "right," etc., as more adequately expressed by "desirable" or "pref-

but a proposal to take pleasure as the ultimate end and hence as the distinguishing mark of goodness. Whatever a proposal may be, whether in philosophy or in courtship, it is not simply a statement about one's feelings or about any other existing state of affairs.

It is unfortunate that Moore and his followers have based their criticisms entirely on the popular treatise, *Utilitarianism,* and have ignored Mill's more technical handling of the matter in the final section of his earlier work, *A System of Logic.* There Mill states as forthrightly as possible:

Now, the imperative mood is the characteristic of art, as distinguished from science. Whatever speaks in rules or precepts, not in assertions respecting matters of fact, is art; and ethics or morality is properly a portion of the art corresponding to the sciences of human nature and society.

The method, therefore, of Ethics, can be no other than that of Art, or Practice, in general. . . .

Mill declares clearly that a judgment of Art or Practice is not itself a descriptive or cognitive assertion:

The relation in which rules of art stand to doctrines of science may be thus characterised. The art proposes to itself an end to be attained, defines the end, and hands it over to the science. The science receives it, considers it as a phenomenon or effect to be studied, and having investigated its causes and conditions, sends it

---

erable"—*i.e.,* in conative terms—than by such affective notions as pleasure and happiness. Those empirical theories which stress the conative rather than the affective do so, as I shall argue in Chapter 11, because of their sense that conative terms, being more active than are the affective, are better fitted to express the prescriptive force of normative words.

back to art with a theorem of the combination of circumstances by which it could be produced. Art then examines these combinations of circumstances, and according as any of them are or are not in human power, pronounces the end attainable or not. The only one of the premises, therefore, which Art supplies is the original major premise, which asserts that the attainment of the given end is desirable. Science then lends to Art the proposition (obtained by a series of inductions or of deductions) that the performance of certain actions will attain the end. From these premises Art concludes that the performance of these actions is desirable, and finding it also practicable, converts the theorem into a rule or precept.

Far from wishing to reduce the "ought" to the "is," Mill distinguished them explicitly:

A proposition of which the predicate is expressed by the words *ought* or *should be,* is generically different from one expressed by is or will be. . . .

Mill's language itself has an up-to-the-minute ring. He speaks not of proving but of "justifying" normative judgments and principles; and he approaches the problem of justification by examining how we give "reasons." His difference from the contemporary non-cognitivists, however, consists in his insistence that the recognition of a non-scientific or non-descriptive element at the core of ethical assertions by no means excludes the possibility of a systematic investigation and exhibition of the cognitive factors: "Now the reasons of a maxim or policy, or of any other rule of art, can be no other than the theorems of the corresponding science." Mill does not develop this point in detail in a satisfactory way, but the ensuing discussion makes clear that, although he speaks of a "Logic of Practice" distinct from a logic of science, and characterized by its use of the imperative mood, he conceives the two to be, so far as their logical structure goes, isomorphic;

and he does not, like contemporary proponents of a third logic, suggest that the Logic of Practice must seek patterns of inference radically different from the forms supplied by ordinary deductive and inductive logic.

Not only, then, would Mill have rejected *NT 4*, but as the passages just quoted make clear, he explicitly repudiated *NT 3*. Far from being a mere factual assertion, the very distinguishing mark of an ethical judgment is its imperative force. But for him it is not a mere imperative; it has a cognitive significance also.

Although *prima facie* there seem to be better reasons for attributing to Mill *NT 1* and *NT 2*—he does speak of goodness and pleasure as "synonymous," and likewise of happiness and the desirable—it is clear that he did not conceive pleasure and happiness as cold descriptive terms, but as referring to properties which by their nature hold an imperative force, or exert a normative tug upon us. But his position on these points is not developed; he neither concerns himself in detail with defining the good and the right formally nor with analyzing normative terms as distinct from normative judgments.

2. *20th Century Naturalists*

When we consider the leading 20th Century spokesmen for empiricism, we find it doubtful that any of them would have subscribed without many qualifications to any of the four theses stated at the beginning of this chapter. For example, in Santayana's *The Life of Reason* (1905) which was widely influential in fostering a naturalistic position in value theory during the first part of this period, we find: "Rational ethics is an embodiment of a living volition, not a description of it. It is the expression of living interest, preference and categorical choice. . . . The rational moralist is not . . . a mere spectator [but] represents a force energising in the world."

Recognition of the expressive or prescriptive force of a moral judgment was not, however, for Santayana, a ground for denying that there could be a "science" of normative principles, and consequently he did not feel it inappropriate to include his discussion of ethics in Volume 5 of *The Life of Reason*, entitled *Reason in Science*. The science—indicated rather than elaborated by Santayana—consisted in a body of principles constructed by dialectic out of human impulses and feelings as its materials and its guiding strings.

The chapter on "Moral Truth" in Santayana's *The Realm of Truth* (1938), is a more explicit effort to grapple with the relation between cognitive and non-cognitive factors. For example: ". . . The nerve of moral judgment is preference: and preference is a feeling or an impulse to action which cannot be either false or true." The term morality refers most appropriately, not to a set of maxims or other judgments, but to "actual allegiances in sentiment and action to this or that ideal of life." There would remain a "descriptive science to be called ethics or the science of manners." It would not be suitable, however, to restrict the term "truth" to the propositions of such a psychology or anthropology of morals. Although moral judgments resemble imperatives in many of their uses —"For that which creates morality is not facts, nor the consequences of facts, but human terror or desire feeling its way amid those facts and those consequences"—a judgment can be said to be "true morally" if "it will express the bias of human nature. . . . This Socratic self-knowledge is not scientific but expressive, not ethical but moral." Ethical theory may consist in the search to define the common human tendency, but moral judgments proper, according to Santayana's version of moral relativism, are true when they express the sincere preferences of the individual who has made himself representative of human nature. The chapter is brief, and passes jauntily over many thorny issues, but it makes abundantly clear that Santayana does not hold a moral judgment to be merely a descriptive assertion.

The first section of Chapter I of R. B. Perry's *General Theory of Value*, the most detailed and most systematic exposition of a naturalistic theory of value yet written in the United States, is headed "Criticism vs. Description," and theory of value is assigned to the domain of the former. His working out of the theory, however, does not keep the distinction clearly in mind. Value, as "any object of any interest," is defined in descriptive or factual terms alone, and the various types of value judgments are treated as ordinary cognitive assertions. Thus an interest judgment, by stating the "expectation" involved, "mediates" between the interest and its object by stating the means of its realization. It is evident, however, that the total function of the interest judgment for Perry is not merely to state something about the object but also to express and to convey the urgency of the interest itself and hence has an imperative force. In a "judgment of value"—which Perry distinguishes from an interest judgment—the interest expressed by the former is explicitly characterized, so that it is relative to the uses of the judgment whether we forthrightly refer to, or merely assume and "express," the non-cognitive factors that are operating.

We would expect pragmatic ethical theories, with their emphasis on action and vital equilibrium, to be very explicitly concerned with the non-cognitive context of valuation, and indeed we find in Dewey and Lewis sustained efforts to take them into account; although because of the commitment of pragmatists to a general scientific orientation, there is a more central emphasis upon the cognitive element. But Lewis says plainly: ". . . That to which value terms apply is always characterized by something holding an imperative for action. Thus if one says, 'The good is pleasure,' then either his statement explicates correctly the nature of that which gives direction to rational conduct or else it is false and has consequences which may be devastating." And again: "the primary and pervasive significance of knowledge lies in its guidance of action: knowing is for the sake of doing." In fact, empiricists of other schools would take this to be an overstatement of the subordination of knowledge to other functions.

Far from conceiving ethical judgments as detached descriptions or predictions, Dewey iterates to the point of tedium the thesis that they have the practical function of reconstructing the "situation" and restoring harmony to experience. In fact, he emphasizes so much the practical and transforming role of all judgments that the tendency is to absorb even so-called scientific judgments as instruments of valuational activity, so that the distinction between "scientific" and "normative" becomes blurred, not by reducing the normative to the descriptive but rather in the opposite way: through insufficient recognition of the partial independence of the descriptive or cognitive from its normative uses.

Even this hasty sampling of representative empirical or naturalistic positions indicates that an injustice is done to them when they are reduced to a simple syllogism which smuggles into the conclusion an element that has been omitted from the premises, or when they are treated as holding ethical judgments to be derivable from purely descriptive observations without the aid of principles that acknowledge the normative element proper. We must recall that naturalists themselves have never defined naturalism in slogans that invoke the fallacies with which they are charged, even though they may have unguardedly lapsed into these fallacies.

The recent criticisms, however, have created a quite legitimate demand that empiricists in the detailed development of their theories should make clearer than they have done the precise relationship of the cognitive to the non-cognitive factors, and should explore more fully than they have done the logic of normative reasoning. A good deal of the effort of empirical theories has gone into the search for definitions of ethical concepts, and here the cognitive element alone is usually mentioned in the definition. This tendency is understandable, granted the conception of a definition held by these writers, but it has reinforced the impression that empiricists have mutilated the total meaning and concentrated unduly on the cognitive elements.

The critics of empiricism have at least directed our attention to certain important logical and semiotical questions which empiricists have not sufficiently considered, and to which none of the parties to the controversy have found an adequate solution. There is equally good ground, however, for believing that the intuitionists and non-cognitivists, for all their contributions, have reached the limits of advance by the methods they have used hitherto, and that solution of the riddles in which ethical theory is bogged, and in particular a more precise determination of the relation between knowledge and the other factors, can be made only by renewed attention to the larger natural and social context of valuations, emphasized by naturalism and largely neglected by recent schools of analysis for more restricted questions of logic and meaning.

6

The Matrix Meaning

1. *The "Warm" and the "Cold" Language of Valuation*

On the most disputed issue, that of the cognitive versus the non-cognitive, the upshot of the foregoing is that at least one of the cognitivist schools, the empiricists, not only would, when pressed, agree with the non-cognitivists that normative judgments have other important and central functions besides the conveying of information and the altering of beliefs, but actually at various points in their systems have so insisted, even though they have not carried out the analysis of the non-cognitive functions systematically.

The intuitionists have perhaps been less forthright in making such admissions than the empiricists, tending to make the expressive or prescriptive uses of ethical terms merely a consequence, or some other kind of subsidiary accompaniment, of their cognitive reference to non-natural properties rather than a direct intention of the ethical judgment, and hence the intuitionists are less disposed to admit the non-cognitive functions into the "meaning." Thus Moore, replying to Stevenson, writes:

I am still inclined to think that there is no 'typically ethical' sense of 'It was right of Brutus to stab Caesar' such that a man, who asserted that it was right in that sense, would, as a rule, be *asserting* that he approved this action of Brutus'. I think there is certainly a 'typically ethical' sense such that a man, who asserted that it was right in that sense would be *implying* that at the time of speaking he approved of it, or did not disapprove, or at least had some kind of mental 'attitude' towards it. ("A Reply to My Critics," *The Philosophy of G. E. Moore*, edited by Schilpp.)

This sense of "imply," Moore goes on to make clear, is not the ordinary logical sense, and in any case is incidental to the main purport of the assertion. But Moore writes that he also has a conflicting "inclination" to accept an emotive theory, and that he does not know which inclination is the stronger. For many years Moore has refrained from writing about ethics in detail, and it appears that he is no longer disposed to defend intuitionism, though he is equally unprepared to repudiate it.

It makes a good deal of difference just which of the various types of non-cognitive meaning we are considering and in what specific kind of normative judgment; so that even though the "expressive" function may be held to be of subsidiary importance, it is hard so to treat the prescriptive or imperative function. Moore devotes considerable space, in the writing in question, to the issue of whether goodness has a synthetic or analytic connection with the "ought" or the normative, and speaks as though one of the crucial marks of the "ought" is the compulsiveness or prescriptiveness that it exerts upon action and decision.

But it would be unprofitable to pursue further the question of the presence, or comparative importance, of the cognitive and the non-cognitive in general, without trying to exhibit with some precision the exact roles that the two play, and their relation to each other.

When we first try to treat this question systematically, we

find ourselves plunged into the middle of things. The ethical language that we have to analyze has been long in process of formation; the process has been largely haphazard, but not wholly uncritical. We are forced to begin with the assumption that our current uses of the terms are the result of a gradual selection, social and experiential, and that the terms in use are not totally unfit instruments for the jobs they are called on to do. We must assume likewise that these jobs are in large part necessary jobs, and there is an initial presumption that no kind of function that language serves is to be discarded until it has been shown to be worthless. On the other hand, there is no justification for assuming either that we have a full realization of what the jobs are, or that we have finally perfected the linguistic instruments for their accomplishment.

A word like "good" or "ought" does multiple duty. It may serve to call attention to certain properties of objects or acts; it may serve to convey a threat, naked or veiled; it may relieve pent-up feeling or express a personal preference; it may command, or cajole, or recommend, or incite revolt, or further cooperative activity; it may seek to shackle the individual to iron custom or liberate him for realization of a unique personal possibility of being; it may enforce the brutality of a selfish desire or urge the furtherance of the most disinterested aspirations of the human community. It may do these and a thousand other things, singly or in combination.

How can we speak of "the" meaning of such a term? Is it even necessary to seek for "the" meaning?

We are in practice aware that the term has a multiplicity of uses, and we may be less unclear about this multiplicity in our working understanding of the term than in our theoretical analyses. We are often not bothered about the ambiguities, because the term's context renders the application clear in the particular case; and we are aided by the grammatical form or the tone of voice.

Such considerations—urged most emphatically by Philosophy of Ordinary Language among the four schools under examination—should remain with us throughout any theoretical inquiry into the language of ethics. They should remind us that it is extremely unlikely that any set of definitions or analyses upon which ethical theory may seize can be final, complete and adequate to the subject matter. Valuational situations are indefinitely complex and various, and a flexible language is necessary to take account of these nuances. For this reason, "ordinary language" can never be wholly replaced by a language whittled, sharpened and dovetailed by philosophers or scientists. With all its patches of vagueness and ambiguity, ordinary language has the necessary plasticity to reach out and grasp new subtleties in the subject matter and new shadings of need, attitude and feeling in the human enterprises that valuational language serves. Somewhere in our language, or languages, of valuation we must make provision for the aptitude of the poet—and of the plain man who is not wholly dulled by conditioning to clichés through the newspapers, radio and group pressures—to grasp the flavor of the novel and the unique. Nor should we lose that equivalent of the actor's "running comment by tone, look and gesture" which, according to Coleridge, makes discourse dramatic when it retains a sense of the context.

Our valuational discourse oscillates between two poles of linguistic utterance, which we may refer to as a "warm" and a "cold" language of valuation, though without equating this with the dichotomy of emotive-cognitive. The "warm" is poetic, dramatic or religious; it has an expressive character. It realizes, by foretaste and pantomime, the fulfillment of the value. It effects a mimesis or an enactment. It gives us a "knowledge" of the values to be expected from the act by presenting them in their concreteness, their ambiguity, their massive and vivid quality. It gives us their texture, rhythm and resonance; it evokes contexts and, being metaphorical, makes comparisons and elaborates archetypal myths. It can be highly deceptive, for by itself it has little predictive value. It abstracts partly, though not wholly, from conditions and consequences, and realizes by foretaste consummations in disjunction from much of the labor that earns them. (Though this labor may be conveyed in foreshortened form, much of its daily tedium and constriction is diminished by ellipsis.) The poet and the prophet confront us with love or beatitude or torment realized so that, if we take these as real possibilities for our lives, an act of faith is demanded of us.

When we have followed the poet or prophet and been disappointed, as so often happens, we shall be wary in future. We shall say at most: this is how it *might* be, and we try to test the vision. We seek to pass from mere faith to experientially confirmed anticipation: the vision becomes an hypothesis. We wish to know if the hypothesis rests on an illusion about the way things are, or on a delirium created by the poet's fever, or on a rare conjunction of circumstances not available to us in our own impoverished life situation. For all this fallibility and potential trickery, the warm language is indispensable to the envisagement of values in their fullness; who lives with sensitivity to the possibilities of experience if he has not been tricked by the poets?

We can indeed to some extent achieve, without the poetic articulation, the consummations that it prepares us for and points us toward. But the enactment of values, like any other skill, requires rehearsal. For one thing, we need practice in subduing the will, in yielding to the consummatory moment when it arrives, in setting at rest the conations that hound us. For another, we need practice in taking many things in at once, in holding them together in a design and bringing them to a focus. Without complexity mastered, the consummatory experience will not have resonance. The complexity can stir a resonance only if its components are held together in expression by a symbolic pattern: only so can their conditions or constituents in our organism be set vibrating and reinforce each other. Full apprehension and enjoyment require some measure of symbolization, and the inarticulate man symbolizes only in a rudimentary fashion. The arts and religion are the chief means of implanting skill in symbolizing immediate values. Without the rehearsal they give us, life would come only to a stunted flowering.

But a life that is nurtured only by the presentations of immediate values in the arts will not come to flowering at all; it will be cut short by frost and drought. The hard business of survival, of weeding and tilling, is accomplished by a tougher and colder language: "This is good" and "That is wrong." Consequently the language of morals has for the most part a different timbre from the language of poetry. It means business, even though the business should be conducted ultimately to provide the things of the spirit. What we have, at any rate, are two opposed directions of language, each with its own type of controls: the one devised for presentation, expression and suggestion of values and disvalues in their full immediacy, the other stripped and trimmed to suit the purposes of their attainment in an existential context that resists and frustrates.

The distinction does not exactly coincide with that between ends and means, or intrinsic and extrinsic values. In fact, the indispensable terms "end" and "intrinsic good" are themselves part of the cold language; and we can use coldly descriptive or analytic language in defining or characterizing them. Conversely, the warm language of poetry and ritual can incorporate the working of means and their interpenetration with ends. If poetry gives us a paradigm of the experience in its wholeness, it cannot concentrate on ends in divorce from means. In fact, only by conveying the constriction of the yearning and the labor can it suggest the massiveness and the fierce ecstasy of the fulfillment.

The ordinary language in which we talk about values is a blend of warm and cold discourse, neither being developed to its limit. Hence the strength of ordinary language: it mediates between the two extreme developments, and brings them into relationship with each other. Philosophy, being itself a mediating activity, must retain the flexibility of that language.

But there still remains a job for the ethical theorist to do in the way of precise and systematic statement and definition. Like poetry, ordinary usage and everyday moral thinking have their imperfections in the way of obscurity and indeterminacy; and in morals as elsewhere it is sometimes desirable to know what we mean as exactly as possible. This need is answered by the refinement of a cold language, though the elucidation of such a language requires warmth and plasticity of expression at the edges.

The theorist must carve out local areas of precision; and he soon finds that he cannot do so piecemeal by *ad hoc* analyses in this region any more than in science. It is the very fact that one thing in experience is related to many others that leads him to seek some kind of general pattern, to construct a system however provisional and tentative. Then he not only becomes critical of ordinary language but seeks to replace it for certain purposes either by neologisms, or by old words, in novel juxtapositions, to which a sharpened meaning has been assigned. To the extent that he is successful, these new terms or meanings may pass into "ordinary language" itself, though they often slip into it imperceptibly to all but historians of ideas and lexicon-makers. Just as the language of common sense knowledge is the language of dead—or partially surviving—metaphysics, so the language of everyday valuation bears the impress, however blurred, of moral philosophers.

2. The "Ought" as a Trigger

To begin with, what we have to do is to find the central and indispensable jobs that ethical terms have to perform, to relate these to each other in orderly fashion, and then to make allowances for the marginal and exceptional functions.

We can get at these central functions by examining the structure of the ethical or valuational act, and the structure of the situation in which this act takes place. Whatever other functions such terms as "good" and "ought" have performed, these terms find their appropriate uses in relation to the inescapable necessity for *choice* or *decision*.

Man, like any other animal, must act, and he is faced with alternative ways of acting. He is driven by needs and desires, some of which he must satisfy and some of which he must renounce; he apprehends various possible goals that promise to satisfy these needs and desires, he becomes aware of different alternative paths to these goals, and he is faced with a choice of responses by which he may take a given path to a given goal. All these factors are potentially present even in the case of a rat at a "choice point" in a maze, where he hesitates before making, at a primitive behavioral level, the rat's nearest analogue to a "decision." He may choose whether to satisfy hunger or thirst, whether to take the path that leads to one kind of food or to another, whether to eat or to starve to death, whether to trust one set of perceptual signs rather than another, whether to gallop confidently to his chosen goal or to sniff along cautiously. Morally sensitive human beings have to choose among many other factors in the situation, but in any complicated perplexity they always have to include the kinds of factors that confront the rat.

Rats always, and human beings often, make such choices without verbalizing the process. But when the human being does formulate fully in language the process by which he

reaches the decision, the last utterance he makes before performing the action on which he has decided is ordinarily "This
is the right thing to do," or "I ought to do this," or some
equivalent. The "ought" or the "right" therefore *expresses the*
fact that a choice has been made, and serves as a signal to
release the action. This, which we may call the trigger function, at any rate is the indispensable function of the "ought."

The term may be used with a slightly different effect in
certain preliminary phases of the process; and it may not in
fact release the act, because of weakness of the flesh, or some
other inhibiting factor. But this is its primary use, even though
the utterance of the word may not always suffice to execute
it. Some of these related uses of the "ought" may be compared
to the loading, cocking and aiming of the gun rather than to
the pulling of the trigger. Indeed the "ought" in the *question*
"Ought I to do this?" usually serves as a safety catch, checking
decision until the aim has been calculated more carefully. Yet
all these operations are useless unless they eventuate in the
firing itself. And in a practical context even the question
"Ought I to do what I ought?" if it is to have significance at all
contemplates for the first ought an eventual categorically imperative function, though the second is imperative only conditionally.

The "ought" thus includes what is conveyed by the gerundive—it embodies the recognition that an act is the one *to be*
done—and sometimes is limited to this; but at its maximum
effectiveness it has a stronger force. The notion of the "gerundive," with which Toulmin equates it, is a shade too weak,
too merely contemplative, to convey this. The "ought" not only
expresses the apprehension that this is to be done, but prompts
the doing of it. Consequently, if we are to treat the matter in
grammatical terms, the force of the "ought," when it is operating most effectively, is imperative and not merely gerundive.
When it is fully performing its function, it serves as a com-

mand—whether given by someone else or by the agent to himself—and leads directly to the act. It signifies that the bridges have been burned, and that the moment to take the plunge of acting has come irrevocably. In this sense the moral imperative is *categorical:* it depends upon many conditions, but these conditions are either resolved or shoved aside when the moment of decision arrives.

The imperative of the "ought" is not categorical in the sense that it carries with it an assurance of certainty, or that it is derived from an indubitable moral law. Often it is accompanied by the most harrowing doubts about the rightness of the decision. Its categorical character resides in the recognition that the time has come to act, that further deliberation and delay would carry with it greater risks than those arising from the semi-darkness in which the act is made, that the moment has come to move into the irreversible future. It is fully compatible with the awareness that many conditions which ideally would be relevant have not been explored or are not practically knowable, and even with the awareness that we are far from confident as to the adequacy of the very standards on which the decision is based.

3. *Finding the Aim*

Although the full-fledged "ought" thus serves a function ordinarily expressed in the imperative mood, so to characterize it nevertheless has misleading suggestions. In its moral uses, the "ought" conveys a special kind of imperative. If it were a mere imperative, we should say simply, "Do this!" or, as does the army sergeant, "March!" rather than "I ought to do this."

One of the elements—and for our present purposes the crucial one—left out by the naked imperative is the suggestion that the command follows from knowledge and commitment. We use the "ought" to conclude a process of investigation or deliberation. Even the rat, when he chooses his path, has taken account of the situation in the way of perceptual cognition. The human being has done this, and usually more. He has taken account of the situation perceptually, and further has symbolized, to a greater or less extent verbally, the relevant features of the act and the situation, and has submitted them to test by the moral standards to which he is committed. The ought, therefore, not merely serves as a signal for the performance of the act, but connotes that this act has been decided on as a result of taking thought. The term "prescriptive," consequently, is better fitted to convey this element in the meaning of the ought than is the term "imperative." For a doctor's prescription ordinarily follows from a diagnosis (at any rate if we are optimistic about doctors). As Charles Morris has put it: "The term 'ought' is complex in its signification; it is a general sign that the prescriptor in which it appears can be grounded, though the grounds are not themselves signified. . . ." (*Signs, Language and Behavior*, 1946.) Even though the sentence containing the word "ought" does not itself state the grounds or reasons, it suggests that there are reasons, that they have been weighed, and that the conclusion is dictated by them and not by the whim of the speaker. The squeezing of the trigger has a *raison d'être* only if we have rationally chosen our target, estimated the trajectory, and steadied our aim.

But in one respect "prescriptive" is less suited to convey the full force of the ought than is the term imperative. For a prescription is not ordinarily penultimate to the act, as is a command. We use our discretion about having the doctor's prescription filled after he has given it to us, and after that about actually taking the medicine. The terms "imperative" and "prescriptive," taken in combination, come nearer to expressing the central force of the ought than either of them singly. But there is no need to rely on either a single or a double synonym, since we can make the matter clear in a preliminary way by saying that the central force of the ought is to set in motion an act after a process of deliberation and to do so with the sanction afforded by knowledge of the situation and by submission of the act to our standards of conduct.

Now what has preceded is far from a complete analysis of the moral ought. For one thing, it does not express the variety of the derived and otherwise related uses which the term has in the context of living language. There are many cases in which the "ought" does not directly release action, and is not so intended—as when I ask whether Brutus ought to have stabbed Caesar, or what the President of the United States ought to do about Indo-China, or what I ought to do next year if such-and-such a situation arises. Here the descriptive meaning is to the fore rather than the prescriptive, but the "ought" nevertheless makes a statement *about* a contemplated prescription, past, present, or future; and it may retain some prescriptive force, even though conditionally.

Secondly, it does not convey the complexity of meaning that the term "ought" in its distinctively moral sense has for a highly reflective and highly sensitive moral agent, who is the product of many centuries of ethical experience and ethical reflection. The analysis offered so far simply describes the central job the "ought" does, without telling us how it does that job, or giving us the criteria for the term's application. For a full understanding of the meaning of the term, we must know not merely *that* it prescribes, but *who or what* does the prescribing—whether God, or the mores, or a bully, or our impulses, or the ideals that express our life-involvements. In other words, we must deal with the difficult question of the nature of the moral authority; and the whole vexing problem of motivation enters here. Nor does it tell us what kind of knowledge is relevant to moral decisions; it simply tells us that the decision expressed by the "ought" professes to have taken account of such knowledge as is available and pertinent.

The trigger function by itself, therefore, corresponds roughly to that basic sense of the "ought" which Ewing equates with "fittingness" and not to the more inclusive notion of the "morally obligatory." The notion conveys the distinctive normative force of the term, its triggering of the act; but the full moral ought also invokes, among other things, the sanction of the moral authority. We shall see more precisely what is the relation of the two when, in Chapters 13 and 14, we try to put the pieces of our analysis together into a rounded account of the structure of the term's meaning in its various connected aspects.

We can justify the analysis we have given so far of the core of the "ought" in terms of the trigger function, not only by reference to the structure of the normative situation, but historically. Take any of the assumptions on which men have based their moral behavior—that the authority is God, or society, or the individual conscience, or the reason, etc. The authority is held to be a moral one, first, because it is the final voice in moving us to act, and second, because we accept God, or society, and so on, as affording *knowledge* of what is the right thing to do.

The trigger function of the term "ought," then, can be called its *Matrix Meaning*. It expresses in the valuational situation the broad general function of the ought out of which the more detailed meanings we assign to the term develop and crystallize. The more detailed meanings are discovered in the process of locating the acceptable authority, and in sifting out the properties of objects and of acts which fit them to evoke the prescriptive function.

It is promising, furthermore, to work on the hypothesis that the Matrix Meaning of "ought" is the basic Matrix Meaning for normative terms, and that the Matrix Meaning, or noncognitive function, of "good" in most of its uses is a function of it. "Good," in other words, usually conveys a *conditional prescription* (or in Kant's language a hypothetical imperative). When we say that apple pie, or Beethoven, or altruism, or representative government, is good, we are not ordinarily trying to pull a trigger and elicit an immediate act, though the word in many cases is used in this way. We are preparing a prescription to be executed if and when certain conditions are fulfilled, conditions which are expressed or unexpressed, fully explored or only partially explored.

The word "good," indeed, is often used with a categorical force, not only in such expressions as "You'll do this if you know what's good for you," which convey a threat. When a mother says to her child coaxingly, "This spinach is goo-ood," the child understands the admonition not merely, or primarily, as a statement about certain properties of spinach—such as that, if he wished to be a baseball star, it will help to make him strong—but as a parental injunction to eat it now. For this reason "good," sometimes with the adverb "morally" prefixed, is often treated as synonymous with "ought" or "right," and serves to release the trigger function.

Distinctively, however, and more commonly, "good" is used in preference to "ought" in a different kind of situation or at an earlier phase of moral deliberation. In a detached contemplative mood, we use it to point to certain properties of objects and acts, where even a conditional imperative is not under consideration. But the press of life is such that most goods are estimated when a decision is in the offing, even though it is not imminent. When we ask if a new play is good, we usually have some intention or hope of going to the theatre sooner or later, even though the time has not come to buy a ticket. The conclusion, "It is a good show," thus does not have the finality of a categorical imperative: we are not ready to put down our money. It means rather, "Buy a ticket for this play, *if* you wish to see a show, and *if* you can afford it, and *if* you have nothing better to do with an evening, and *if* you do not hear of a better play," etc. Thus "good" ordinarily plays a role in the preliminary phase of exploring the situation, of estimating in disjunction from each other the several values which are to be compounded and weighed when the moment of decision arrives. When we have once formulated an opinion explicitly or tacitly studded with such "ifs," then we can rationally proceed to the decision only provided that we have further explored the conditions to be satisfied and removed the "ifs."

The notions of both the intrinsically and the extrinsically good have this conditionally imperative force. The intrinsically good, indeed, is a step nearer to an unconditional prescription, but by itself it is still hypothetical rather than categorical. Leaving aside the question of what specific properties are referred to, "This is intrinsically good" means in part "Choose this in so far as you are concerned with it without regard to its feasibility and its consequences. . . ."; and "This is extrinsically good" means in part "Choose this in so far as you are concerned with it as a means of achieving intrinsic good or avoiding intrinsic evil. . . ." We may call these the Matrix Meanings of these species of goodness. Before the object is prescribed unconditionally, not only must the means and consequences be considered in the first case and the ends in the second, but still further conditions must be satisfied, such as the values of the alternatives in the particular situation, and the place of the object in the total context of the moral economy. The intrinsically good is a step nearer the ought only in the sense that questions about ends must always be resolved before the decision is taken, whereas in some rare cases the object presents itself for the taking without need for concern about means.

But the relation between "ought" and "good" cannot be fully stated until we have pointed to the other ingredients in the functioning of ethical terms besides the Matrix Meanings. These include the cognitive or descriptive element.

7

Principles and Maxims

1. Conferring and Identifying Properties

The Matrix Meaning by itself is empty and blind. It tells us to go, or to be ready to go, but not where to go. Although in the context of its normal use it suggests that the prescription is based upon knowledge, it does not tell us what this knowledge consists of. It prescribes an act, but leaves open the question what characteristics an act must have in order that it may be prescribed, and under what circumstances the act is suitable. These are cognitive questions, and we do not have a full understanding of the "ought" or the "good" unless we are able to "describe" such characteristic properties of the act or the situation. Consequently, in addition to the non-cognitive functions expressed by the Matrix Meaning, we are impelled to try to discover and state the nature of the knowledge elements.

When we examine the ways in which moralists and philosophers have sought to specify these cognitive factors, we find that they seize upon two kinds of properties. At the proverbial or what Santayana calls the "pre-rational" stage of moral reflection, the descriptive properties which elicit notice consist of characters having a comparatively low degree of generality—

those which confer goodness or badness, rightness or wrongness, upon objects and acts within a certain kind. Speaking the truth is morally right, breaking a promise is morally wrong. A balanced shaft makes a spear good; eloquence in counsel makes a good chieftain. Rules formulating such properties, and prescribing these for the attainment of certain ends or for the production of certain kinds of objects, remain of greater or less usefulness in the most developed practice of valuation. Of such a nature are prudential maxims, rules of social policy, recipes, medical prescriptions, technological formulae. We may say that they symbolize *Conferring Properties* of goodness or rightness, or one type at any rate of what various analysts, of the intuitionist persuasion, have referred to as "goodmaking" or "ought-implying" properties.

The general scheme for such rules, where CP_1 stands for a given Conferring Property, is as follows: If x has CP_1, then x is good (right, etc.) under conditions c; where c states the use of x, or its kind, or the circumstances under which it is to be employed. Such rules are empirical generalizations, based on practical experience or scientific computation; they are usually not intended as absolutely universal, but admit exceptions, and are therefore rather of the nature of probability statements or statistical tabulations.

Some of the informalists hold that maxims of this sort are the only generalizations of a cognitive sort that can legitimately be invoked in normative reasoning. Such maxims are "criteria" for the application of a term, and practical rules for guidance of conduct. Any attempt to state more general principles, such as definitions, upon which such maxims rest is held to be based upon a false analogy with the exact sciences.

It will be noticed that goodness or rightness is not defined by the informalists and is in effect held by those writers, such as Hampshire, who reject normative definitions, to be indefinable. We have what amounts to a *working knowledge* of what goodness or rightness means, and this working knowledge includes a grasp of the non-cognitive function of the term. So that the analysis of an ethical term is exhaustively reducible to the grasp of what I have called the Matrix Meaning together with the ability to furnish "reasons" consisting in the assertion that the x in question has certain Conferring Properties and therefore satisfies the criterion.

But ethical theory since Socrates has until these recent developments not rested content to leave the cognitive element at this level. It has assumed that it is possible to give definitions, or to state principles, having a higher degree of generality. Such principles do not assert the characteristics that confer goodness within a kind, but express properties common to all the things or acts of which any normative term, such as "intrinsically good," or "morally obligatory," can be asserted. The utilitarian principle, Perry's definitions of value in terms of interest at various levels, and Kant's formulations of the Categorical Imperative, are attempts to do this.

If it is possible to achieve such principles or definitions, what we have are general statements of the cognitive element in the meaning of normative terms. Such principles formulate the property—often a rather complex one—by which the presence of goodness, etc., can be identified. So we may speak of such characteristics as *Identifying Properties*. Sometimes ethical principles have an even stronger force: they may be construed as asserting that such properties do not merely identify the necessary and sufficient conditions of goodness, etc., but actually *constitute* the property of goodness. In this case, they would better be referred to as *Constitutive Properties*. But let us base our discussion on the search for Identifying Properties, which supply us with a somewhat more modest goal, leaving it for the time being an open question whether it may also be possible, at least in some cases, to find properties that have a claim to being constitutive.

We shall not even prejudge the issue as to whether there are Identifying Properties. Our concern at this point is simply to obtain clarity and precision in stating the problem of the meaning or analysis of normative terms. We want to know what Identifying Properties would do if we could find them.

For this purpose, our three-fold terminology (Matrix Meaning, Identifying Property and Conferring Property) has certain advantages over distinctions now in use, such as that between the "good" and the "good-making" and the "ought" and the "ought-implying." Such dichotomies conceal a number of problems, and the three-fold terminology may help in sharpening the points at issue. The intuitionists, for example, hold that there is an Identifying Property for ethical terms, but that this property is a non-natural property, known by intuition. Natural properties, of whatever degree of generality, are lumped together simply as "making" or "implying" properties. Yet one reason for invoking a non-natural property seems to be the normative tug, the obligatoriness or prescriptiveness, of the terms or concepts in question. We shall consequently ask whether this problem cannot be adequately cared for by treating a value-concept, so far as its general force goes, as dual in its nature, consisting of a Matrix Meaning which is non-cognitive in its force, and an Identifying Property which is a natural property. On this view, the Matrix Meaning will also be a natural property—but a property directly of the term itself, rather than of the object or act referred to, whereas the Identifying Property is a natural property of the things denoted by the term.

Similarly, the non-cognitivist schools treat the "meaning" of good or right as consisting in what I have called the Matrix Meaning alone. The cognitive elements consist entirely of Conferring Properties, and though they come into the "analysis" of normative expressions, they do not constitute part of the meaning of the ethical term itself. Or, if they are included in the meaning as in Stevenson's second-pattern models (persuasive definitions), they are a miscellaneous lot whose role is subsidiary. Some of those whom I have included under non-cognitivists, such as Toulmin and Hare, though in general they restrict the meaning of the term to its non-cognitive force, nevertheless in the process of the analysis do offer, as has been shown in Chapter 4, properties of a higher degree of generality than we have included in Conferring Properties. Our chief question about the non-cognitivists, then, will be whether this rejection, or admission through the back door, of Identifying Properties is tenable.

If the three-fold analysis we have suggested can be upheld, then the following schematic position is indicated. The *general* meaning of a normative term consists in its Matrix Meaning (non-cognitive) plus its Identifying Property (cognitive), if one can be found. Such a linkage of a Matrix Meaning and an Identifying Property would constitute a *principle* for ethics or value theory, and might be summed up in a definition; and there may be other "principles," for example those having the logical force of "postulates" rather than of definitions, in so far as these can be distinguished. The chief problems, then, would consist in the selection of the Matrix Meaning and the Identifying Property in the case of the various terms, and in justifying their linkage.

Since Conferring Properties are indefinitely numerous, it would be impossible to include the maxims formulating them in the *general* meaning of a normative term. Their discovery would be a problem for applied ethics rather than ethical theory, though the latter has to deal with the questions of the logical status of such maxims, and their relation to principles.

The proposal to take the meaning of a normative term as consisting of Matrix Meaning plus Identifying Property is at variance with the usual practice of all four of the schools in question. The cognitivists often in practice take the meaning of the term to consist solely in the Identifying Property, whether natural or non-natural. This alone is formulated in definitions when definitions are given; and, when they are not given, it forms the center of reference in the analysis, and the Matrix Meaning if recognized at all is taken for granted or treated as subsidiary. For the non-cognitivists, on the other hand, the meaning of the term consists in its *use*—in which the prescriptive or emotive force is central, and such cognitive elements as are recognized are factors in the "analysis."

Our proposal assumes a tolerant and inclusive view with respect to the term "meaning." There would, indeed, be advantages in avoiding the term entirely. The semanticists have made us abundantly aware of its vagueness and slipperiness as used not only by philosophers but by others; and for certain purposes it may be cleansing to take a fresh start and base the discussion, for example as Charles Morris does, on a less infected concept such as "sign-behavior" or "signification." But since the same problems recur in whatever terminology, and since no substitute for the term "meaning" has succeeded in crowding it out of our vocabulary, we shall continue to use it with, let us hope, profit from the lessons taught us by those who would reject it.

2. *The Logical Structure of Ethical Reasoning*

We shall assume, then, that at least some elements in the descriptive reference of the term, and also some features in the "use," can be included in the general meaning of the term. This procedure will permit us to exclude incidental or accidental descriptive properties from the general meaning; and also to exclude secondary uses, such as those that are not intended or presupposed in the normal functioning of the term.

Let us assume further, for the time being, that it is possible to achieve principles or definitions or theories formulating

Identifying Properties for normative terms, more general in scope than maxims or rules prescribing Conferring Properties; and let us ask what kind of structure our normative reasoning would have *if* we made use of such principles and maxims. It will be helpful to know what the use of such rules would commit us to, before we ask whether and how they can be "justified," and before we try to justify any specific set of them.

We have suggested that such a principle would link, for each normative term, its Matrix Meaning with its Identifying Property. The most important type of principle, a definition or criterion for the use of the term, would have some such form as, to give an oversimplified version: "This is good" means "This has the Identifying Property of goodness; do or seek this under conditions *c!*"

"You ought to do this" means "This has a certain Identifying Property; do this!" (where it is assumed that the conditions have been satisfied).

In both these types, the Matrix Meaning consists in, or includes, some kind of prescription or imperative, whether conditional or unconditional, and not merely states that there is such a prescription but, in its strongest use, has the force of prescribing or triggering the act.

For example, on a hedonistic theory of the Identifying Property, "This is intrinsically good" means "This experience is pleasant; seek it or hold on to it, in so far as the experience is considered without regard to its consequences, and if no pleasanter experience is available." On an intuitionist theory, it would mean "This has the non-natural property recognized by ethical intuition; seek it, etc."

On an interest theory, "This object is generically good" means "This object arouses interest; seek it unless something else is feasible which arouses more interest."

On a Kantian theory, "You ought to do this act" means "This act is one whose maxim is capable of being universalized, one which regards all persons affected by it as ends and not merely as means, and one which the will prescribes to itself; do it!" The Identifying Property here is three-fold, including the properties specified in each of the formulations of the Categorical Imperative.

As so far stated, these principles correspond roughly to Stevenson's second pattern of analysis, that of the persuasive definition. But the account here offered differs from Stevenson in the following respect, among others.

It is assumed that, for a normative theory to be possible, such principles are not all on the same footing, that for each ethical term it is possible to arrive at an Identifying Property which is more adequate than alternative Identifying Properties offered by competing theories. In other words, the linkage (inadequately symbolized above by a semicolon) between the Matrix Meaning and a specified Identifying Property is not arbitrary, not a matter of mere conditioning or stipulation or effectiveness in persuasion, but is justifiable or self-justifying. That is to say, the principle is accepted as authoritative, however the authority may be conceived; and its imperative force derives from this, and not, as apparently in Stevenson's view, from the naked desire of the speaker or the suggestibility of the hearer.

The general schema for the meaning of a definitory principle, as it has just been formulated, is, where "E" stands for an ethical term, "IP" for an Identifying Property, and "MM" for a Matrix Meaning:

"x is E" = "x has IP_1; MM!"

Or, to recast it in a form that is more suitable for use in discursive reasoning:

"x is E" (where the Matrix Meaning is absorbed into the

ethical predicate, "good" or "right," and hence the statement
has a prescriptive force) $\equiv$ "x has IP$_1$." [1]

The simplest case of an ethical inference, then, would have
the form:

"x is E" $\equiv$ "x has IP$_1$."

"This has IP$_1$."

"Therefore this is E"—a conclusion which in turn comprises
an injunction to seek this provided the assumed conditions,
if any, are satisfied.

The principle or major premise is established or justified in
whatever way we may decide that such principles can be
justified. The minor premise is an empirical statement, since
the Identifying Property is empirically discoverable. The conclusion follows syllogistically, but is itself an empirical statement since it rests upon an empirical premise (although of
course on an intuitionist theory such would not be the case).
The fact that the major premise is not itself an empirical statement—since on the view I shall propound its "justification" is
not the same thing as empirical "verification"—does not render
the conclusion non-empirical, for no basic principle in any
field, on this view, is an empirical statement in the same way
that subsidiary propositions are empirical statements. No primary definition, in fact, not even in the admittedly empirical
sciences, is strictly speaking verifiable empirically, although

---

[1] This latter model is put into the form of a material equivalence
(three bars) rather than a conceptual identity (two bars): whenever something is good it has the Identifying Property, and conversely; even though the two are not identical, goodness has the
prescriptive force invariably associated with it, and supplying the
distinctive normative element, whereas the Identifying Property
can be conceived in disjunction from the trigger function which, by
the ethical theory that adopts the principle, is linked with it.

the acceptance or rejection of most definitions is subject to empirical controls.

Generally we have to use more complex methods of confirming ethical judgments than the simple model given above. We can rarely go straight from the principle to the conclusion by finding the Identifying Property, but must do so via maxims stating Conferring Properties. What Mill said of the principle of Utility is applicable to principles in the revised form in which they are here conceived:

The corollaries from the principle of utility, like the precepts of every practical art, admit of indefinite improvement, and, in a progressive state of the human mind, their improvement is perpetually going on. But to consider the rules of morality as improvable, is one thing; to pass over the intermediate generalisations entirely, and endeavour to test each individual action directly by the first principle, is another. It is a strange notion that the acknowledgment of a first principle is inconsistent with the admission of secondary ones. To inform a traveller respecting the place of his ultimate destination, is not to forbid the use of landmarks and direction-posts on the way. The proposition that happiness is the end and aim of morality, does not mean that no road ought to be laid down to that goal, or that persons going thither should not be advised to take one direction rather than another. Men really ought to leave off talking a kind of nonsense on this subject, which they would neither talk nor listen to on other matters of practical concernment. Nobody argues that the art of navigation is not founded on astronomy, because sailors cannot wait to calculate the Nautical Almanack. Being rational creatures, they go to sea with it ready calculated; and all rational creatures go out upon the sea of life with their minds made up on the common questions of right and wrong, as well as on many of the far more difficult questions of wise and foolish. And this, as long as foresight is a human quality, it is to be presumed they will continue to do. Whatever we adopt as the fundamental principle of morality, we require subordinate principles to apply it by; the impossibility of doing without them, being common to all systems, can afford no argument against any one in particular; but gravely to argue as if no such secondary principles could be had, and as if mankind had remained till now, and always must remain, without drawing any general conclusions from the experience of human life, is as high a pitch, I think, as absurdity has ever reached in philosophical controversy. (*Utilitarianism*, Ch. II.)

The application of such a principle as that of utility, particularly where "ought" or "right" is in question, requires an elaborate forecasting of means and consequences. Often we have neither the time nor the detailed knowledge of the situation that would enable us to do this. Consequently, we fall back on maxims such as those enjoining promise-keeping or truth-telling, which in our past experience we have found on the whole to promote the realization of such an Identifying Property as the general welfare, even though we may have encountered exceptions to their tendency to do so. In such a case, where a maxim is taken to consist in the assertion of a Conferring Property, we have a complication of the inference:

"If x has CP_1, then x probably has IP_1."

"This has CP_1."

"Therefore this (probably) has IP_1."

From this argument, together with the preceding one, we infer that the object in question is probably good or right.

Actually, even these schemes in combination oversimplify greatly the reasoning involved in arriving at most considered ethical decisions, since the circumstances may be extremely complex, a choice between alternative Conferring Properties may be required, the Conferring Properties themselves may have to be investigated by indirect means, and we may even be forced to call in question our fundamental rules or principles. And conversely, maxims are sometimes lacking or obviously irrelevant, so that we must investigate directly the conditions and consequences of the occurrence of the Identifying Property in the particular case, without relying on our general confidence in certain Conferring Properties as productive of it.

It is not suggested, moreover, that we always use explicitly such a scheme as the above. We often make even complicated ethical decisions while short-circuiting certain phases of this procedure: we may rely on a working knowledge of a principle or a maxim, using it as an assumption rather than a premise, without articulating it in language. But this is the case with all "logical" reasoning. If men were logical before Aristotle, they were ethically rational in some degree before Socrates, and they continue to be so without benefit from his successors. When we undertake an analysis of their procedures, however, we must make their implicit assumptions explicit.

3. *The Limits of Formalism*

The analysis just outlined would be vigorously repudiated by the contemporary non-cognitivist schools, and particularly by moral philosophers of the informalist persuasion, like Hampshire and Toulmin. The informalists see clearly that definitions and principles cannot be used as *formulae* for the immediate solution of practical problems. And so they advise us to turn away from a "logic" which would deduce the judgment in the particular case immediately from the principle; it is obviously futile to hold that any principle, whether it be the greatest happiness of the greatest number, or the possibility of universalizing the maxim, can serve as a cybernetic machine into which we can feed particular data with the expectation that the machine, operating through the formula together with the rules of logic, can click out the answer. The uses of principles and logical forms are otherwise.

On the other hand, we cannot expect great results from a "logic" or methodology which, like that of the informalists, simply describes specimens of logical reasoning and fails to exhibit any specific connection between reason and conclusion, but leaves our awareness of the connection to our unanalyzed sense of relevance.

Let us consider the very close analogy of ethics to the law. Not even the highest rules, such as a Bill of Rights—which may be considered as a list of maxims of high generality, only slightly below the principles of political ethics themselves— afford magic formulae from which, together with the facts of the particular case, the judge can deduce a solution. There is always the problem of interpretation and application in the particular instance. What the Bill of Rights does supply is a general orientation of attitudes, a general prescription of ends, necessarily somewhat loose and vague. But despite the margin of vagueness, and the consequent uncertainty as to the application in the particular case, the general orientation is indispensable. The First Amendment may not tell us what freedom of speech is in the particular case, but it serves to orient us toward the search for it, and instigates a multiplication of maxims and analogies by means of which the courts seek to specify its range of application. Likewise with such supreme principles of the law as the general welfare clause in the Constitution. Bentham's greatest happiness principle, its philosophical equivalent, by itself will not enable any judge to make a correct decision. Yet it has sufficient clarity to produce quite a different direction of general attitudes from such a principle as precedent, or existing privilege, or "natural right." It tells us to look forward to the consequences of institutions in the lives of men—of suffering, enjoying men—and not backward to accidental status or upward to supposed eternal laws which pure reason strains to glimpse. Such an orientation of general attitudes may be called a *structural presupposition* of our valuation, and it is this that a principle makes explicit. The principle itself may be crude and vague, but all that the choice requires of it in order that it may supply guidance is that it be less crude and vague than the alternatives themselves. The greatest happiness of the greatest number, or the regarding of persons as ends and never merely as means, may be terribly obscure to a trained philosophical or legal analyst, but they are clear enough if espoused to permit us to deduce from them, in conjunction with other data, that we should not torture violators of the law, without regard to their rehabilitation; and it even led the utilitarians, when they overcame certain hastily chosen economic principles, to reject a system which forced children to work fourteen hours a day.

Ethical principles—at any rate, as we have been able to exploit them so far—do not give us detailed guidance in our decisions, much less enable us to deduce with precision any course of action in hard cases. What they do offer, along with general orientation, is criteria of choice among the rather broad and crude alternatives with which life usually confronts us. The hope for a considerable measure of rationality in living springs not so much from any prospect of applying logic to its subtler problems (where a sensitive empirical intuition with all its fallibility is usually the best we can aspire to) but from the very broadness and crudity of the alternatives. The alternatives are to marry this girl or not to marry her, or to marry her rather than some one of two others, or to achieve some measure of bliss without any of them. Or they are, for the politician, to vote for or against this piece of legislation; for the citizen, to flout a law, or to put up with its indignities, or to work for its repeal.

Most commonly it is possible to make the choice without raising the question of principles explicitly: when there is a well-established custom, with which both the moral agent and the community are satisfied, a maxim will do, or even a moral habit which is below the reflective level of a maxim.

Acknowledging this, however, does not render chimerical

the search for principles. The philosopher is kept at this search partly by speculative curiosity: *he cannot be finally convinced that the domain of values is chaotic*, that it will ultimately resist his passion for finding or making intellectual order. And men who are not philosophers are recurrently impelled to philosophize, or to look to theorists wistfully for guidance, when an acute and persistent conflict seizes them: when their only hope for life, or a decent life, is to think the conflict through. Here custom and habit have failed, and intuition, whether *a priori* or empirical, is too frail an instrument to risk everything upon it.

A society, like an individual, usually seeks help from philosophy only when in serious trouble: then it expects too much. The most that philosophy can offer here is a general re-direction of attitudes and assumptions; the detailed answer, so far as one can be found, is a matter for the social scientist, the publicist and the politician. But without some benefit from philosophy, even though they are not conscious of it, these latter are likely in a time of troubles to make the inadequate response of temporizing or, at the other extreme, of fear-driven violence.

Somewhat similar observations may be made about maxims, as distinguished from principles. Whatever the usefulness of recipes in cooking, medicine, painting, law or bridge-building, it depends on our ability to grasp and control the conditions, and this is limited where the ingredients are complex and variable, the circumstances largely unpredictable, and the ultimate product fitted to a unique situation or, as in the fine arts, directed to the creation of a novel Gestalt-quality.

In morals, where the complexity, variability and unpredictability are even greater, maxims are of still more restricted use and must be held even more tentatively. Many of the rules that we invoke are not specifically "moral" maxims: they are the formulae of medicine, or political science, or psychology, or nuclear physics—which tell us what are the Conferring Properties of goodness with respect to the attainment of a specialized type of end. The moral maxims proper—as contrasted with technological rules—refer to features of acts that recur frequently in the individual's organization of his life to achieve a variety of ends, personal and interpersonal. They point to certain major pitfalls to avoid and certain dispositions that must be cultivated for the sake of this general organization. Principles, on the other hand, deal with the basic structural features of this organization itself—the structure of means-end relationships, the "existential" confrontation of the self and the other, the inventory of man's common resources including his motivation, his capacity for feeling, his necessity to act, his ability to reflect and to guide his action by symbols.

Casuistry is the effort to systematize maxims. It seeks to produce a rule-book, or manual, which will foresee all possible combinations of circumstances and prescribe rules-of-thumb for meeting them. Although an engineer's manual may serve well the humble builder of culverts on county roads, and is indispensable for the practitioner with little theory, the George Washington or Golden Gate Bridge, as we are reminded, was not built in this way. And the complexities of moral conduct are much greater than those of bridge-building. For this reason, a manual of morals would be less adequate than an engineering manual to our living in an intricate civilization that is permeated with change and full of surprises.

Yet it may be that a renewed attention to the possibility of achieving moral maxims, even though it did not support an effort at casuistic systematization, would disclose that maxims are more useful than we now generally recognize. The analogy with jurisprudence and with the conduct of institutions of a number of kinds can help here. With all its rigidities, the rule of law when that law is at all adequate is preferable to the arbitrary rule of men: such is the obstinate burden alike of the Anglo-Saxon, the Greco-Roman and the Hebraic elements in our political heritage. Whether the maxims of law be legislated explicitly in statutes, or extracted inductively from cases by judges and first made into generalizations by them, such maxims put a check to the capricious and tyrannical license of the wielders of executive, legislative and judicial power; and they also have the essential function, as jurists have insisted, of shaping "expectation" so that men may act with some measure of confidence in their ability to predict the social acceptance or non-acceptance of their acts.

There is always a margin of vagueness or indeterminacy in the law itself, so that some scope is permitted for correction of the rigidity of maxims on the score of equity or of "interpretation"; and in any decently organized society, there is provision for alteration of the law itself. This is true even on "positivistic" theories of jurisprudence, which appeal to the customs or social habits of a community. When the maxims are offered as formulations of the customary valuations of the society, it is always possible to hold that the formulations are inadequate, rather than the customs themselves, so that a restatement of them is necessary. Thus we may catch a habit or custom at the moment of re-direction—for social habits no more than personal are wholly rigid and stereotyped patterns of response but are always more or less adaptive to the particular situation. Even with such qualifications, however, juristic "positivism" is an inadequate theory for dealing with legal reform. It is at best a fiction and at worst an imposture to claim that valuational habits, even at the focal point of re-direction, supply a sufficient guide for changes in the law. Consequently jurists, in order to avoid what amounts to a premonition of the Naturalistic Fallacy, commonly seek to support proposed changes in the law, not by a simple appeal to a change in prevalent habits but by recourse to the "moral sense of the community," or to eternal principles such as natural law or natural rights, or to the future consequences of the reform in improved social habits and mechanisms. But on whatever theoretical assumptions the reform may be justified, the altered law always seeks new maxims to replace the old, and to provide clearer guidance in specific situations.

The contemporary disfavor with which moral maxims are regarded springs not only from a somewhat questionable sense that the conditions of living have changed so rapidly in recent centuries as to make the old maxims often seem blunt and outmoded instruments, but also from the awareness that moral maxims by themselves never suffice to offer direction in a society where the crucial consideration may hinge more upon new impersonal mechanisms—technological, medical or administrative—for the achievement of the ends in question than upon the volitional attitudes of the personal agents of change, which constitute the traditional domain of morality.

Yet moral maxims do not necessarily represent platitudes or fossils of outgrown attitudes. The maxims urged by the great prophets were revolutionary in their time, and had the power to orient a saving remnant toward life rather than toward death. And we must remember that "moralists" include such unconventional figures as Montaigne, La Rochefoucauld and Nietzsche as well as partisans of the entrenched angels. The neglect into which the trade of moralist has fallen is especially great in emancipated circles of the Anglo-Saxon countries, where a kind of empirical intuition of the particular case has tended to be trusted more than generalizations about conduct at any level. In a country like France, however, "moralist" is not necessarily a term of reproach, but a characterization of a legitimate role that is expected of philosophers and literary men as at least one of their professional functions.

We may see both the possible utility and the limitations of moral maxims when we recognize that the valuational situation includes at the same time personal agents and impersonal elements. The maxims are, for the most part, attempts to specify more or less general features of the personal element— the kinds of acts that are on the whole to be approved and which it is wise to make habitual, and the motivational attitudes and affective rewards and punishments that accompany these. Often we may take such facts for granted, and the problematic element consists in the more external features of the situation. To this the invocation of maxims is usually irrelevant.

So the logic of valuation—still on the assumption that principles enter into the matter—may involve justifying the particular judgment by invoking a maxim, which in turn is justified by invoking a principle. Or, the decision may bypass the maxim entirely and go directly from the singular judgment to the justifying principle. The principle itself in the latter case is a criterion prescribing the most general and ultimate end; and decision on the means may require no alteration in personal attitudes of the agent, and no perplexing choice among alternative habits, but hinge upon the nature of the "objective" elements in the situation.

Principles, if we could get reliable ones, would then seem to be indispensable, though not by themselves sufficient factors in a thoroughly reflective attitude toward valuation. But how can we justify the principles themselves? Here we seem to hit the ceiling. There must somewhere be a limit to the extent to which we may proceed in this appeal to ever more general criteria. If we seek to justify the principles by deduction from still higher principles, we are caught in an endless regress. So this process of logical justification would seem to have limits. Either principles are not justifiable at all—in which case they would seem to be illusory props for ethical reasoning—or else they are justifiable by some radically different movement from that which we have described in the ascent from singular judgments through maxims to principles. This is the major puzzle for a cognitivist theory in the present state of the discussion.

8

Valuation and Language

1. Sub-Discursive Valuation

Our explicit ethical reflection, like our explicit knowledge of the world and of ourselves with which it goes hand in hand, is a late and precarious development both in the human individual and in our culture. In their developed forms, both knowledge and valuation depend on a highly sophisticated and highly self-conscious use of linguistic symbols. But this should not blind us to the fact that a good deal of our knowledge, and a good many of our valuational decisions, take place without the use of language, and that even when explicit reflection occurs it usually intervenes only at crucial phases in processes that are largely non-discursive or non-symbolic but enable us to take account of the world, to adjust ourselves to it, to dominate it, and to guide our conduct more or less rewardingly both for ourselves and for others affected by our acts.

It has been said that we always understand more than we can symbolize; it is likewise true that we understand in some measure before we can symbolize.

There are two stages of sub-discursive comprehension: one is pre-linguistic or non-linguistic, the kind of understanding that animals have; the other consists in the non-discursive or operational comprehension of language itself, that is to say, the more or less effective use of language without capacity to analyze or criticize that use—the stage of discourse without discourse about discourse.

In the first stage, cognition is wholly perceptual. Animals respond to certain features of their environment, and of their own behavior, as signs, and they develop fairly reliable expectations accordingly. The psychological studies of animal learning deal with the "how" of this process. Along with non-linguistic cognition goes non-linguistic valuation. Under favorable conditions animals are highly successful in ensuring their own survival, in satisfying their needs and in working out a rewarding pattern of conduct.

But non-linguistic valuation, like the non-linguistic cognition that is bound up with it, is fallible, and limited in its scope. A study by O. H. Mowrer and A. D. Ullman ("Time as a Determinant in Integrative Learning," *Psychological Review,* vol. 52, 1945) has shown that it is particularly difficult for animals—just as according to K. Goldstein it is for humans suffering from lesions of the frontal lobe, who are unable to abstract—to grasp the time factor in conduct without explicit symbolism. If an electric grill is placed between a group of rats and their food, and the current is turned on for a few seconds after a buzzer signifies the presence of the food, some of the animals after several trials can learn to wait the required number of seconds until they are able to cross the grill without shock. These are the so-called "normal" rats. Others, dubbed the "neurotic" rats, are so disorganized by the shocks that they never learn to cross the grill, but cower in their corners till they starve to death. Still others persist in barging across the grill to their food as soon as the buzzer sounds, regardless of the severe punishment this causes them to take. These rats are appropriately called "delinquent." The experimenter, in his detachment, comments that the normal rats have developed the "right" habits of valuation—or, as we might say, they show an operative grasp of the "prudential ought" in this situation; the delinquent animals manifest less effective habits, and the neurotic ones totally wrong habits. The rats, if they could discuss the matter among themselves, would probably agree.

Similarly, common observation of animal behavior—we don't even need to go to the laboratory for this—shows that various animals manifest greater or less capacity to harmonize their needs by co-operative activity with other animals. We can say that they exhibit at least a rudimentary behavioral analogue of the "moral" or "social" ought.

Adult human behavior is always influenced to a considerable extent by a previous stage of learning in which reflective activity, mediated by language, has played a part. But we often make intricate and adequate valuational responses—in playing tennis, in driving a car, in creating works of art, in "intuitively" sizing up people, in spontaneously considerate treatment of others—without verbalized judgments or processes of discursive reasoning directly leading to them. People who never learn to think straight about matters of conduct may do better not to try. And as Santayana has remarked: "It takes a wonderful brain and exquisite senses to produce a few stupid ideas." Ideas—particularly the ideas of philosophical moralists —can easily mix us up more than they straighten us out. But after having tasted of the fruit of discursive knowledge it is impossible to go back to the Garden of Eden; we are committed to language, for better and for worse.

The second stage—that of discourse without discourse about discourse—never dispenses entirely with the purely perceptual responses operating in the first stage. And the second stage likewise has its effectiveness on its own level. Even those whose business it is to use linguistic symbols often have a working grasp of their use without being able to analyze how they use them or to justify their ways of using them: great scientists who are innocent of logic and inarticulate about scientific method, such business men as really have their much-vaunted "know-how," parliamentarians who rely on "parliamentary sense" without definitely formulated rules of strategy, prophets who affirm new values without arguing for them, poets who know when a line or an image is right without being able to tell why, statesmen who have a feel for the destiny of the nation or the needs of the people without being able to offer an articulated program or rationally justified goals. Just as we did not learn our native language out of a textbook, and many of us use it correctly with little benefit from grammars and dictionaries, so some persons are able to get along quite well—and even to rise to positions of eminence—by verbalizing only their conclusions and letting their nervous systems operate directly in recording and weighing the evidence on which these conclusions are based.

But sub-discursive knowledge at either of these levels has its limitations. When it fails us, and we run into serious trouble, our only recourse is to work the hard way—through language and the critical use of language. And so, at some time, most people begin to find and to articulate "reasons" for the conclusions that are expressed in such judgments as "This is good," "That is wrong" and "So saith the Lord. . . ." Some go still further and engage in explicit reasoning, following more or less closely the patterns of logical inference, in order to reach these conclusions.

2. Three Kinds of Reasons

When we give reasons, these may be at three different levels:

(1) The reasons may be singular propositions attributing some quality or some relational property to the act or to some other feature of the situation. Thus, at this level of normative

reflection we may say: "This is a good spear, because its point is sharp and hard, and its handle well balanced"; or "This is a good poem, because its words interanimate each other"; or "I ought to teach summer school this year, because my family needs expensive medical treatment."

Thus we symbolize two things. In the conclusion, we symbolize and prescribe, conditionally or unconditionally, the act or object as a whole about which the decision has to be made. In the "reason," we symbolize some selected feature of the situation on which our previous non-discursive experience has focused our attention, as a feature relevant to this decision; and we assert the presence of this feature as described.

(2) In the second type of reason, we not only assert singular propositions of the types indicated above, but we assert also general maxims of which the singular proposition is an instance, or, in some cases, where the singular proposition has a more indirect logical relation to the maxims. Thus, "This is a good spear, *because* its point is sharp (etc) . . . *and* a good spear must have a sharp point . . ."; or "This is a good poem, *because* its words interanimate each other, *and* the interanimation of the words enhances the aesthetic goodness of a poem that tries to evoke a mood." Or, "I ought to teach summer school, *because* my family needs medical care *and* my family's health takes precedence over my relaxation or my writing." The maxim then is offered as a reason for the relevance or evidential force of the singular judgment in relation to the conclusion.

(3) But the process need not stop here. We may have to justify the maxim itself, or to show the relevance of the singular judgment where no maxim is available, or to find some ground for choosing between two maxims which support alternative conclusions in the case in question. Here our reasons, if we continue to offer such, in addition to types 1 and 2, include principles or definitions or theories. Consequently, besides the reasons previously given in our judgment of the poem, we would support our reasons and our conclusion by, for example, distinguishing aesthetic value from other kinds of value, and showing that interanimation of words satisfies the general criteria invoked in the distinction. Thus we would add: ". . . And aesthetic goodness is satisfaction derived from contemplation of the sensory pattern of the work in interplay with its immediately grasped meanings."

Now acceptance of this principle may lead me, in the particular case, to decide that the poet has been too successful in making the words interanimate each other, and that the poem in question would, by the principle, be aesthetically better if the poet had, as in an Imagist or Chinese poem, sharpened his visual imagery at the expense of its verbal texture. Or the ethical principle which I would adduce to test the judgment about teaching summer school might lead me to find consequences that outweighed the urgency of medical care for my family. Thus the principle, if we can get a reliable one, takes logical precedence over the other two types of reason, and these reasons depend for their probative force on their relation—explicit or implicit—to the principle.

Now it is possible to go on to a fourth stage—that of meta-aesthetics or meta-ethics—where we seek to test or justify the principles themselves. But before we consider this stage, let us reflect on what we have done so far.

When we give reasons of type 1 (singular propositions), we point to the presence of certain Conferring Properties taken as *relevant* to the predication of goodness within the kind of object or situation under consideration. At this stage we do not justify our conclusion by appeal to explicit generalization at any level, but simply point to particular properties—which, however, from the necessities of language itself, are characterized in terms of predicates or "universals" such as "sharp" or "hard." We do not venture the maxim that all spears, or most of them, in order to be good must have sharp points; we simply say that this one has, and suggest that our conclusion is "reasonable" in the particular context.

But when someone first gives a singular reason of this kind, it is usually safe to assume that he, or his group, has already observed (perhaps non-discursively) on a number of occasions previously, that goodness in spears goes with sharpness in points. Our aborigine who gives the reason has never defined goodness, and has had still less occasion to define sharpness, but he has some kind of sub-discursive working understanding of what both mean. He or the group has been in the habit of choosing sharp-pointed spears, and it is only an aborigine who was challenged as to his choice of this spear—say from somebody's still unformulated insight that a blunter but heavier spear might be more appropriate to stun a large, thick-skinned animal—or a loquacious savage who enjoyed verbalization for its own sake, or a reflective one who liked to understand what he was doing, or one who liked to instruct children in the rudiments of his craft, who would take the occasion to state the reason.

The reason, consequently, in its initial use, simply verbalizes one factor in what was already an operative habit. And in this case it is a cognitive factor, at the perceptual level: the reason points to the presence of a Conferring Property that was perceived to have been present in the case of similar operations of the habit that were successful and is perceived to be present in this one also.

When the speaker goes on to offer a maxim, or reason of type 2, and say "*All* good spears must have sharp points" (perhaps mentioning the purpose or circumstances also), he is formulating in words the habit itself, and not simply one perceptual factor in it. He is making explicit what amounts to both a valuational habit and a semantical habit. For he has habitually chosen sharp-pointed spears, and he has also habitually applied the term "good spear" to one with a sharp point.

But notice that his interlocutor, in the case of a genuine dispute, might likewise go on to offer a competing maxim, or a revised set of maxims: "A sharp point is good for hunting rabbits, but a heavy point for hunting iguana." Here, too, he is simply formulating habits—either giving a more adequate expression of the habits shared by both speakers, or voicing habits that rest on a wider experience of hunting than the first speaker has. (For the sake of simplicity, we can ignore at this point the case where the reason expresses insight into a novel situation rather than simply voices an established habit.)

A similar account is plausible in the case of moral maxims proper, as distinguished from technological rules. Proverbs and moral commandments rarely express entirely novel insights into the conduct of life: they simply put into words practices that have long been habitual in the group, or in a considerable segment of it. Even when, as with the great ethical prophets of Judea, maxims are offered as the word of God thundering against existing practices, they usually express habits of conduct that were common to the group at some earlier stage and still persist weakly, and they are frequently offered as such. Thus historians of ancient Hebrew thought often interpret the social morality preached by the herdsman Amos as the reaffirmation of conceptions of justice and mercy that had been practiced unquestioningly within the patriarchal group of an earlier nomadic stage, and still persisted in the semi-nomads across the Jordan, but were vanishing among the more individualistic farmers and town-dwellers of Canaan. At some point such maxims must be articulated for the first time, even though the habits which they formulate had previously functioned so generally and so adequately that no need was felt to make them explicit. The prophets and sages are geniuses in uttering the hitherto assumed but unuttered.

The supply of available maxims is limited in any society; they fail to cover all the situations in which a decision has to be made, or they pass out of use from their failure to correspond with the tacitly or non-discursively recognized needs of contemporary practice; or they conflict among themselves. Consequently, just as recourse is made to a maxim to "back up" a singular evidential judgment when the latter is challenged, so we are tempted to seek a definition or ethical theory when a maxim fails or becomes doubtful. And at this point moral theory, or what Santayana calls rational ethics as distinguished from pre-rational morality, is aborning. Here for the first time is raised seriously the question what goodness or justice or obligation means in general, and not merely questions as to what things or what kinds of things are good or just. Our operative understanding of the term goodness itself has broken down, and needs to be replaced by a discursive understanding.

Here, as analogously in the previous stages, we do not at first set up novel or altered meanings of normative words. We seek merely to make explicit the more general assumptions of our valuation which have led us to hit on the maxims themselves. We seek, in other words, for the implicitly recognized Identifying Properties which have led us sub-discursively to seize upon certain Conferring Properties rather than others as relevant to our choices in particular acts, and as the properties to be formulated by our maxims.

Just as the maxims are attempts to formulate valuational *habits* that are accepted in practice as "successful" or "adequate," so principles and definitions try to make explicit the *structural presuppositions,* constituting implicit cognition, which underlie the maxims themselves and govern the choice of them. They perhaps can themselves be called habits, but express general ways of acting and knowing that precipitate a variety of the more specific types of response usually designated by that name. Again, at this third stage, it is our *working sense* of their adequacy that leads us to formulate the presuppositions as principles, and not any explicitly formulated criteria of adequacy. When we raise the latter question, which is that of *justification* of principles, we go on to still a fourth stage, the stage of meta-ethics or theory of value.

This genetic account of the crystallization of our different kinds of reasons out of the matrix of action and assumption can be represented schematically as follows:

Implicit (Operative) *Understanding*	*Explicit (Discursive)* *Understanding*
1. Valuational perceptions	1. Singular evidential judgments
2. Valuational habits	2. Maxims
3. Structural presuppositions of valuation	3. Valuational principles
4. "Global sense" of adequacy	4. Justifying reasons

The kinds of "reasons" which are listed in the second column are, initially, simply symbolizations of factors that were operative in the non-discursive or sub-discursive practice of valuation.

3. *Structural Presuppositions*

Let us ask what is meant by the "structural presuppositions" which become formulated as principles. And let us examine three different sets of principles offered by various moral philosophers: the consequentialist principle, the hedonist principle, and the three formulations of the Kantian Categorical Imperative.

The consequentialist or teleological principle—which in one form can be stated as "The right act is that which will produce the greatest good and the least evil"—is one which was at least partially adhered to in moral practice long before any ethical philosophy formulated it. In a loose form, it is written as a tendency into the nervous system at birth, and operates implicitly when the child learns to avoid the flame and the animal to pursue a path which leads to its food. It is presupposed by innumerable cases where we point to reasons of type 1 to back up our judgments, and by maxims that enjoin thrift, industry, caution, observance of law or custom. Since the distinction between a principle and a maxim permits of gradations—at any rate as we have roughly sketched them so far—we even find maxims that state the principle itself in a rough and metaphorical way: for example, the proverb, "Look before you leap." But this proverb states the principle imprecisely, for it contradicts the aphorism, "He who hesitates is lost." As reformulated in more general terms, the principle covers both cases and adjudicates the conflicts between them. It tells us in theory when to leap and when to hesitate: namely, that we should do the one or the other depending on which will produce the greater good in the particular situation or kind of situation. Even the second maxim, which appears to conflict with the principle, actually presupposes it, for it points to being lost as a consequence of hesitation. That we cannot always apply the principle in practice to resolve a dispute reveals no shortcoming in the principle itself, but is entailed by the recurrent squeeze of life's situations which force us to make decisions without adequate time or data for reflection.

As this example illustrates, the principle in the more abstract form does not serve the purposes for which maxims are often invoked: it does not enable us to deduce what we should do in the particular case from appeal to the formulation alone. But, though the principle seems empty when it is expected to supply an answer by itself, it serves a purpose which provides a still more useful lesson, and corresponds better to our sense of adequacy as that is knocked into us by experience: it prescribes examination of the consequences in the particular case, or the specific kind of case, and it tells us about all that we can find for guidance on this kind of topic, however indeterminate it may be. Above all, it points to a structural feature that is universal to the normative situation, namely, the fact that acts are not complete in themselves, but have fruits in good and evil that are germane to the choice of acts.

But the consequentialist principle by itself is obviously incomplete. It assumes that we know independently what good and evil are, perhaps through an operative understanding of the terms, and of course it has to meet more serious challenges on its own ground from competing principles, such as those which prescribe acts "for their own sakes" without regard to consequences. A partial attempt to supply the first of these lacks is made by the Xenophontic Socrates and the Platonic Socrates of the early *Protagoras*, where it is supplemented by the hedonistic principle. That the Identifying Property of experiences that are good in themselves is pleasure, and of those that are bad in themselves is suffering, formulates a structural presupposition that covers an immense range of experience, whether it can be made absolutely universal or not as a law of motivation. Not only is it the presupposition of the action of most men most of the time, but it is one which they, on the whole, try to persist in from their sense that it is "adequate."

Likewise with the three formulations of the Categorical Imperative. Kant arrived at them initially as simply expressions of the "common rational knowledge of morality," that is, as the assumptions of moral conduct on which men act at the stage of moral reflection which he considered adequate. Kant did not profess to be inventing these principles, but rather to be giving precise expression for the first time to the general features of the moral situation which people whom he considered "rational" had long taken into account implicitly. A morally meritorious act is one which is in some sense capable of being universalized, one that involves the consideration of human beings as ends and not merely as means, and one whose maxim a man has espoused as a result of his own reflection. Many persons—at any rate, many of the conscientious, theologically liberal if morally rigorous Protestants whom Kant assumed to have a full working knowledge of morality—had been acting habitually more or less in conformity with these principles, and using ethical language accordingly, long before Kant put their assumptions into abstract language.

Whereas, in the first section of the *Metaphysic of Morals*, Kant is simply trying to make explicit these implicit assumptions of moral action and reflection, in the remainder of the treatise he goes on to do something different—namely, to try to "justify" them by showing that they are *a priori* in the structure of practical reason, and ultimately that they spring from the noumenal self.

All the candidates for the status of ethical principles that we have noticed so far profess to supply Identifying Properties by which we may recognize a good thing or a morally right act, and consequently offer tests for the applicability of normative terms. Such principles are conceived as having imperative or prescriptive force, but they also single out certain general properties—often in the situation or the context of the moral agent's reflection—which things or acts must have in order that the judgment may correctly prescribe them. Thus, in order that an act should be morally right, according to Kant, it must either have been chosen because of a maxim that has been tested by universalization ("performed from duty") or be capable of meeting this test ("be in conformity with duty"). This is a property of the act, though a rather complex and indirect one.

Let us ask, then, what ethical theories that reject principles are committed to. Some current positions would restrict "reasons" to type 1, others to type 2. The former hold that we can say "I ought to do this, *because* (reason type 1)"; or, in other words, that a reason of type 1 is a reason *for* the conclusion. Now this use of language would suggest that there is *some* relation between reason and conclusion; the words "because" and "for" ordinarily designate a relation, and in expressions of these forms—at any rate, outside of ethics—they designate a logical relation. The proponents of the view under examination, however, either deny that what is meant is a relation at all, or else while admitting that it is a relation deny that it is a logical relation; or, sometimes, they call for a "third logic" to cope with the situation.

The view that a reason can be relevant to the acceptance of a conclusion without being related to it at all is totally unintelligible to me. If, however, there is a relation but not a logical one, what kind of relation could it be? The only other sort of relation I can think of that might possibly be meant would be a psychological relation, such as the relation between a motive and the act that springs from it, or between a stimulus and a response. The reason indeed stimulates us to reach the conclusion. But since this happens when we are misled by bad reasons as well as when we are led by good ones, I take it that such a psychological relation is not what is primarily intended by the informalists, though it does seem to be the view of the emotivists.

The person who insists on freezing reasons at type 1 may back up his stand in one of two ways. He may say: "I know that the reason justifies the conclusion, and I know what justification is, but I can't—or won't—tell." This position is impregnable: it amounts to the declaration of an obstinate intention to persist in a language habit or a habit of valuation. But this attitude is equally open to upholders of reasons of types 2 and 3, who can produce their maxims or their principles and then proceed to sit tight upon them after proclaiming them "reasonable." When someone adopts such a position, further conversation becomes impossible. The politic thing to do is to begin to talk about the weather.

Another way of tackling the matter is, however, open to us. This is to go back to consider the relations between sub-discursive and discursive valuation. What are we doing when we first offer reasons of type 1? We are singling out and symbolizing features of the situation which, pre-discursively, we took account of, and responded to as stimuli, but did not symbolize. The conclusion of a process of valuation is the prescription of an act, an act as a whole. Now an act is: (a) cognitive, (b) purposive, (c) skilled, (d) motivated, (e) affectively toned. When we give a reason of type 1, we are singling out a feature of the situation that has a bearing on one of these five aspects of the act. The reason may state, for example, some feature of the situation, cognition of which is pertinent to our decision; or it may state the goal upon which our purpose is directed; or it may call attention to the motive, such as the attitudes that lie behind my concern for my family's health. The feature symbolized will ordinarily be one that at the beginning of the inquiry was uncertain, or whose relevance was problematic.

When we restrict ourselves to reasons of type 1, as we often do, we choose to symbolize precisely those features of the situation because in what we recognize non-discursively to have been successful or adequate acts of valuation we have taken account of specific features of the situation similar to those Conferring Properties which we symbolize in reasons of type 1. By "successful" or "adequate" acts of valuation we mean—putting the matter in a preliminary way—subjectively, those which correspond to our global or working sense of "good" or "right," and objectively those which have not got us into serious trouble, have furthered our purposes, organized our conduct, eliminated suffering and given us satisfaction.

This is a rough indication of what we mean by calling such features "relevant" and by calling "reasonable" the reasons which describe or express such features.

But the burden of proof is on those who would require us to stop with reasons of this type. If symbolizing these features of the situation helps to further the valuational process, why stop there? Why may it not help also to symbolize the successful habits of valuation themselves—that is, to state maxims —and to symbolize the general structure of the kinds of valuational act that have been found to be adequate—that is, to articulate principles? If our valuational processes are corrected and improved by getting particular features of the act out in the open, as in giving reasons of type 1, why may it not help likewise to exhibit the more general and structural features of the valuational situation?

Such, at any rate, is the assumption of those philosophers who have sought definitions, principles or theories. The assumption is simply that the normative domain is not chaotic, at least potentially: that if we seek hard enough and think hard enough we can find in it or make for it a general pattern, just as we do in the realm of physical nature, or of economic behavior, or of logic. It is not, usually, the assumption that such a pattern has been achieved, even implicitly, but rather that it can be approximated.

This assumption, we must admit, is not too triumphantly borne out by the results hitherto. Nearly a century later, we must still confess what Mill acknowledged in the opening paragraph of his *Utilitarianism:*

There are few circumstances among those which make up the present condition of human knowledge more unlike what might have been expected, or more significant of the backward state in which speculation on the most important subjects still lingers, than the little progress which has been made in the decision of the controversy respecting the criterion of right and wrong. From the dawn of philosophy, the question concerning the *summum bonum*, or, what is the same thing, concerning the foundation of morality, has been accounted the main problem in speculative thought, has occupied the most gifted intellects and divided them into sects and schools, carrying on a vigorous warfare against one another. And after more than two thousand years the same discussions continue, philosophers are still ranged under the same contending banners, and neither thinkers nor mankind at large seem nearer to being unanimous on the subject than when the youth Socrates listened to the old Protagoras, and asserted (if Plato's dialogue be grounded on a real conversation) the theory of utilitarianism against the popular morality of the so-called sophist.

If the attainment of a set of ethical principles on which agreement may be secured is still very much of a pious hope, on the other hand the contemporary analysts have not given us conclusive grounds for abandoning the attempt.

The current opposition to principles and definitions springs in part from two considerations. First, these philosophers dogmatically limit analysis to the explication of ordinary usage; and here the ambiguities of a term are more salient than any basic or central descriptive meaning that may be assigned to it. But empiricists have been proceeding on the assumption that *creative* thinking in morals as elsewhere refuses to limit itself to ordinary usage, however much this should be respected, and so empiricists feel free to propose modifications in the accepted meanings in such a way as to make moral thinking more exact and more effective. Such a process is happening all the time in the admittedly empirical disciplines such as the natural and social sciences.

Secondly, the informalists are understandably bewildered and disgusted by the conflicting array of definitions that ethical theorists have flung at them. They see that the man in the street and even the moral philosopher himself manages to make shrewd valuations, and usually to avoid total disaster in the business of living, without direct benefit of ethical theory, and that a moralist's definition may befuddle as much as it enlightens. They possibly have in mind such a field as the common law, whose "growing edge" serves with some rough success the purposes of social morality in coping with novel situations, and yet does not proceed by deduction from constitutional legislation of universal principles, but rather works by empirical intuition from clear-cut case to clear-cut case, at most restricting itself to such low-level generalizations as that which consists in formulating analogies between cases. Yet we know that the common law itself tends toward some measure of codification (or, as the current term has it, "restatement") and, where conflicts and uncertainties are acute, to be replaced by statutes prescribing definitions from which deductions can be made. In ethics as in jurisprudence, it seems that a prudent policy would be to keep on seeking definitions, but to hold them always in suspicion.

The only conclusive answer to such embarrassments would be to offer a set of principles for the normative studies and to defend them convincingly in detail, by whatever method of "justification" may turn out to be permissible. And later chapters will attempt to do this sketchily. But we are still in the stage of having to be largely concerned with writing prolegomena to ethics, and we are far from clear as to what we are looking for in the way of principles. Before we can fill in the pattern in detail, we must keep on trying to get its main outlines straight, and we must ask how one might try to "justify" such a pattern if he had it.

9

Pragmatic Justification

---

1. Two Ways of Supporting Principles

The two preceding chapters have tried to show, first, what could be expected of normative principles if we had them, and second, how the demand for such principles arises out of valuational activity that has not yet achieved them. In dealing with this second question, Chapter 8 has indicated certain broad features in the emergence of principles which a genetic treatment of them would have to include. It has not attempted to give anything like a full causal account of moral principles, which would have to be left to the history and psychology of morals. This is, notwithstanding, a matter to which we shall have to return frequently, since the problem of origin and the problem of justification, though distinguishable, are not wholly separable.

However intimately they may be bound up with each other, the problems of origin and justification make different cross-sections of normative phenomena. When we raise the matter of justification, we cannot take the detached scientific and speculative attitude that is appropriate to the question of origins. We are in the thick of the battle. However principles may have arisen, the question of our espousal of them arises when two of them conflict, or when none seems to carry us far, and yet we must act, wishing to act rationally. Even if we knew how they had come to be presupposed and then formulated, we would still have to seek procedures for deciding among the candidates for our allegiance, whether these procedures ultimately rest upon an appeal to rational or non-rational factors.

The chief difficulty that has arisen here centers about the question of the "limits of justification." By the process described in the preceding chapters, roughly speaking we first seek to justify valuational conclusions by "singular" reasons, then we go on to offer maxims under which these may be subsumed, and finally we back up our maxims—or by-pass them—in an appeal to principles. The principles serve as the major premises, or postulate set, of ethical reasoning; and here we seem to hit the ceiling. If we should try to go on to derive the principles themselves from still more general principles, we would land in an indefinite regress. It seems necessary to call a halt to the process somewhere, and the indicated stopping place is at the principles themselves. So runs the argument which holds that there are limits of justification.

Intuitionism, and other forms of rationalism, have an easy way of dealing with this difficulty. The principles are held to be self-evident axioms; they carry their own truth with them, and neither admit of proof nor require proof. They are said to be *a priori*, or we "just know" that they are true, or we "see" their truth by a mysterious intuitive faculty called by some such name as "the eye of the mind." When the deliverances of intellectual intuition vary, there seems to be no recourse except to retreat into dogmatic assertion, or wait for greater "moral maturity" and hope for an ultimate convergence of certainties by the mature. Intuitionism has derived its persistent appeal from its recognition that first principles cannot be "proved," together with a stubborn conviction that some principles must be "true"—or, if this is not quite the right word, they are held to have some kind of "objectivity" comparable to that of truth, so that they are to be sought with the same tenacity with which we seek truth. Intuitionism's weakness has lain in the assumption that the ground of their truth lies in the kind of self-evidence that mathematical axioms were once (but are no longer by most students of mathematics) supposed to have.

Anti-rationalist theories which hold to a belief in principles usually adopt a similar strategy and encounter an analogous impasse. The principles are justified not by intellectual intuition but by some affective or non-rational agency such as conscience or divine grace. When disagreements arise and have been clarified semantically, all we can do is in some sense to wait and pray, working while we pray.

Even ethical systems that profess to be empirical often succumb to the same difficulty and abandon their empiricism when they reach the level of principles. Once given first principles, defined in such a way that they can be made meaningful empirically, then moral questions can be decided by getting the relevant observational evidence, whether that be garnered by external observation or by introspection or by a combination of the two. But the principles themselves cannot be treated, in the ordinary empirical way, as "hypotheses" to be verified empirically. For they define the meaning of basic terms, and prescribe the methods to be employed in the process of verification itself. A definition of the kind in question does not have the form of an empirical assertion, but is frequently a proposal or a decision, hence cannot be verified in the same way that hypotheses can be verified. To deal with this difficulty Sidgwick, for example, had to have recourse to a methodological eclecticism which made particular ethical judgments dependent on empirical evidence but justified by intuition such principles or axioms of distribution as those of prudence, benevolence and justice, as well as the principle of utility itself. One is, in other words, an empiricist on rationalistic grounds.

Other empiricists, seeing more or less clearly the difficulties in treating principles either as self-evident axioms or as empirical hypotheses, have groped for different methods of justifying them. In so far as these methods do not recur to intellectual intuition or to a moral sense view in various disguises, they can be treated as variations of one of the following two types of justification, or a more or less muddled combination of them both:

(1) A defense of principles as "a priori" (or what amounts to this, though the term is not often used here) in some sense distinct from the usual rationalist or intuitionist interpretation of this notion, and usually appealing to a congenital basis in human nature. This strategy, of course, has to meet the charge that it is committing the Naturalistic Fallacy.

(2) A position which seeks to support the principles by some doctrine of "pragmatic justification," or "vindication," distinct from the ordinary methods of empirical verification. Whatever such vindication is held to consist in, it must have a way of showing that it escapes the vicious regress indicated above.

A naturalistic kind of *a priori* justification can be found in Hume, though this is less fully elaborated in his ethical theory than in his general theory of knowledge. Hume held that such epistemological and metaphysical presuppositions as those of causality and an external world could not be established either deductively or inductively, but rested on nature's having determined us to think in these terms, and to act accordingly, in the same way that she has determined us to breathe or feel. Similarly he rested our moral sentiments such as benevolence, self-love and justice upon a foundation in our natural affections, though these, he held, were elicited and shaped by our contacts with the world and our fellow men, which crystallized them into conventions; and he recognized a woeful incompleteness in this mode of justification.

Bentham in general professed to base his doctrine of utility on "the natural constitution of the human frame." He stopped short, however of treating it as a psychological law, in the sense in which he held the allied principle of psychological hedonism to be a "law," perhaps scenting the danger of incurring such objections as those raised in the later doctrine of the Naturalistic Fallacy. In so far as the principle of utility is independent of the hedonistic principle, it is supported by Bentham (*Principles of Morals and Legislation,* Ch. I), in a more indirect and dialectical fashion, involving ten steps, which amount to recommending that anyone who rejects the principle of utility should ask himself in the course of a thoroughgoing analysis of moral problems if he is not presupposing it or if he could get along without it. Bentham here takes a tack that, as we shall see, more closely resembles the method of pragmatic justification though, in him as in other naturalists, this functions in alliance with the appeal to the congenital *a priori.*

Mill, too, recognized clearly that ethical first principles, like the first principles of any branch of philosophy, were incapable of proof "in the ordinary and popular meaning of the term," *i.e.,* by the usual procedures of deduction and induction. And like Bentham, he vacillated between a naturalistic line of justification which traced them back to a foundation in our psychological make-up, and an attempt to show dialectically that our accepted moral beliefs are due to "the tacit influence of a standard not recognized," which he further supported by a quasi-pragmatic appeal to our continuing involvement with pleasure as the ultimate end and a spontaneous or socially created imaginative concern for the welfare of other people.

Twentieth century empiricists, though their concern with

ethical methodology has been more central and more elaborate
than that of earlier writers, usually seek to justify principles
by a similar combination of the two appeals—at times, as we
shall see in the case of C. I. Lewis, falling back on an intuitionist mode of speaking when they get into especially rough
going.

That Lewis sometimes seeks to justify valuational principles
by the strategy we have referred to as that of the congenital
a priori is evident from a number of passages. Thus in seeking
to show that values, intrinsic and extrinsic, as he has characterized them hold an imperative for action, he writes:

Life is temporal; and human life is self-consciously temporal. Our
ultimate interest looks to possible realizations of value in direct experience; but the immediacies so looked to are not what is immediate now but extend beyond that to the future.

It is thus that human life is permeated with the quality of concern. The secret of activity is to be found in such concern; of
activity, that is, so far as it goes beyond unconscious behavior and
animal compulsions, and attempts some self-direction of the passage of immediacy. It is only by such concern and such attempt of
self-direction that we entertain any clearly conscious interests and
seek to make appraisals. This is also the root of what we call our
rationality and of that imperative which attaches to the rational.
It is through such concern that we are constrained now to take that
attitude, and now to do that deed, which later we shall be satisfied
to have taken and to have done.

If we inquire what it means to be rational, the reply is likely to
be given, in terms of our tradition of western thought, by some
reference to inference and logical validity. But perhaps we should
do better to consult our own sense of ourselves, and should then
find an answer in terms of our capacity for foresight and the direction of our action by it. To be rational, instead of foolish or per-
verse, means to be capable of constraint by prevision of some
future good or ill; to be amenable to the consideration, "You will
be sorry if you don't," or "if you do."

Rationality, in this sense, is not derivative from the logical: rather it is the other way about. The validity of reasoning turns upon, and can be summarized in terms of, consistency. And consistency is, at bottom, nothing more than the adherence throughout to what we have accepted; or to put it in the opposite manner, the non-acceptance now of what we shall later be unwilling to adhere to. . . .

To act, to live, in human terms, is necessarily to be subject to imperatives; to recognize norms. Because to be subject to an imperative means simply the finding of a constraint of action in some concern for that which is not immediate; is not a present enjoyment or a present suffering. To repudiate normative significances and imperatives in general, would be to dissolve away all seriousness of action and intent, leaving only an undirected floating down the stream of time; and as a consequence to dissolve all significance of thought and discourse into universal blah. Those who would be serious and circumspect and cogent in what they think, and yet tell us that there are no valid norms or binding imperatives, are hopelessly confused, and inconsistent with their own attitude of assertion. . . .

The validity of this categorical imperative to recognize genuine imperatives of thought and action, does not rest upon logical argument finally. Because presuming that the one to whom the argument is addressed will respond to considerations of consistency and inconsistency, presumes the validity of precisely what is argued for. *The basis of this imperative is a datum of human nature.* . . .

That the good life represents the *summum bonum* is, as we have said, not to be argued. *It is the universal and rational human end;* the end we aim at so far as we approve of our aims and of ourselves in aiming, and do not recognize some perversity or foolishness or weakness of will in our motivations and our doings. *That fact is a datum of the human attitude to life. It is not a datum of the sort commonly called psychological:* we recognize in ourselves the perennial liability to the weaknesses mentioned, by which we are solicited to depart from this ideal of ourselves which still we cannot set aside. It is that norm which can be repudiated only by repudiating all norms and the distinction of valid from invalid in general; by reducing all that we can purpose or accept with the sense of rightness or correctness or validity, to the status of the non-significant—to mere 'psychological data.'. . . . (*Analysis of Knowledge and Valuation*, Ch. XVI.)

As the passages I have italicized show, with respect to some but not all of the basic assumptions of valuation, Lewis holds that the only way they can be justified is to show that they are elements in the construction of human nature. They are part of the structure of the human act, and "essential" to the human make-up. If there is a pragmatic factor here it consists in the relation of such assumptions to action, and particularly in the fact that we discover the assumptions themselves, and their necessity, in the course of coming actively to terms with experience.

But Lewis treats this congenital factor in justification as closely bound up with a linguistic-conceptual *a priori* which dictates the meanings of valuational terms.

Thus, in his preface to the volume, he writes: ". . . What is knowable *a priori* is certifiable by reference to meanings alone." He holds the *a priori* in this sense to be intermediate between two extremes: a transcendentalist view which bases the *a priori* on "some metaphysically significant character of reality," and assumes that "universals have some peculiar mode of being, obscure to sense but disclosable to reason"; and the nominalist extreme, which regards meanings as "no more than the creatures of linguistic convention. . . ." In opposition to nominalism Lewis holds that, "Once the conventions of language are fixed, one can no more affect these meanings or alter their relations than one can alter the facts of existence by talking about them in a different dialect. On that point Platonic realism is nearer to the truth." In this vein Lewis subsequently says of valuational principles, including definitions, that they "are not empirical statements at all, but are analytic and knowable *a priori* or else false."

2. *Validation and Vindication*

Whether Lewis has successfully combined these three approaches to justification—by way of the congenital *a priori*, by way of the linguistic-conceptual *a priori*, and by way of pragmatic justification—is a matter for subsequent discussion. At this point, let us note that another contemporary writer on value theory, Herbert Feigl, who has worked away from the type of emotivism offered by the earlier logical positivism to a view more closely resembling the empirical position, also arrives (in "De Principiis Non Disputandum . . . ?", *Philosophical Analysis*, edited by Max Black, 1950) at a doctrine of justification not far from Lewis' on two of these approaches, namely the congenital *a priori* and pragmatic justification, though he holds a position considerably different from Lewis' on the question of the linguistic-conceptual *a priori*.

Feigl writes that principles, whether those of ethics, logic, epistemology or semantics, are not capable of theoretical justification or "validation," but only of pragmatic justification, for which he has devised the useful synonym, "vindication." Yet as we shall see, in the process of elaborating the latter, he also has recourse to what I have called the congenital or structural *a priori*.

The regress mentioned previously is offered by Feigl as the reason why principles are not capable of deductive-inductive validation. Given rules or principles, specific normative judgments can be validated, but when we reach the principles themselves we have attained the limits of justification along this line of procedure. Principles within any domain constitute the standards that "formulate the system." They also have the function of "implicitly defining the critical terms of the domain in question"—such terms as "valid" in logic, "meaningful" in semantics and "right" in ethics. Feigl differs from the school of Ordinary Language by holding that philosophers must continue to try to achieve precisely formulated principles: "Full awareness of the basic principles of knowledge and evaluation can be attained only by a systematic analysis of the 'rational reconstruction' type." He seems, further, to be closer to the older logical positivism, which held a nominalist view combated by Lewis, in holding that "the status of validating principles (in logical reconstruction) is that of stipulations, definitions or conventions. . . . Like all definitions or conventions the justificantia are *a priori* precisely and only because they are analytic." Yet he insists that meanings are not assigned to such terms arbitrarily or by *fiat*—a view usually held by those who take a "stipulative" view of principles and definitions. On the contrary, the meanings of the basic terms in knowledge and evaluation are controlled by our purposes, and:

Far from being "arbitrary" or "capricious" in the usual sense of these words, our terminal purposes are usually held with the most serious and profound conviction. The only sense in which the misnomer "arbitrary" could be sensibly interpreted here is in the sense of "ultimate," *i.e.*, nonvindicable and resting on the (logically) contingent traits of human nature. Such standards as those of justice and kindliness, as well as of self-perfection, are the counterpart of goals such as those of a harmonious, peaceful, and progressive humanity. The goals or purposes are in turn *resultants of the nature of man* and his needs and interests in ever widening and ever more interdependent social contexts.

It is to be noticed that in this account of pragmatic justification there is a reference to the "nature of man" as the source, or partial source, of our ultimate goals and purposes. But this appeal to a congenital *a priori* is qualified by the statement that such goals and purposes "emerge" only in the course of "the broadest experience," and, consequently, that the needs and interests which constitute the nature of man are disclosed only as they manifest themselves in response to expanding social contexts. It looks, therefore, as though any justification of principles other than by validation must in some way appeal both to the congenital and to the pragmatic element, and that these two are closely interrelated. It appears, furthermore, that the "stipulations" (according to Feigl), like the grasp of the "essential" meanings of terms (according to Lewis), on which definitions are based are for both these philosophers in some way controlled by the congenital and pragmatic elements, though neither elaborates this recognition as fully as could be desired.

Before we go on to try to unravel this puzzle, let us examine briefly some other features of Feigl's conception of vindication. He writes: ". . . A pragmatic justification amounts to showing that something serves as a means toward an end. It thus requires a prior agreement (1) as to the desiredness of the end and (2) as to the method or type of reasoning by which the appropriateness of the means to the end is to be shown." Principles, therefore, for Feigl are means-end propositions—though they are not to be understood as purely descriptive statements, since they also have a prescriptive thrust derived ultimately from espousal of the ends.

But if principles, so far as their cognitive element goes, simply state connections between means and ends, then by Feigl's own criteria they are subject to *validation* rather than vindication. For Feigl nowhere suggests—nor would it be compatible with his general theory of knowledge—that we discover the relation of means to end in any other way than empirically, *i.e.*, by a combination of induction and deduction. The means are chosen simply through factual knowledge of their comparative fitness to promote the ends.

The general ends of life themselves, it must be inferred, are not for Feigl justifiable at all, either by way of validation or by way of vindication, but are in some way adopted by "prior agreement." And here, despite Feigl's disclaimer of a "vicious" type of relativism, he replies to the question "What is the purpose that is fulfilled by adoption of, *e.g.*, The Golden Rule, or a principle of impartiality?"

To answer clearly depends on the individual's personality. Perhaps he obeys the golden rule because of sheer prudence and "enlightened egoism." Perhaps he has by training, education, experience, or reflection developed genuinely altruistic interests and thus holds the ideal of the greatest satisfaction for the greatest number.

Even though he eventually goes on to place limits on the variability of the needs, interests and aspirations of individuals through appeal to socially emergent purposes, we are still puzzled to know: (a) whether the needs, interests and aspirations justify (vindicate) the "purposes"; or (b) whether the purposes are at the same logical level as needs, etc., and therefore are likewise unjustifiable. The second alternative seems on the whole to be Feigl's view, though he may wish to have it both ways. If however (a) does represent his position, we are forced to ask whether this tendency of needs to generate purposes is not itself a factual proposition, so that the purposes likewise are to be validated rather than vindicated.

But his position seems on the whole to be the contrary, as shown by the statement that "terminal purposes," being ultimate, are "non-vindicable" because they rest on "the (logically) contingent traits of human nature." So the appeal to what I have called the congenital *a priori* is not for Feigl a "vindication" of the purposes though it is assumed in the vindication of the means to them, and hence the purposes themselves (and likewise the principles expressing them) are not justifiable.

It follows that the notion of vindication becomes superfluous if we thus render Feigl's position consistent. Expressions prescribing general ends are not for him justifiable at all, nor are those ends themselves; expressions prescribing the means to them are validated rather than vindicated. Hence there is nothing left for vindication to do.

But there is one major flaw in Feigl's treatment of the problem, which if remedied may make it possible to save the notion of vindication. This flaw consists in the assumption, quoted above, that principles state and prescribe means to ultimate ends rather than those ends themselves.

The Golden Rule, for example, is conceived as commanding means to such alternative ends as "sheer prudence" on the one hand or "genuinely altruistic interests" on the other. And the standards of justice and the like are treated as formulating such a goal as that of "a harmonious, peaceful, and progressive humanity." But—at any rate on Feigl's own view of them— such so-called principles clearly constitute what I have called maxims, stating properties which lead to the ends in question under stated or assumed conditions. I see nothing here that requires anything more than validation, except the terminal goals themselves, which according to Feigl are neither validable nor vindicable. Vindication therefore seems superfluous on his own view if we render it consistent with his empiricism.

What has just been said applies also to logical principles. Thus, vindication of a rule of induction "concerns the choice of means for the attainment of an end." And "our end here is clearly successful prediction, more generally, true conclusions or nondemonstrative inference."

A place, however, can be made for the notion of vindication if we apply it to the acceptance of the "general ends of life." This view would require us to conceive principles in the primary sense not as prescribing means to the goals but as *characterizing and prescribing the goals themselves*. And what are ordinarily called principles do this. It would be impossible to exclude from any formulation of the ultimate assumptions of inductive logic the general end of "successful prediction," and a characterization of what would constitute this. Likewise in ethics: our maxims or rules would have no applicability unless we also had a characterization of the end which they serve, such as the Utilitarian principle or Feigl's conception of a harmonious, peaceful and progressive humanity.

If the point just made were taken into account by Feigl, he would avoid the suggestion of a vitiating cultural relativism which has exposed him to criticism. Such means-end propositions as Feigl discusses, or most of them, are culturally variable like all maxims; but this does not mean that the general ends of life which are formulated in principles, or would be if we could get the right principles, would be similarly variable.

Before something like a constructive and systematic treatment of the justification of principles can be attempted, it is necessary to indicate briefly the present state of controversy with respect to two questions which are closely related to the subject under discussion and to each other: (1) the logical status of definitions of the kind at issue; and (2) the dispute over the nature of the analytic and synthetic.

Principles, not only in ethics but in the other domains in question, are definitory. They define—according to my view— the ultimate ends of conduct and of thought, or—according to Feigl—the general means to these ends.

Whatever may be the case in such a domain as that of pure logic and mathematics, the definitory principles of ethics, epistemology or semantics cannot be conceived adequately in any of the following three ways, each of which has its strong proponents in contemporary discussions of definition. They cannot be conceived (a) as mere factual propositions reporting usage; nor (b) as sheer arbitrary stipulations as to the substitutability of one set of symbols for another; nor (c) as analyses of ready-made equivalences in meaning (Lewis).

They cannot be (a), because usage in these fields is usually more or less vague and groping, and the formulation of definitions seeks to remedy this. They cannot be (b), because their acceptance is under the control of existential and experiential considerations, even though in strict logic these considerations do not confirm or infirm them. They cannot be (c), because in the fields in question the hard problems concerning definition arise when equivalences of meaning are not well established, or not sufficiently clear, so that we must tinker with such partial equivalences as we have and try to sharpen them into exact equivalences, even though that requires in some sense a legislation. It does not follow, however, that the legislation is merely a verbal stipulation, any more than the legislation of political bodies is this. Congressional legislation, when it is responsible, is preceded by fact-finding and guided by considerations of use and value, even though it is not a report on any of these nor an inference from them alone.

Definitory principles have their peculiarities which distinguish them from lower-level definitions, but what has just been said applies also to the hard cases of the latter. It applies, for example, in a critical or reconstructive phase of a science— whether a factual or a normative science—when accepted definitions, whether explicit or implicit, have broken down and a revision of the terminology and the principles of the subject is required. It would be easy to illustrate this point from any revolutionary situation in physics or art criticism.

3. *Principles as Analytic or Synthetic*

It is in part the perception of this characteristic of definitions which has led to the current view that the distinction between the analytic and the synthetic is, at least in certain domains, a shifting and relative one.

An analytic statement, according to the older view which rested upon a subject-predicate logic, is one whose predicate is contained in the meaning of its subject; the statement itself, consequently, follows simply from an analysis of the subject's meaning. With the development of the new relational logic in the past century, it was seen that most statements are not fully analyzable by treating them in the subject-predicate form, but can be more adequately analyzed as consisting in the assertion of a relation between two or more subjects. The notion of an analytic statement was accordingly revised to conceive it as one which follows deductively from the set of definitions and postulates assumed by the system to which it belongs, *i.e.*, from analysis of their meaning, together with the accepted rules of inference. A synthetic statement, on either the older or the newer view, is one whose truth rests on something outside the meanings of terms; this appeal may be either to experience or to some kind of *a priori* other than what we have called the linguistic-conceptual.

A distinction of kind between the analytic and the synthetic can be supported only when the so-called definition is either an arbitrary stipulation or when, to use W. V. Quine's phrase, there is a "pre-existing synonymy," based on use or established definition, between the term defined and the set of terms by which it is defined. As Lewis himself says, "Once the intensions of language are fixed, one can no more affect these meanings or alter their relations than one can alter the facts of existence by talking about them in a different dialect." In such a case, a definition can with some plausibility be treated as strictly analytic; it formulates an established equivalence in meaning. But the crucial problem over definitions arises when the intensions or meanings of the terms are not fixed, when there is at least a margin of indeterminacy and fluidity in them, whether that lie in explicit formulation or in implicit linguistic practice. And this is certainly so in the present confused state of

ethical controversy, whatever may be the situation with respect to the definitions in such a subject as logic.[1]

Quine bases his view that the distinction between the analytic and synthetic is a relative one on an examination of "a
variant type of definitional activity which does not limit itself
to the reporting of pre-existing synonymies" ("Two Dogmas
of Empiricism," *From a Logical Point of View*, 1953). In such
a case "the purpose is not merely to paraphrase the definiendum into an outright synonym, but actually to improve upon
the definiendum [the term to be defined] by refining and
supplementing its meaning." Such, at any rate, is Quine's
professed aim, but he modifies it when he goes on to state that
although such a definition "does not merely report a pre-
existing synonymy," it "does rest nevertheless on *other* pre-
existing synonymies," which are those of the term's context
in use: "Any word worth explicating [a term Quine takes over
from Carnap for this purpose] has some contexts which, as
wholes, are clear and precise enough to be useful; and the
purpose of explication is to preserve the usage of these favored
contexts while sharpening the usage of other contexts." This
requires according to Quine not a synonymy between the
terms, but a synonymy between contexts. The latter notion is
an odd one, for symbols, terms and statements are the kinds
of things that can be synonymous rather than contexts; and
the notion is not clarified by Quine.

---

[1] In the brief treatment of the problem here, I shall not try to
deal with the question whether the view that the distinction between the analytic and the synthetic is a shifting and relative one
can be applied to propositions of pure logic and mathematics. This
is the point on which the position of Quine and Morton White has
been most strongly attacked. I shall limit myself to considerations
pertinent to the analytic or synthetic character of ethical and
valuational statements and principles.

This view does not tell us what to do when we must invent a new term to express a new distinction, nor does it tell us how to "sharpen" the usage by co-ordinating references to contexts. In discussing explication, Quine limits himself to "natural" languages and does not deal with the problem of definition most crucial in ethical theory; namely, how to deal with a situation where the natural language must be improved or supplemented by a terminology that goes as far as it can with pre-existing usage, but is forced for the sake of clarity and adequacy to introduce an "artificial" element along with the "natural." Furthermore, he does not give any analysis of "synonymy," the notion on which, for him, the solution of the problem of definition ultimately hinges.

Though Quine consequently leaves the problem of definition hanging in the air, his general way of dealing with the distinction between the analytic and the synthetic nevertheless is of aid in tackling this problem. He writes:

The totality of our so-called knowledge or beliefs, from the most casual matters of geography and history to the profoundest laws of atomic physics or even of pure mathematics and logic, is a man-made fabric which impinges on experience only along the edges. Or, to change the figure, total science is like a field of force whose boundary conditions are experience. A conflict with experience at the periphery occasions readjustments in the interior of the field. . . . But the total field is so underdetermined by its boundary conditions, experience, that there is much latitude of choice as to what statements to re-evaluate in the light of any single contrary experience. No particular experiences are linked with any particular statements in the interior of the field, except indirectly through considerations of equilibrium affecting the field as a whole.

And to deal with the problem of the analytic and the synthetic, Quine advocates a more thoroughgoing pragmatism than that of Carnap and Lewis, who

. . . take a pragmatic stand on the question of choosing between language forms, scientific frameworks; but their pragmatism leaves off at the imagined boundary between the analytic and the synthetic. In repudiating such a boundary I espouse a more thorough pragmatism. Each man is given a scientific heritage plus a continuing barrage of sensory stimulation; and the considerations which guide him in warping his scientific heritage to fit his continuing sensory promptings are, where rational, pragmatic.

By this view it is implied that definitions, like the other conceptual tools of knowledge, are part of the apparatus for predicting further experience in the light of past experience. They are tools which are not indefinitely flexible to experience, but are revealed to impose stubborn requirements arising from the progressively evolving nature of language and thought, so that experience, up to a certain limit, must conform to them as well as vice versa.

It follows that at no level are primary definitions validated or "verified." [2] A primary definition expresses a decision or proposal to assign, stabilize or retain the meaning of a symbol or term. Being a decision or proposal rather than a statement (whether of fact or of established equivalence of meaning), this act, and the definition it sets up, are justified by their power to organize experience, their fruitfulness in clarity, coherence and successful prediction. A definition is thus under the control of experience in the broadest sense, but it is not strictly speaking rendered true or false, more probable or less probable, by the specific predictions which it helps to generate. The definition may be maintained in the face of negative results, and the system of which it forms a part is

---

[2] A fuller treatment of the logical aspects of this problem is to be found in the author's "Definitions in Value Theory," *Journal of Philosophy,* vol. 44, 1947.

rendered less acceptable by such negative results if long sustained. But inadequate definitions are not "disproved" by developing knowledge but repudiated in some other way; usually, like the Greek gods according to Comte, by being forgotten. The remote control by experience, therefore, can be said to provide a pragmatic justification of definitions, in the sense that action—the action of practical thinking—supplies the ground for their acceptance or rejection. We are, then, using "experience" here in a sense which, like Aristotle's, includes participation as well as observation.

An easy way, sometimes currently taken, of disposing of this problem is to make a sharp distinction among: (1) analytic statements, (2) synthetic statements, (3) imperatives, (4) rules, so that the question whether imperatives and rules are analytic or synthetic does not arise. It is clear that what we have called a naked imperative—a command that is not backed up by rational justification—is neither analytic nor synthetic by any criterion. A rule, however, contains both a cognitive and a prescriptive element. It is then legitimate to ask whether, granted the legitimacy of the prescription, the embedded cognitive element is analytic or synthetic. And, indeed, when the rule is derived in part by deduction from a principle, its descriptive content may follow analytically from the principle. It is, therefore, quite pertinent to ask whether the cognitive element in such a rule as a definition rests, directly or indirectly, on sheer stipulation and is thus analytic, or whether it is established through pragmatic control by experience and, therefore, when regarded apart from the context of its functioning, has the ambiguous status between the analytic and the synthetic we have been considering.

When we come to the highest-level definitions in any field, that of principles, this remote control by experience seems itself to be dependent in part on basic structural features of human nature and the human situation which do not vary with the shifting disclosures of specialized knowledge and the specific actions involved in getting it, but rather provide a control of a different kind. This control constitutes what we have referred to as the congenital or structural *a priori:* a difficult notion which we must now proceed to try to clarify and assess.

10

The Appeal to Human Nature

---

1. *The Structural and the Linguistic* A Priori

When empiricists attempt to justify principles by invoking an experiential control that is still not verification or validation, they are often impelled, as we saw in the preceding chapter, to appeal at some stage in the process to "human nature," or to the way we are built. This is usually offered not as a complete justification, but in support of certain selected principles or certain elements in them. We have called such an appeal the invocation of a congenital or structural *a priori*, as distinguished from the linguistic-conceptual *a priori*, though it may in some cases be advanced as the ultimate source of the latter.

To call such a foundation for principles an *a priori* may sound like an abuse of language. Yet I believe that the usage can be supported historically. *A priori* in general has meant "prior to experience," and this in turn means logically independent of experience. Something may be independent of experience either because it rests on established or accepted meanings of language, or because it springs from the ultimate make-up of the knower or agent, in so far as that is not alterable by experience. Even here, however, we must say with Kant that all knowledge *begins* with experience, and the congenital *a priori* is disclosed only in the process of experience and critical reflection on it, where alone if at all we can learn what our make-up contributes and what we receive from other sources.

Such a conception lay at the basis of Leibniz's and Kant's views of the *a priori,* though we have to disentangle it from the language and the methodological assumptions in which it was embedded in order to make it pertinent to our own problems. Consider, for example, Leibniz's well-known defense of innate ideas against Locke in the *New Essays on the Human Understanding:*

The question is to know whether the soul in itself is entirely empty, like the tablet on which nothing has yet been written (*tabula rasa*) according to Aristotle and the author of the *Essay,* and whether all that is traced thereon comes solely from the senses and from experience; or whether the soul contains originally the principles of several notions and doctrines which external objects merely awaken on occasions, as I believe, with Plato, and even with the schoolmen, and with all those who take with this meaning the passage of St. Paul (Romans: 2, 15) where he remarks that the law of God is written in the heart. . . .

After having employed the whole of the first book in rejecting innate knowledge (lumières), taken in a certain sense, [Locke] nevertheless admits at the beginning of the second and in what follows, that the ideas which do not originate in sensation came from reflection. Now reflection is nothing else than attention to what is in us, and the senses do not give us that which we already carry with us. This being so, can it be denied that there is much that is innate in our mind, since we are innate, so to say, in ourselves, and since there is in ourselves, being, unity, substance, duration, change, action, pleasure, and a thousand other objects of our intellectual ideas? . . . If there were veins in the block [of marble], which should mark out the figure of Hercules rather than other figures, the block would be more determined thereto, and Hercules would be in it as in some sort innate, although it would be necessary to labor in order to discover these veins and to cleanse them by polishing and by cutting away that which prevents them from appearing. It is thus that ideas and truths are innate in us, as inclinations, dispositions, habits, or natural capacities, and not as actions; although these capacities are always accompanied by some actions, often insensible, which correspond to them.

What Leibniz is saying, in other words, is that we are not wholly malleable to experience, that our congenital structure inclines us to actions of one sort rather than another, and that we discover this by acting rather than by a detached study of our make-up which rests on inductive inference from observation of our states and our behavior. Whether human nature, as Leibniz suggests, is in its turn an adequate expression of the nature of reality in general, is another question. Nor does Leibniz give us an adequate answer to the question how we grasp this inalterable core of potentiality in ourselves, or how we can sift the alterable from the inalterable with any precision.

Kant explicitly recognized a connection between the conceptual *a priori* and the structural *a priori,* and in his doctrine of the forms of intuition and the categories attempted to found certain elements in the former on the latter. The method which he offered for grasping the elusive structural element in knowledge was his famous "transcendental method," the method of asking what is presupposed by experience but not found in experience. When he went on from cognitive principles to moral and religious principles, he had to abandon even this mode of justification and appeal to the noumenal self, as the source of "postulates" which were on quite a different footing from the principles of the understanding or the forms of intuition, though these postulates, too, were held to reveal in a different way the structure of our being.

Contemporary empiricism, in rejecting the rationalistic methodology and the transcendent metaphysics on which these positions rested, is nevertheless being forced to come to terms with the notion that our most general presuppositions are based, at least in part, upon our ultimate structure as thinking, feeling and acting beings. It has scarcely begun, however, to unravel the perplexities to which this concern leads. Nor do the non-naturalists, if their unanalyzed "intuition" be taken as the mode of grasping the structural *a priori*, carry us far: what they offer us is not a mode of advancing the solution of the problem but a counsel of despair and an invitation to dogmatism.

Some of the basic presuppositions of our action to which we cling obstinately seem to be capable of no other justification than by appeal to our congenital make-up; in the case of others, this appeal falls short. The appeal is plausible in the case of presuppositions like "we ought to seek ends" or "we ought to choose the means to our ends." These seem tautological or trivial, because we can't help acting on them; and so to ask for a justification becomes superfluous and even meaningless. Yet they do express a fundamental feature of animal existence, and such a recognition has to be dealt with.

At the other extreme is such an altruistic principle as that in our conduct we ought always to regard the well-being of others. To this principle there are genuine alternatives; we are built in such a way that as individuals or as a species we can act otherwise, and if the principle is justifiable at all, it is only through the accumulation of commitments in prolonged moral performance. For it is equally consistent with our nature to be altruistic or to be selfish.

In between the two kinds of principles are other principles whose justification requires a blend of nature and commitment: *e.g.*, "Other things being equal, we ought to avoid suffering wherever possible." This is partly *a priori*, in the sense that there is built into us a very strong tendency to act in accordance with it; but there is also ground for doubt that this principle can be erected into a universal law, for it seems that on the particular occasion it is possible for us to act against it. And so there appears to be, along with a strong natural predisposition toward it, an element of choice in its adoption.

In one sense, the congenital factor does not supply a justification: in so far as we cannot act otherwise, no justification is possible or needed. As Kant held, ought implies can and is incompatible with must. Instead of offering the basis for a justification, then, this factor establishes the limits of justification. It is through action that we find out what these limits are, and test that area of activity where there are alternatives. Consequently, positive justification always occurs in a pragmatic context; the *a priori* functions only negatively in this process by setting bounds to the possibility of choice. Even the bounds, however, are disclosed in action when action exhibits its iron pull upon us.

We shall see, however, that there is another level at which the dichotomy again arises. This is at the point where we ask whether the modifications forced by action are themselves due, as a whole or in part, to the way we are built.

But let us first explore further the status of such principles as seem to be indisputably *a priori* in the above sense, such as the prescription of normativeness or goal-seeking. This principle is genuinely a principle: it formulates a basic structural presupposition of our actions, even though we may never in practice flout it and, consequently, do not feel a need for its justification. We espouse it, then, we may say, because we are men, and man is by nature a normative animal. This is in some sense a *fact*, a fundamental datum. All living beings are loaded and cocked when they come into existence. We can put the matter either metaphysically by saying that the

Platonic Eros is of their essence, or scientifically by saying that the goal-seeking urge is thrust upon them by their metabolism, life being a generation of energy that must be expended. It is of their nature that men—not to mention children—are trying to go somewhere. Their perplexities arise, not from the need to justify the fundamental restlessness or vectorial character of existence, but from the doubts knocked into them in the process of learning where to go in order to fulfill their innate purposiveness, and how to get there. The problem is not how normativeness gets into the make-up of the human or sub-human animal but how to channel it in such a way that it furthers the realization of those properties of objects and experience on which normativeness seizes in the developing process of experience, how to organize the various specific ends adopted in this process, and how to make the individual's normativeness compatible with the goal-seeking orientations of other living creatures.

There is, as we have suggested, undoubtedly *some* sense in which purposiveness—goal-seeking, the disposition to pursue ends—is congenital to human nature. But in precisely *what* sense? Only if we can answer this question can we decide whether the question "Ought I to seek ends?" is meaningful and justifiable.

There are three alternative ways of formulating the matter. Goal-seeking may be called: (1) a *law*, (2) a *tendency*, or (3) a *structural feature*, of human nature or more precisely of the human act. If it is either (1) or (3), it is a universal feature of the act; if it is (2) merely a tendency, it characterizes only some acts or characterizes acts under certain conditions.

Now the answer obviously depends in part on how we define an "act," either explicitly or implicitly. If we define an act in such a way as to exclude the notion of purposiveness from the defining property, then the principle is either a law or a tendency. If a universal characteristic of the act, it is a law. If it characterizes only some acts, or permits of exceptions, it is a tendency.

If an act, however, is defined in such a way that something is not an act unless it is purposive, then purposiveness is a structural feature of the act, impacted into any adequate definition of it.

Now it has become customary, even among behaviorists such as E. C. Tolman and C. L. Hull, to define an act, or the term behavior itself, in such a way that it includes purposiveness. If a segment of a living thing's process is not directed toward a goal, then it is not a behavioral act but something else.

By calling such a pervasive property of the life situation a *structural feature* of that situation, we have a terminological device for keeping the logical problem about laws and tendencies from popping up at every crucial phase of the argument. We can become "more purposive" or "less purposive" in the sense that we can adopt the rule that we will devote more, or less, thought and effort to the definition and attainment of specific ends. But this maxim itself presupposes the more general principle that we seek goals—for being "more purposive" or "less purposive" is itself a goal—and whichever of these more specific goals we choose, the maxim formulating it cannot be "justified" by the appeal to our congenital make-up alone; it involves experiential considerations.

With respect, at least, to such principles as that we should seek ends, we must say that if to justify them by an appeal to our nature is to commit the Naturalistic Fallacy, so be it. But to call it a Naturalistic Fallacy, or any kind of fallacy, would be to treat as a logical inference what is an existential necessity. The "justification" which we have suggested at no phase of the process rests upon an inference such as: "we are built in such a way that we must seek ends; therefore we ought to seek ends"; for the "ought" in the conclusion, when we analyze its meaning, is not the common type of moral ought which applies to the kind of situation where choice is possible. Here no choice is possible: the function of the "ought" is simply to rule out the alternatives which make choice possible, because there are no alternatives. The plausibility of the "ought" form here arises in part from the theoretical raising of the possibility of alternatives, a possibility which is quickly excluded by the pressures of existence, so that it is not a real alternative for action. The "ought" in question has whatever genuine, if truncated, meaning it retains from the fact that both it and the "ought" which applies to a choice-situation possess a prescriptive force. In the one case, end-seeking is prescribed by the iron necessity of our nature; in the other case, a particular end is prescribed by our reflection upon the actual alternatives and the prescription is incorporated into the principle which we espouse. Both share the feature of the "ought," in its most characteristic use, that it is a prescriptive sign.

The theoretical perplexities of naturalism arise, then, not from a need to justify this elemental normativeness of the human being, but, first, in trying to understand in detail how it develops from its primitive form to its complex operations in the sensitive moral conscience and the subtle processes of valuational reflection; and secondly, and for our subject more important than any such genetic considerations, in seeking to discover how the complex and unstable creature, ensnared within the process in which his own developing nature involves him with the world, can find guidance in the midst of the moral struggle. These questions cannot be answered by any counter-syllogism to Moore's naturalistic paralogism, but by a detailed examination of the phenomena of moral experience.

The recent anti-naturalist schools have been so fortified by their supposed discovery of the Naturalistic Fallacy that they have felt themselves to be absolved from what naturalism has felt to be one of its major obligations: namely, to square the ethical theories to which one gives allegiance with an account of the existential context out of which ethical phenomena arise. It is quite true that ethical justification is not identical with causal explanation, and that normative knowledge is not identical with descriptive knowledge. But the course of intuitionist ethics has shown us the impasse into which the attempt to cultivate one kind of knowledge—normative knowledge at the phenomenological level—lands if it is sought in complete independence of the other kind of knowledge. The non-naturalist predicament is more frustrating than the great puzzle of the Naturalistic Fallacy. The non-naturalist establishes an absolute cleavage between value and fact, the normative and the descriptive, the ethical and the natural. He sees quite correctly that the normative judgment is something more than a mere characterization of an existing object, and that it cannot logically be derived from descriptive statements alone. But he is so overwhelmed by this insight that he makes it the final boundary of ethical understanding.

2. The Natural Basis of Ethical Thinking

Faced with such a predicament, all the philosopher can do is to take the line of procedure that he follows where other apparent blocks to intellectual advance are encountered; i.e., to continue in the search for understanding. Just as the idea of "intuition" boils down to an injunction to stop analysis, so the idea of the "non-natural" is an injunction to cease trying to fit goodness or the ought into the natural process or to account for its origin in any other way. We cannot prove that values generally have a natural cause, any more than we can prove the law of causality in general. All we can do is to keep ahead in the search for those conditions which are stable accompaniments of the manifestation of values, meanwhile being on our guard against the genetic fallacy of mistaking the cause for the effect, or confusing the statement of the conditions of the occurrence of the value with the justification of the value judgment.

A genetic explanation is not identical with a justification either in ethics or in logic; yet we have a right to be suspicious of any justification that invokes factors whose genesis is unintelligible or which are described in such a way that, like non-natural properties, they cannot be conceived as having originated at all, except by an *ad hoc* miracle. To distinguish between justification and causal explanation does not at all require us to hold that the factors which supply the justification are uncaused or causally unintelligible. On the contrary, the presumption is that, if we cannot give such an explanation with plausibility, the factors in question do not occur. And we cannot justify the real by the illusory. There are some explanations which "explain away"; and others which resign us to the inevitable. It is the latter which are under consideration here.

The procedure suggested is applicable whether we conceive the justification of normative judgments to require principles or not to require them. Both the anti-definist and the definist, if they try doggedly to account for the prescriptive force of normative judgments without invoking intuition, are forced to have recourse to the ineradicable normativeness of the human creature. This situation is often concealed, for the anti-definist of the Ordinary Language persuasion, by his refusal to carry the genetic method beyond a dogmatically chosen limit. He holds that the history of language is relevant to its meaning, but refuses to carry his genetic inquiry beyond the question, how did or can the individual learn to use a given word correctly in the course of his own training in the language. He leaves unexplored the larger question, how the habit of correct usage thus acquired by the individual was itself forged in the saecular or millennial experience of the community that settled upon a certain usage as correct.

For a genetic approach to the question, the great divide, as suggested earlier, is the point of contact between pre-discursive valuation and discursive valuation. The animal and the human infant, without language, make choices with respect to the satisfaction of needs, the avoidance of suffering, and the organization of their conduct. The possibility of making these choices more effective, and also the possibility of bringing error and confusion into them from new sources, is greatly furthered by the acquisition of language. But we must conceive the first stage in discursive valuation to consist in simply making explicit through language features of a situation that have already been hit upon by the trial-and-error, resting upon the sub-linguistic selectiveness of the organism, previously undergone by the individual and by the group.

Just as the creature needs no one to teach him the supposed rule that he ought to seek ends, likewise with the supposed general thesis that he ought to employ means to achieve his ends. The earthworm or the rat adopts means to his goals without having to be taught to do so. The tendency to employ means is built into his cell structure, developed in response to the life-situation. When a philosopher first tries to formulate a distinction between means and ends, he is, at most, making precise a distinction that long before found its way into the language and produced distinctive linguistic forms to express it; and this first discursive expression itself in turn simply formulated features already operative in pre-linguistic valuation. What language bestows upon him is not the lesson that in order to achieve the end you must find the means—a principle of which he already has a working knowledge, despite its lapses in fantasy-life—but a much greater ability to grasp the possibility of alternative specific means, and to forecast the detailed operation of the means.

E. C. Tolman has shown that a rat has a working understanding of the meaning of the choice-situation ("The Determiners of Behavior at a Choice Point," *Psychological Review,* vol. 45, 1938). When a rat reaches a choice point in the maze, he may halt and run a little way into each of the alternative paths. This "running-back-and-forth" Tolman takes as the primitive behavioral analogue of reflection or of "consciousness" itself. What releases the eventual choice—and therefore serves as the behavioral analogue of the prudential "ought"—is presumably a lessening of tension in the rat's muscles when he enters the alley that has previously led him to food. The perceptual pattern governing the choice—a central neural Gestalt linking sensory and motor elements—Tolman calls a "strip map." When a human being makes a similar choice at a cross-road by use of a highway map, he has a much steadier, less fallible and better tested instrument than the strip map that flickers through the rat's perceptions. The acquisition of explicit symbolism thus confers greater capacity of control over the valuational situation, but it does not abolish the broad features of the situation that were present in pre-discursive behavior; nor, except in the ultimate scrutinies of philosophers, does it ever question them. When questions are raised about these fundamental features, the answer can do no more than make explicit what we—and the rat—knew already by way of *savoir* rather than *connaître,* or *wissen* rather than *kennen.*

Now, when fairly adequate language habits and reliable habits of reflection have been acquired, it is not indispensable to be able to state these explicitly. This is the partial insight behind the insistence of informalists that we ordinarily give "reasons" only when a judgment is challenged, and that we have an immediate grasp of the relevance of certain reasons and the irrelevance of others, so that we do not need to reach these by a formal pattern of logical reasoning. The skillful bricklayer knows where to cut a particular brick in order to fit it into a wall, without invoking the theorems of geometry, and the faithful mother knows when to change the baby's diaper without deriving this conclusion from the premises of a syllogism. But the architect who designs the building, or the doctor who is trying to cure the baby of a rare ailment, must proceed discursively, and on hard occasions must invoke specific formulae of physics or specific maxims of biochemistry.

Morally and valuationally speaking, man is always, as Hegel called him, the sick animal. So that his normative habits are not altogether adequate. But man is also the animal that is always trying to get well, or when that has proved to be hopeless, to come to terms with his sickness. He is therefore impelled constantly to call one factor or another into question. The moral philosopher, impressed by the perennial human sickness, must be prepared to raise doubts about all the factors. He seeks to make all valuational assumptions explicit, and thereby to conceive the possibility of changing any of them. When we express in language any presupposition on which we have been acting, that presupposition at once comes to seem manipulable, so that we contemplate the possibility of changing it. For language is our greatest instrument of control, and ordinarily when we can name a thing we become able to dominate it. But some features of our conduct prove to be recalcitrant, just as do some features of the world. In practice, we soon learn that we can no more abolish our tendency to seek ends in general than we can repeal the law of gravitation. All we can do is to accept such structural facts of existence, and shape our specific ends and means in accordance with the detailed knowledge that our increased understanding of the structure gives us.

Wilfrid Sellars has made a useful distinction between "tied" behavior and "rule-regulated" conduct. The former is "action which merely conforms to a rule," and the latter is action "which occurs because of the rule." Action of the first type occurs without knowledge of the law or presupposition which governs it, or proceeds in accordance with it whether we are aware of the rule or not. In the second type, the knowledge of the rule is itself a causal factor in the process, and whether the action will be performed depends on whether or not we grasp and adopt the rule. (W. Sellars, "Language, Rules and Behavior," in *John Dewey, Philosopher of Science and Freedom*, edited by S. Hook, 1950.)

It is still a matter of debate whether certain of the most disputed principles are really of the second type. For example, the psychological hedonist or the psychological egoist holds that we are "tied" to pleasure-seeking-and-pain-avoidance, or to selfishness, and therefore there is no genuine possibility of altering the rules by becoming conscious of them. If they were right, then hedonism and egoism would be just as *a priori* as the principle that we should seek ends, and as little in need of justification. Justification becomes a serious problem only when there is a genuine possibility of change in an assumption of conduct.

The tendency to regulate behavior by rules, though we do not share it with other animals, nor even with many humans, can itself become so constant and pervasive a feature of our moral activity that it is "second nature," *i.e.*, it is a structural feature of our moral attitudes as these have been shaped by long buffeting from the world. (Cf. Pascal: "I fear greatly that this nature may be only a first custom, just as custom is a second nature." *Pensées.*) We can then, if we like, say retrospectively that it was *a priori* not as an actuality of our "first" or congenital nature, but as a potentiality of it to be realized when we are plunged into social relationships as they await us. To call it *a priori* in this qualified sense is, as previously, to rule out practical alternatives.

3. *Nature and Experience*

When we consider such principles as those advocating prudence or altruism, or the auxiliary principle that we should guide our conduct by principles, we cannot treat them as natural in the same sense as the principles prescribing that we seek ends, or regard the means to them. Yet the appeal to "nature" in justification of principles is a recurrent one even here, and survives the equally perennial refutations of it. Its initial plausibility resides in the fact that nature itself exhibits strong normative urges. Its initial implausibility consists in the equally salient facts that nature also exhibits vast areas of indifference to norms, that it contains destructive urges, and that the normative urges themselves can miss the mark. The problem at this general level may be summed up by saying that man is by nature a normative animal, but an imperfectly normative one. So it may appear that some normative principle itself not discoverable in nature must be sought in order to correct the imperfections of nature; or, if this solution is ruled out, that the appeal to nature must be more selective than the above general statement suggests and than it has usually been in the history of naturalistic doctrines.

Let us first consider the broad grounds for the plausibility of the justification by nature. It is not plausible at all unless it is restricted to living nature. For non-living nature is, except in a few tiny cosmic oases, either too hot or too cold to be benign to norms. It has indeed generated them when it generated life, and it supports life precariously. But the partial hospitality to norms is relative to life and sporadic. Living nature, on the other hand, is always on the whole striving toward an apparent good or a virtual good when possible, and when impossible away from evil. Even the amoeba ejects substances which will be harmful to it. The human body, as we know, is the great healer, and usually the most the doctors can do is, gently or drastically, to remove impediments to its curative tendencies. Madness is itself a natural device for coming to terms with intolerable strain and eliminating it by extreme exclusion.

But the normativeness of nature, when conceived in this broad way, also has its limitations. Whether we speak of the death wish, the demonic in man or original sin, the individual at times seems bent on his own destruction. He also is generally content with less good than he is capable of achieving. And he tends to be less regardful of rules, and of knowledge in general, than his well-being would require. When we consider the relations between individuals, furthermore, we find less of the subconscious and automatic tendencies toward health than in the case of the single organism. Societies, even more than individuals, can stabilize themselves for long periods in a kind of living death.

Naturalism must at best, then, appeal to some element in nature, not imposed fatefully by nature, for the redemption of the rest of nature. Its general support for such a selective procedure is the prime article in the naturalist faith:

> Yet nature is made better by no mean
> But nature makes that mean. . . .
> (Shakespeare: *Winter's Tale*)

Nature as a whole is a very mixed affair, but it contains the good as well as the bad, the better as well as the worse. And any means that may arise for furthering the good or the better would itself by this faith be a natural product whether the instrument be a charismatic man who sets an example of noble conduct, or a moral rule that crystallizes slowly out of the experience of the race.

190

Although by this faith there is no appeal to anything outside nature, here is where the justification by nature fails us, and some naturalists invoke the pragmatic justification, or as it is sometimes called, justification by involvement or commitment.

The justification by nature is invoked when we stand outside the process and seek to understand it. The justification by involvement occurs when we are caught up in the normative process and participate in it. They are two phases of the same thing, and mutually contributory, but they have a different direction. And the justification by involvement is the crucial phase. We may speak of both of them together as constituting vindication as distinct from validation.

Vindication may appeal to the human make-up, but it must finally be the human make-up as shaped by a social situation, including social procedures of reflection, and as confronting with urgency the possibilities of change in the established structure of that situation itself.[1] It is prospective as well as retrospective. If we identify it, in part, with the deliverances of the "moral consciousness" of "reasonable" men, this moral consciousness itself must be conceived as consisting in a global sense of directedness which is partly expressible in principles but in its totality eludes formulation, because it is the ever-

---

[1] This dual character of vindication is emphasized in traditional political philosophy by natural law or natural rights theories, which appeal to a congenital *a priori*, and by social contract theories, which invoke pragmatic justification. Both are one-sided, and although we may learn something by examining the functions these theories have been devised to serve, little can be gained by trying to base a complete theory of law or government on the one or the other. We have tried here to get a foothold on the problem by avoiding the terminologies of both types of theories, needing as they do a thorough recasting.

expanding matrix of working assumption out of which principles crystallize. To call it "intuition" would be to suggest
that the limits of expansion have been reached—and of this we
can never be sure—or that the principle which it recommends
is complete in itself, and not dependent on further shifts in the
matrix as that encounters new situations. To call it *a priori*
connotes a salutation to the coerciveness of our developing
and self-disclosing nature, but ignores the partial plasticity of
that nature with respect to the external situation which is
equally a factor.

To call it pragmatic is not to appeal to action excluding
thought—as in the cruder versions of pragmatism—but to
action incorporating thought. The question is one as to the
level where our pragmatism comes in. To justify a particular
judgment by an appeal to its "working" is to misplace our
pragmatism. When more or less reliable habits of reflection
have been developed, the judgment "works" effectively only
as it fits into a context of theoretical justification, and the
working consists in the interplay between the theoretical system and action.

When we speak of the moral consciousness as a global
"sense" of directedness, furthermore, we are not referring to
a mere passive feeling. The introspective glimpse that we get
of the working of such a Gestalt is only a fragmentary cross-
section of its total nature, which includes active pressures,
having wide ramifications into past and future, and into our
subconscious and physiological processes. The introspective
sense of reasonableness, then, is simply the phenomenal resultant and sign of this compounding of active forces; but it is
these as summed up in the overwhelming sense of moral compulsion—*"Ich kann nichts anders."*

Whatever fixity may be found in human potentialities, it is
also true that our make-up is somewhat indeterminate, somewhat plastic to experience, so that we cannot call our most

vexatiously debated principles wholly *a priori* in the existential sense, and hence we must acknowledge our global moral awareness ("conscience" or "intuition") itself to be indefinitely educable. However we may be built, we are subject to further *Bildung*. It is above all the actualities and potentialities of the social structure that shape us, so that the working presuppositions which moral principles and maxims formulate are the expression of human nature not in isolation but in its normative responses to the pressures of social relationships. The more specific maxims and codes are highly relative to the culture; when we seek general principles that are less variable, they try to express the human make-up as it manifests itself under the universal conditions of social living, and to exhibit the structure that persists through the variability of the particular manifestations. We do not know what our make-up is until it reveals itself in response to the tasks and opportunities with which society and our personal involvements confront us; and this is an unending process, so that we never know fully who we are and what we are. We cannot deduce or induce principles from our best verified theories as to what human nature is, though these exercise restraint upon us and offer guidance. Our principles voice commitments and devotions espoused in the thick of the battle, and it is here, as well as in our reflective moments, that we reject or modify the presuppositions that have guided us hitherto.

After we have made a commitment, we can turn upon it and cognize it. We may call the commitment so formulated a moral *law*. The commitment itself, however, consists in assuming a direction while we are within the process of action, and not in standing off and describing or explaining that direction. The commitment, we assume when we reflect upon it in detachment, springs from the structure of human nature in interaction with the human situation. But since this structure,

while limited as to its potentialities, is more or less plastic, we
can't know in advance what the limits of this plasticity are,
nor what new directions we shall be impelled to take when
we are confronted with radically novel configurations of the
situation, though at a reflective level we can bring to bear
upon the decision all the knowledge we have acquired concerning human nature and the human situation.

We cannot say outright, then, that ethical principles are
a priori either in the linguistic sense or in the existential sense.
They may express adequately the structure of the linguistic
and normative habits that to date have withstood the buffeting
of experience through a variety of conditions. But these habits
are never completely comprehensive and completely precise,
and both they and the principles which formulate their general structure are subject to change. Furthermore, principles
may express common human nature, but this is not wholly
prefixed, or if it is, its potentialities are never wholly known.
There is always the possibility of a radical mutation in the
human structure, or a cataclysmic change in the structure of
the natural or social world; but even apart from these there
is always the possibility of discovering new capacities for experience and new ways of integrating conduct. So that principles voice our "second nature" and not merely that shadowy
and elusive primary nature presumed to lie behind it, which
impels us in certain directions in our response to experience
and sets fixed limits to our ultimate potentialities. And this
second nature is one in which our congenital make-up and
the formative influence of experience are compounded, perhaps inextricably. It is also capable, up to a point, of being
altered.

One of the basic commitments of what we regard as the
enlightened moral conscience (become second nature) is to
rationality so far as it can be attained. This is itself vindicated

rather than validated, but in so far as it is accepted as vindicated it commits us to validation up to the limits of that mode of justification.

In one meaning of final, the final vindicating agent for the validating principles may be called our global sense of well-being or directedness, as that manifests itself in feeling and action as well as in thought; and in behavioral tendencies as well as to self-observation. For some such synoptic capacity is required to compound or to integrate the multiple and disparate factors. Such a global sense voices not only our direction upon our individual well-being but also upon that of others in so far as it has been incorporated into our concern. It is pounded into us by social compulsions, but it is also critical of them, so that in its social aspects the moral authority for the enlightened conscience comes to be not that which society commands but our ideal of what is demanded for the good of society. The global sense of directedness shapes our ethical principles, and conversely admits its particular manifestations to scrutiny by them.

It follows that, in so far as this global sense can be called non-rational, it is no more final than the rational or cognitive factors which articulate it and make it explicit. For, by this articulation, we get its purport out into the open, exhibit its implications, test it for consistency and square it with other knowledge whose criteria and presuppositions may themselves rest back upon a pragmatic justification, but have survived the close screening of experience in domains such as those of the factual sciences.

Conscience then—or this global sense—may be our guide, but it is a guide that needs a map. And in the territory of morals, there is always an unexplored frontier where both guides and maps are fallible.

The major hazard in the view I have suggested is the ever-present possibility that the global sense itself may be distorted or diseased. It has to judge not only lesser principles but its own terrible aberrations; it has to ask itself whether it is normal or abnormal. Psychological science can give us no short cut for dealing with this matter. There is no direct factual validation of our criterion of normality such as would be afforded by equating it with the average, or with *de facto* social adjustments. Normality or health has been defined by Georges Canguilhem as *normative capacity*, the capacity to live well and live better (*Essai sur quelques problèmes concernant le normal et le pathologique*, Clermont-Ferrand, 1943). And our awareness of what this consists in is expressed, when we articulate the global sense, by our ethical principles themselves, and hence is vindicated as they are vindicated, with all the tragic hazards that accompany this mode of justification.

The best mode of justification we have been able to find is, then, a slippery and far from satisfactory one. But before we pass judgment on it, let us try to see how it can be applied in the case of some specific normative principles. As the foregoing account suggests, such principles cannot be fully justified in a book; in so far as a justification is possible, it is finally carried out in the white heat of living. A book, however, can be of use in some phases of the process. It can sharpen the statement of the principles, test them for scope and consistency, square them with the observed deliverances of experience. It can also point us toward the experiential test itself. After we have explored these uses, we can then return to the tragic or tragi-comic character of the situation and ask if there is any escape from this.

11

Intrinsic and Extrinsic Goodness

———

1. Conative vs. Affective Theories

If such "principles" as that we should seek ends or use means to them are justifiable only by reference to the way we are built, other principles including those which characterize and prescribe intrinsic and extrinsic goodness, aesthetic value or the moral ought, cannot be dealt with so summarily.

The Matrix Meaning of "intrinsic goodness" is fairly clear from an analysis of usage, together with that of the structure of the normative situation. What we have to do, after it has been clarified, is to make a decision whether to link the Matrix Meaning with one Identifying Property—such as enjoyment or capacity to arouse interest—rather than another. Here alternative structures are possible and actual. The major disputes in value theory arise accordingly.

No analysis of the structure of the normative situation, and of the language that is fitted to deal with it, can omit inclusion of the prescriptive factor. Unless such terms as good and ought prescribed something, conditionally or unconditionally, they could not release action and guide conduct; i.e., they would not be normative. This is the function which normative language is devised to serve, and that which distinguishes it from other kinds of language. It is also a structural feature of the situation that we need some terms to prescribe conditionally and others to prescribe unconditionally. For valuational reflection proceeds by grasping and removing conditions. The preference of one *word* over another is a matter of usage—unless a neologism is required for a distinction not already firmly rooted in a semantic habit—and we have earlier given reasons for holding that when "good" has been distinguished from "ought," the former expresses a conditional prescription and the latter in its crucial use an unconditional one.

An important distinction with respect to the conditions springs from the need to distinguish between things in so far as they are prescribed without and with regard to their consequences or effects. We cannot take in all the properties of objects at once, and this distinction likewise is structural to the normative situation. The world is such that objects are both causes and effects, and our valuation of them must take this into account. The distinction between intrinsic and extrinsic goodness is not identical with the distinction between cause and effect, nor with the related one between means and end, but it rests upon these distinctions which, as we have already seen, are themselves structural. The words "intrinsic" and "extrinsic" goodness are those most commonly used, at any rate by philosophers, to make the distinction in question, whatever the other respects may be in which their usages diverge.

We may, then, have a considerable variety of views as to what properties make something worthy to be prescribed; and yet these tend to agree that when we call it intrinsically good or extrinsically good we are in the first case prescribing it only in so far as we abstract from its consequences, and in the second case only in so far as we abstract from its value properties that are exhibited in its direct presentation. Both empirical and intuitionist theories are generally so far in agreement, when they have carried out the analysis to this extent, and so are the different varieties of such theories that make the distinction. They can also agree that when an object is unconditionally prescribed, this can be done rationally only if both its intrinsic and its extrinsic values have been explored and weighed against each other, so that the abstraction of the one or the other is remedied. If a theory should base the prescription of an object in a particular choice-situation on either its intrinsic or its extrinsic values alone, it would have surveyed the situation incompletely.

Where the theories diverge is upon the nature of the Identifying Property whose presence releases the prescription, provided the other conditions are also fulfilled. The intuitionists say in effect that it is the recognition of the presence of a non-natural property that releases the prescription, the empiricists the recognition of a natural property. Since few people have been able to find such non-natural properties and no one has told us clearly how we could recognize them, we have earlier suggested that the supposed non-naturalness of the property may spring in part from the dimly recognized prescriptiveness lurking in the sense of the normative term; having recognized this element we can go on to consider the fitness of alternative empirical properties to release the prescription.

Affective theories hold that the Identifying Property of intrinsic goodness is a feeling, or feeling-component, such as pleasure or enjoyment; conative theories that it is a relation to interest or striving, such as the capacity to arouse or satisfy desire. As a matter of fact, conative theories make much less use of the distinction between intrinsic and extrinsic value than affective theories, preferring, as with Perry, to take some other notion such as that of the *generic* good as basic rather than intrinsic goodness. But the distinction nevertheless can easily be made in the conative language: the intrinsically valuable is that which is *desired*, or capable of being desired, for its own sake, and the extrinsically valuable that which is desired (etc.) for its consequences; or, on a "satisfaction" version of the conative theory, the intrinsically valuable is that which, apart from interest in further consequences, satisfies the interest immediately operating; and so on.

How is the choice of one type of Identifying Property rather than the other to be justified? Generally speaking, an answer would have to be along these lines: the Identifying Property must be chosen in such a way that the resulting definition [1] would constitute part of a system of normative principles that, because of its clarity, its fertility in empirical reference and its comprehensiveness, is fitted to make the multiple distinctions forced upon us by our confrontation with the various aspects of the normative situation; and it would have to enlist and fulfill our general sense of directedness, as that manifests itself progressively in our buffeting by the world and our effort to articulate the process. The assumptions disclosed in ordinary usage, and by the "reasons" we habitually give when we defend the assertion that something is good in itself, are im-

---

[1] As previously suggested, empirical theories hitherto have usually included the cognitive element, or Identifying Property, alone in the definition, and ignored the Matrix Meaning. Since the definition ordinarily is used as a criterion for determining which objects are properly identified as good, etc., and the specification of the Identifying Property serves this purpose, no harm is ordinarily done in practice. But if the definition is expected to give the full meaning of the term, of course the Matrix Meaning must be included, and failure of naturalistic theories to do so explicitly has been, as also indicated previously, at the root of a good many perplexities over the Naturalistic Fallacy.

portant clues to the fitness of a definition to satisfy the criteria, since they are witnesses to its rough success in meeting these tests in the past. But they are not decisive. Ordinary usage is not clear and distinct. Nor are all the "reasons" compatible with each other, nor is it always clear which reasons are "relevant" and which are not. Consequently, these clues by themselves cannot suffice to guide us in our present and future involvements.

Both conative and affective theories encounter difficulties in satisfying the criteria stated at the beginning of the preceding paragraph. The two main versions of a conative theory are: (a) what I have called the "teaser" theory, which holds that the good is that which arouses interest or desire, and (b) the satisfaction theory, which defines the good as that which reduces or terminates it.

Neither of these definitions will perform fully the job that an analysis of "good" is required to do in an ethical theory that seeks to give reflective guidance to conduct. The "teaser" theory suffices roughly to characterize the things that we *call* good at a pre-reflective or imperfectly reflective level. It does not, however, allow us to make in any useful way the important distinction between things that initially *appear* good and things that after experience and reflection are decided to *be* good, or the distinction between *imputed* value and *actual* value. We often find that objects that aroused our interest initially are, when thoroughly tested and understood, not worthy of our continued commendation. Consequently, to the extent that the need to make this distinction between appearance and reality, or imputed and actual values, is itself vindicated by the persistent impact of experience, the definition must be rejected.

The satisfaction theory appears, with some plausibility, to escape this objection. If the object not merely aroused our interest but proved in our further commerce with it to allay

the unrest of our striving toward it, what more could we ask
in order that we should forthright call it good?

But here the object is called good not because of a realized
quality but because of one of its consequences, namely the
consequence that it terminates striving, and hence whatever
plausibility the theory possesses accrues to it as an account of
extrinsic value and not of intrinsic value.

The basic difficulty with both versions of the conative theory lies in the fact that any objects whatsoever, except those
"mental objects" which we call experiences, are manifest to us
through their effects and can be judged only by reference to
those effects in us. Consequently the goodness of non-mental
things consists precisely in this relational property of producing certain kinds of consequences in experience, and so is
extrinsic.

2. *Goodness in Experiences*

If we wish to preserve the distinction between intrinsic and
extrinsic goodness, then, we must look for the Identifying
Property of intrinsic goodness in experiences only.[2] Those who
have looked have come up with a variety of candidates for the
honor. That range or "dimensionlike mode" of feeling qualities
which we more or less inadequately designate by the terms
pleasure and enjoyment has been the most popular single
candidate not only with philosophers but above all with in-
tellectually less hag-ridden men. Others, however, have been

------

[2] This point has been argued most fully by C. I. Lewis in *Analysis of Knowledge and Valuation*. I have dealt with it at greater
length than here in "Science, Humanism and the Good" (Lepley,
op. cit.), where I have examined the psychological assumptions
which give conative theories their plausibility.

proposed: vividness, complexity, variety-in-unity, etc. None of these latter by itself has succeeded in enlisting the allegiances of those to whom it has been proposed. Vividness is possessed by bad smells; complexity and variety-in-unity by some of our most frustrating and harassing experiences which after having them we prize only because of their consequences. But these qualities are sometimes defended in a pluralistic way: by arguing that though vividness or complexity is not always by itself a mark of intrinsic value, nevertheless when it is present in an "organic whole" it *enhances* the intrinsic goodness that is constituted by pleasure alone, so that we have not a single Identifying Property, but a disjunction of them so that when they occur together they reinforce each other. In order to establish this view, it would have to be shown that these properties can be introduced or enhanced to increase intrinsic value without making the affective tone itself more intense, more choice, more ecstatic. I am unable to conceive how this might be done.

So far as the ordinary practice of valuation is concerned, it seems that we do commonly judge the intrinsic worth of variety, complexity, etc., by their fruits in affective tone rather than vice versa; and that this is the result of inability to make any sort of headway when the opposite procedure is adopted. These properties are often perplexing, distracting, destructive, and consequently painful. When this is the case we seek to make experience more uniform and simpler unless instrumental factors are urgent. Similarly, at the moral level proper, we treat "growth" and "development of personality," so far as their fruits in value are concerned, either as instruments of adaptation or as contributory to a richer quality of experience, or as a combination of the two. Unless these notions can be so analyzed, they seem so vague as to be unilluminating: there is no commoner mysticism today than the mysticism which takes "growth" and "personality" as ultimates.

In short, I can see no advantage in taking these properties as Identifying Properties of intrinsic value that is not outweighed by taking them as Conferring Properties, and hence as themselves under certain conditions extrinsically good. And this latter course of procedure has the additional merit of introducing some intellectual order into the subject matter, which otherwise would leave the choice between the number of alternative Identifying Properties to some kind of intuition.

After such considerations have been adduced in the justification of enjoyment or hedonic tone as the Identifying Property, the last step in vindication of this choice can be taken only by the moral agent himself. When he has clarified the meaning of the alternative conceptual and linguistic instruments, he must ask himself, not just once but repeatedly in the course of his experience: Can I find anything else except positive hedonic tone which can serve as the ground of choice between experiences when I regard them apart from their consequences? And when I consider the chain of the consequences themselves, can I find anything other than joy or suffering in someone's experience to which I can refer my allegiances? Yet he must ask this question, not in isolation, but in the context of a system of normative concepts into which this analysis of intrinsic value must fit, while being itself only a part of the structure. The last vindication, then, is a sort of *argumentum ad hominem,* but the man to whom it is addressed is one who has pushed thought as far as he can carry it, while at the same time he is willing to carry it farther if he runs into more trouble.

The matter would be much easier if we could call the principle of intrinsic value *a priori,* as we have treated the principle that we should seek ends as *a priori.* But the most we can claim is that there is a strong foundation for the choice of this principle in the way we are built.

Traditional hedonism has not always been clear on this

point. Usually it has wished to have the matter both ways: like Bentham and Mill, it has tried to vindicate its basic definitions pragmatically by proposing them to the continuing allegiance of the moral agent, and at the same time to validate them theoretically by deducing them from a psychological law of motivation—e.g., by deducing ethical hedonism from psychological hedonism. If we are built in such a way that we can't desire anything but pleasure and the absence of pain, then the ethical principle no more needs vindication than does the principle that we ought to seek ends. It is, in the strict sense, a congenital *a priori*, and the "ought" reduces to a "must." If a problem of vindication arises at all, it does so not with the principles of intrinsic and extrinsic value but in connection with the prudential "ought," where there seems to be a possibility of choice between a decision to pursue the maximum of pleasure and non-pain or something less than that; and even more clearly, in the case of the social "ought," where there is undeniably a genuine alternative between a purely self-regarding happiness and a universalistic ideal of happiness.

But we are on very hazardous ground when we seek to defend a hedonistic theory of motivation. Being a factual assertion about human nature, it can be defended if at all only empirically. Perhaps better empirical grounds for defending psychological hedonism will be advanced in future than we now have, and consequently we should be open-minded on the subject. Psychological hedonism has no more been definitely refuted than it has been established with high probability. Not only do general hypotheses about motivation seem uncommonly slippery when an attempt is made to verify them, but they resist efforts to state them with enough precision that convincing verification of them becomes feasible in principle.

The most sustained efforts to verify a quasi-hedonistic law

experimentally have been made by E. L. Thorndike and the
C. L. Hull group respectively; the former under the rubric
of the Law of Effect and the latter under that of a highly inadequate behavioristic substitute for hedonism, the principle
of need-reduction. But after a lifetime devoted largely to this
effort Thorndike decided that, despite the wide scope of the
Law of Effect, it needed to be supplemented in certain areas
by the Law of Exercise, which bases reinforcement on mere
repetition independently of its consequences in satisfaction or
dissatisfaction. The experimental attack of Hull and his associates upon the problem has been even more massive, but the
initial assumption, so far as it affects this problem, is highly
questionable: namely that positive and negative hedonic tone
can be equated behaviorally with need-reduction and need-
augmentation respectively. Strictly speaking, then, Hull's is
a version of the satisfaction theory and hence takes conation
rather than affect as central; and indeed Hull once outlined
a value theory on this basis ("Value, Valuation and Natural
Science Methodology," *Philosophy of Science,* vol. 12, 1945).
Even so the work of the Hull group has lately evoked a lively
reaction from other psychological schools, such as that led by
E. R. Guthrie, which have adduced impressive evidence for
their form of the Law of Exercise. Still other principles besides the Laws of Effect and Exercise, furthermore, have their
supporters among experimental workers in motivation and
learning: notably the principles of "expectation" and "interest,"
and the Gestaltist emphasis on insight and problem-solving.

The experimental work encounters the fundamental difficulty that it has not yet offered a plausible behavioral equivalent of pleasure and pain, and it does not seem to have made
a tenable theoretical distinction between *reinforcement of
motives*—which alone is relevant to our problem—and other
types of learning such as the acquisition of skills. The mechanisms by which motor skills are learned is a problem that has

little to do with the question at hand, namely whether it is pleasantness or something else that leads us to adopt anything as an end. Nor do the purely introspective approaches to the problem seem to fare better than the behavioristic, for they constantly run up against the necessity of acknowledging that our motives are often deeply hidden from self-inspection.

The most that emerges with some convincingness out of recent experimental studies—and perhaps also the most that can be claimed for introspective observation—is summed up by E. C. Tolman's remark ("The Law of Effect," *Psychological Review*, vol. 45, 1938) that the Law of Effect is defensible if it can be simply re-formulated as follows: "We can still accept the empirical statement that rats (and of course humans as well) tend in the end towards food and away from shock. But this now becomes a statement not about learning *per se* but about learning plus utilization or performance." On the whole Tolman's view at that time was that the Law of Effect tells us very little about *learning as such*, which "can no longer be envisaged as a matter of the building of stimulus-response connections but . . . must be considered rather as learning of 'what leads to what.'" But the *utilization* of learning, or *performance*, he held to rest upon something very like a hedonistic principle.

In a later, widely influential article, "There is More Than One Kind of Learning" (*Psychological Review*, vol. 56, 1949), Tolman distinguished six types of learning, only one of which he thought could with plausibility be accounted for primarily through the principle of reinforcement by need-reduction, and a second type by this together with traumatic experience. The two types of learning in question, however, are those most closely involved with the operation of motives and the choice of goals; the remainder have to do with such forms of learning as cognitive orientation and acquisition of motor skills.

P. T. Young has recently summarized the evidence that hedonic factors are more important in motivation than experimental psychologists have generally been willing to admit ("Food-Seeking Drive, Affective Process, and Learning," *Psychological Review*, vol. 56, 1949; and "The Role of Hedonic Processes in the Organization of Behavior," *Ibid.*, vol. 59, 1952). He criticizes stimulus-response psychology, for example, for omitting central hedonic processes, and likewise need-reduction theories for overlooking such evidence as that which shows that rats will choose a saccharine solution for its sweetness over plain water or a sugar solution, even though the saccharine has no nutritive or "need-reducing" value.

One who dips into the psychological work is forced to conclude that the problem of motivation is still far from having achieved an experimental treatment which has that "scientific clarity" which it is sometimes hoped will settle the waters muddled by philosophers.[3] The non-psychologist, whether he be a philosopher or some other kind of man, resists efforts of psychologists to convince him that he does not on the whole and in the long run tend to seek that which gives him enjoyment and avoid that which causes suffering. But whether this is a law or merely a tendency he is not sure. We cannot, of course, hold that animals and humans from birth are always motivated by a *conscious* desire to seek pleasure and avoid pain; the defense of psychological hedonism in terms of an unconscious tendency in this direction is more plausible but still far from established.[4] Our drives create in us a restlessness

---

[3] I have tried, though with no pretense at exhaustiveness or *expertise*, to draw upon the psychological materials at greater length than here, in "The Ego and the Law of Effect" (*Psychological Review*, vol. 53, 1946), and "Science, Humanism and the Good" (*Value: a Co-operative Inquiry*, edited by R. Lepley, 1949).

[4] I omit here any discussion of masochism, where people seem to choose suffering for its own sake. What is called masochism can be plausibly accounted for by the tendency to replace a greater

208

which at first fixes on *objects* rather than pleasure and pain; it is certain kinds of objects that become the explicit goals. Gradually we learn to introspect and symbolize in language the hedonic and algedonic tones that accompany the satisfaction or frustration of these drives, so that the objects aimed at are scrutinized in terms of the feelings they will produce; in this way, as S. C. Pepper says, we can "learn to become hedonists"—*i.e.*, a more or less explicit aim to seek more enjoyment or less suffering (whether for ourselves or others) can become second nature. In so far as the adoption of other people's happiness becomes incorporated into our aims, the learning of this principle is complicated and always imperfect. Everyday observation—which is the only kind so far available to us in most instances—is perhaps compatible with the view that many people some of the time are willing to put up with a certain amount of easily avoidable suffering, and even more are content to do dull things for their own sakes. The ultimate factors in motivation—which probably must be conceived in terms of the "unconscious," or physiological mechanisms—are still largely veiled from our knowledge; so that we cannot confidently equate these with a general pain-avoidance or pleasure-seeking principle.

3. *Vindication of an Affective Theory*

But, even granting the case against the universality of psychological hedonism—granting that some people continue to desire, consciously or unconsciously, suffering or dullness *for*

---

suffering by a lesser, as when we incur physical pain in order to distract ourselves from the much greater suffering of anxiety, or when we punish ourselves to relieve feelings of guilt. Whether this is a completely adequate solution to the problem is still far from clear on the basis of clinical evidence.

its own sake (and it is almost impossible to disentangle the consequences here so as to produce a satisfactory test)—it still does not follow that suffering or dullness is good in itself. A decision on this question is not in any case capable of verification by an appeal to a Law of Motivation; it can be established only through a pragmatic vindication; and to anyone who, after contemplating the possibility of both enjoyment and dullness apart from their consequences chose the latter, we could say nothing relevant. We have reached the limits of vindication as well as validation; and the same objections would arise to "forcing anyone to have a good time" that arise to "forcing men to be free." The alternative, however, is not a very serious one in practice, since we are doomed most of the the time to concern ourselves with avoiding suffering or with replacing illusory prospects of satisfaction with genuine ones —and it is not even well established that choice of dullness or pain *for its own sake* is a genuine phenomenon.

We cannot wait for a provisional solution of the problem until the psychologists have drained and plotted the jungles of motivation. Our choice of a principle of intrinsic value will have to rest on a series of "experiments," actual or imaginative. Imagine or arrange or observe an experience, whether your own or another's, that is rich in enjoyment; and set against it one otherwise resembling it as closely as possible but negative or neutral in hedonic tone. Then, after having ruled out consideration of the consequences of these experiences (including the consequences in the lives of others), let your general sense of directedness choose. After having gone through similar comparisons with experiences that are vivid, complex, unified, etc., then perform some more complicated experiments. Observe or imagine or arrange an experience that, again in abstraction from its consequences, is both vivid and agreeable, and one that is vivid and disagreeable; a third that is agreeable but not vivid, and a fourth that is neither vivid nor agreeable. If the first and third, but not the second and fourth, enlist your allegiance, this creates a presumption in favor of agreeableness as the Identifying Property. Then, in the case of experiences that are both vivid and agreeable, enhance and diminish respectively the vividness. If your positive normative thrust increases as the resulting agreeableness also increases, and diminishes as the resulting agreeableness diminishes, then your allegiance to enjoyment as the Identifying Property is to that extent vindicated. The matter cannot be settled by one such series of "experiments"; the vindication is continuing, and rests upon a lifetime's effort to disentangle the immediate characteristics of an experience from its consequences.

We have called this procedure a series of "experiments"; but it is not a *validation* of the definition. Or, though the procedure so far as it eliminates certain Identifying Properties is analogous to, or isomorphic with, inductive forms, the conclusion does not rest upon the cold calculation of a probability relation but on the warm response of your total nature. This does not imply any "third logic," but rather ultimate recourse to something besides logic.

It is very odd that no better method of justifying such an important principle should be available; but where can a more reliable one be found? The vindication in question is consequently a frail one, but the frailty is of a sort which infects all our commitments to basic principles. Yet the method is not without its strength too; for its appeal is to the deepest affinities of the human creature.

In the above we have not done entire justice to a conative theory. But neither have we slighted it entirely. When we refer the vindication of a principle to the warm response of our total nature, we are appealing to human conation, to the Platonic Eros. The trouble with the conative theory is not that it takes as central an element that is unimportant in the normative phenomenon, but that it misplaces the role of one that is important. What I would suggest is that the affective theory gives us a characterization of the *value quality* in the case of intrinsic goodness; whereas the conative theory gives us a characterization of the *act of valuing* which applies to all normative behavior. *The conative theory mistakes the act for the quality, or the hypothetical behavioral correlate of the experience with the immediately given property*; and the confusion is both easy to make and not too far off the track, for the reason that the affective and the conative aspects are closely associated and often concomitant.

The relation between feeling-tone and conation is a complex one. When an experience is enjoyed, there is ordinarily a striving to hold onto it, and a disposition to seek other experiences like it; when it is characterized by suffering, we usually strive to get rid of it, and we tend to avoid similar experiences. So it may look as though an affective theory and a conative theory were simply two sides of the medal. But even if it were possible to resolve the difficulty suggested earlier in finding an exact correlation between positive or negative hedonic tone and the concomitant striving, it would still remain the case that the feeling-tone is the immediate constitutive quality of the experience for its own sake; whereas, on the contrary, a striving to attain the experience is discounted in our final reflective judgment upon it unless it bears fruit in enjoyment. Positive affective tone therefore serves as the identifying or constitutive property of experiences to be sought for their own sakes, whereas positive striving is the structural feature of the act of valuing.

In fact, the conative element is a central factor in the Matrix Meaning; for how does the normative term acquire its prescriptiveness except by transference from the tendency of the object to arouse conation? The conative theory, therefore, may be conceived as *the result of a confused recognition by empirical theories of the need for inclusion of a non-cognitive factor in the description of the valuing situation.* Its mistake consists in trying to treat this factor as the central descriptive element in the meaning. Of course, we can describe the conation when we give a full account of the normative situation: but as we have already seen, every prescription can also be described. The primary role of the striving in the situation, however, consists in moving us, and not in its consequent amenability to being cognized. And recognition of the Identifying Property of the experience is the ground for eliciting both our conation toward the object and the prescriptive force of the normative term.

Conation enters in a similar way, when we treat the problem at a different level, that of justification of principles. The global sense of directedness which, in conjunction with objective factors, ultimately vindicates the choice of one Identifying Property rather than another, is itself a manifestation of conation; for principles engage us as well as objects. The espousal of principles is thus itself an active enlisting of our motivations, and not merely an act of cognizing the properties described and prescribed by those principles. To put the matter in venerable language, the Platonic Eros here attaches to ideas rather than to things. But the ideas in this case are concepts whose special function is to prescribe the things.

An elucidation of the possibility of such a commitment to principles would consist in defense and application of the following assumption: *that man can be moved by anything he can symbolize; and that he can symbolize abstract structural features of his thought and action as well as directly presented sensory properties.* Without this assumption, however, philosophy and science would be chimerical enterprises.

The imaginative experiment we have described is rendered hazardous in practice by the difficulty in disentangling the pull that experiences exert upon us by their immediate quality from the influence which we subconsciously undergo from the connection of these immediate qualities with their regularly associated consequences. Thus, an individual may prize either simplicity or its contrary complexity whenever it bobs up in his experience, and convince himself that he prizes it for its own sake. Yet sustained reflection on experience may show him that a repeated preference for simplicity as such is relative to a phase in his life when his problems tend to be too complicated for him to solve, or that a preference for complexity springs from a predicament which leads him to organize his life by excluding unnecessarily classes of simple goods which would be desirable in themselves if he could fit them in without causing disruption. And so he may come to see that neither simplicity nor complexity is in itself a good, but that the one or the other is a contributory value relatively to the circumstances.

Furthermore, we must recognize the common phenomenon of "functional autonomy" whereby a practice initially adopted as a means comes eventually to acquire intrinsic value. This was recognized long ago by Epicurus (*Letter to Menoeceus*):

Prudence is a more precious thing even than philosophy; from it spring all the other virtues, for it teaches that we cannot lead a life of pleasure which is not also a life of prudence, honour, and justice; nor lead a life of prudence, honour, and justice, which is not also a life of pleasure. For the virtues have grown into one with a pleasant life, and a pleasant life is inseparable from them.

The honest or just act thus has genuinely acquired intrinsic value, but in accordance with the analysis we have been proposing, this is because the individual has come to enjoy its performance; the major part of its justification, however, continues to reside in its consequences, and if acts of the sort did not reliably contribute, directly or indirectly, to the enhancement of happiness or the diminution of suffering, they would no longer retain the intrinsic value which characterizes them.

Such an analysis as here indicated would not deny that honesty, promise-keeping, growth of personality, and the like, are, generally speaking, positive values. The differences arise only over the question whether they are, as such, intrinsic values. An affective theory holds that objects and acts having these properties are ordinarily to be prescribed, but (a) conditionally, and (b) as means to further goods. Such characteristics, then, are to be conceived as Conferring Properties of goodness in specific situations and within certain kinds, and not as Identifying Properties of intrinsic value in general, though the Identifying Property—enjoyment—may become attached to them.

12

Aesthetic Judgment

1. *Criticism and Aesthetics*

The aesthetic domain is one in which the philosopher would be especially well advised to tread softly. If any "principles" are discoverable here, their application to the judging of art is a devious and ticklish matter. Whatever may be the case with moral judgments, our guides in aesthetic matters are likely to rely on taste rather than on deductions from generalizations of any kind; or if they do generalize, we respect them more for their ability to sharpen our perceptions in the individual case than for any general rules they may give us. The critic usually gives "reasons" of some kind for his judgment, yet a subtle guidance of taste may exert itself without offering reasons of any kind:

> The Emperor Saga of Japan [reigned A.D. 810–23] one day quoted to his Minister, Ono no Takamura, the couplet:
> "Through my closed doors I hear nothing but the
>   morning and evening drum:
> From my upper windows in the distance I see ships
>   that come and go."

Takamura, thinking these were the Emperor's own verses, said: "If I may venture to criticize an august composition, I would suggest that the phrase 'in the distance' be altered." The Emperor was delighted, for he had purposely changed "all I see" to "in the distance I see." At that time there was only one copy of Po Chü-i's poems in Japan and the Emperor, to whom it belonged, had allowed no one to see it. (*Translations from the Chinese*, by Arthur Waley, 1941.)

This example illustrates our thesis in Chapter 8 that valuation is possible at a sub-discursive level, where the subsequent verbalization of the process simply formulates a perception. Although no rule of taste was offered by Takamura—and the Emperor arrived at the same critical judgment without need of one—nevertheless an operative habit was at work in both connoisseurs, which (if one can judge adequately from the translation) when articulated and applied would have run as follows: A poem should be economical and suggestive; the phrase "in the distance," which states what is sufficiently implied by the preceding phrase, "From my upper windows," is redundant and therefore should be deleted.

No rules, whether they are at this level, namely, of maxims, or at the more general level of aesthetic principles, can be a substitute for the taste that operates implicitly in aesthetic perception. If the philosopher bulls his way into the china shop of poetry or painting without such taste, he creates nothing but havoc. The artist or critic or connoisseur has a lifelong involvement with the aesthetic that the philosopher (who by profession has more fleas than a dog) can never hope to match. Aesthetic valuation, surely, is a sphere in which a delicate taste, formed and shaped by prolonged immersion in the subject matter, is a prime requisite not only for making valuations but for essaying a theory of valuations. Such taste is of the kind exhibited by the artist or the critic at his best.

This is the Age of Criticism *par excellence*, and never before, perhaps, has there been a body of criticism so massive and so acute. When the philosopher approaches the question of aesthetic standards, it is only at his peril that he by-passes this body of criticism and goes directly and exclusively to the arts themselves. What has been said in preceding chapters about the crystallization of explicit maxims and principles out of evaluative habits already operating in the community receives striking confirmation here. The working critic, who may be innocent of aesthetic philosophy and even contemptuous of it, nevertheless assumes criteria of what is legitimate in art, and of what makes it good or bad, that may correspond closely with the standards formulated and elaborated by philosophers. To the extent that the critic has a consistent point of view, he is tacitly presupposing an aesthetic theory, whether he acknowledges the fact or not; and if he is inconsistent, the philosopher will have no difficulty in exposing a muddled *mélange* of principles.

The philosopher may discover his aesthetic principles by extracting these unformulated assumptions of critics; or, alternatively, through the interaction between his own direct experience of the beautiful and his philosophical categories drawn primarily from other domains of experience. Usually, today, when we have such a lively and insistent body of criticism that the aesthetician cannot escape it, he must shuttle back and forth between the two procedures.

But there is another side to this relation of give-and-take between aesthetics and criticism. Not only may the aesthetician discover and articulate his principles by making explicit the structural presuppositions of the working critic; the only way, finally, that he can test or "justify" them is by a return to the practice of criticism, either in his own person or, in part, vicariously through the success of professional critics in illuminating art, whether this be by applying the explicit principles devised by the philosopher or, as more commonly, by submitting the corresponding working assumptions to the fire of critical practice. And this justification is a pragmatic one, or a vindication by involvement: hence the relationship between aesthetician and critic both supports the general account of justification we have sketched in Chapters 9 and 10 and illustrates its inconclusiveness. For there can be no definitive criticism of a great work of art. Hence the dubiety of the critic's conclusions is transmitted to the aesthetic principles which they may be taken to "justify."

This dual relation between philosophy and criticism is exemplified by parallel developments in both fields, which have led to the major cleavages in current controversies within each. The philosophical conflict between cognitivists and non-cognitivists, or between those who uphold the possibility of aesthetic principles and those who repudiate it, is paralleled by the central dispute between the so-called New Critics and their adversaries. Although the New Criticism is not a "school" but a loose collection of diverse critics, they are usually grouped together because they share a common tendency. This tendency is to distinguish rather sharply the aesthetic attitude from non-aesthetic attitudes, and to make such a distinction the basis of critical practice. Thus the New Critics hold that the focus of critical attention should be on "the poem itself," or the painting itself, etc., rather than on its ambience—historical, biographical, social, moral or political—however much the critic may have to deviate into these fields in order to elucidate the poem. And secondly, criticism is held as by John Crowe Ransom to be "the attempt to define and enjoy the aesthetic or characteristic values of literature." In practice, the New Critics are distinctively concerned with such elements of literature as imagery, metaphor, structure and the linguistic factors in the immediate aesthetic effect.

The most vigorous movement in opposition to the New Criticism objected to what it considered the divorce between the aesthetic and other kinds of attitudes, stressing the psychological, social and ideational context of literature and the mutual dependency of art and "life." Its concern has been with literature as an expression of morals, manners and motivation, and its capacity in turn to shed light on these.

This cleavage within the critical camp—which goes back of the current scene to Coleridge on the one side and Arnold on the other—is reflected by a similar broad division within philosophical aesthetics which has grown up more or less independently. Roughly on the side of the New Critics are Kant and his descendants who try to delimit the aesthetic attitude or aesthetic experience as sharply as possible from such activities as the scientific, the moral and the practical. Thus Kant offered as his criteria of the aesthetic: disinterestedness, the non-conceptual (whether sub-conceptual or supra-conceptual) character of the experience, "purposiveness without a purpose," subjective necessity or universality. And Santayana, in *The Sense of Beauty* (1896), distinguished the aesthetic from the non-aesthetic by the "objectification" of meanings and values in the response to a work of art or of natural beauty.

Aligned on the other side are such aestheticians as John Dewey and (in his early work) I. A. Richards, who emphasize the continuity between so-called aesthetic and non-aesthetic activities, rather than their distinctness, showing how they draw upon each other and shade into each other.

This dispute over the question whether the aesthetic attitude or experience can be distinguished from other types of experience is not directly a controversy over the criteria of aesthetic valuation but, nevertheless, it is a preliminary issue basic to any attempt to define aesthetic value.

In modern aesthetic theory, the two focal questions have been, "What is the aesthetic attitude?" and "What is aesthetic value?" These correspond to the two polar topics of literary criticism, as stated by T. S. Eliot: "What is poetry?" and "Is this a good poem?" (*The Use of Poetry and the Use of Criticism*, 1933).

If both sets of questions are meaningful and legitimate, then in order to establish a principle of aesthetic value we would first (in some sense of first) have to justify a theory of the nature of the aesthetic experience or the aesthetic attitude, and then base a principle of aesthetic value on this together with our general doctrine of intrinsic and extrinsic goodness. Thus: an aesthetic experience is one characterized by properties A, B, C . . . ; an aesthetically valuable experience is an aesthetic experience (as just defined) which conforms to our criterion of intrinsic goodness. Similarly: an aesthetically valuable object is one that is inherently valuable and capable of leading to aesthetically valuable experiences under specified conditions.

The procedure, however, would not in practice be as simple as this, since our analysis of the nature of aesthetic experience itself would be partly dependent on its capacity to fit in with a definition of intrinsic value. The kind of experiences that we would decide to label as aesthetic would in part depend on the fitness of experiences of this kind to satisfy a criterion of valuableness; just as we cannot define art without some conception of what good art would be. Here as elsewhere in philosophy it is hazardous to assign any one principle an absolute priority over related principles.

Furthermore, when we come to aesthetics we cannot simply assume as established certain principles of extrinsic and intrinsic value, and then apply them automatically to the subject matter. For the justification of these principles themselves depends in part on their applicability to special normative domains such as the aesthetic.

2. Aesthetic Principles

The standard aesthetic theories offer a number of competing candidates for the defining property of the aesthetic. They can be classified with rough adequacy into Imitation, Form, and Expression theories: each type of theory has some plausible claim to adequacy for a certain kind of art, but is inapplicable to other kinds. Moreover, within each of these broad types of theories there is a similar partial but incomplete plausibility for its several versions. Imitation theories differ as to what is imitated: whether it is particular objects, or universals, or universals in particulars, or actions in their historical and social contexts. The divergence among formalistic theories as to what is meant by Form is notorious. Expression theories are similarly at variance as to what expression consists in: whether an overflowing of the artist's personality or an evocation of a feeling or image in a beholder, or a communication of psychological responses to an object.

But this situation does not entail any radical skepticism or vicious relativism with respect to the possibility of bringing some intellectual order into the aesthetic domain. It simply demonstrates that aestheticians and critics have been looking in the wrong place for principles; that they have been seeking defining properties of the aesthetic at too low a level of generality. In accordance with the general analysis we have offered in this book, they have been seeking to treat as Identifying Properties characteristics of art that are fitted only to serve as Conferring Properties.

The point needs no belaboring where "canons" or rules appropriate to a specific Kind or particular Style are in question. The most that can be claimed for a set of such canons is that they express good-making properties within a specific type of art—Perpendicular Gothic or Baroque architecture, Imagist or Metaphysical poetry, Impressionist or Expressionist painting. The so-called aesthetic principles of artists themselves, and of the critics who write manifestoes for a movement, are often little more than rules of technique for obtaining an effect of a sort that constitutes the peculiar strength of a school, or for exploiting a newly recognized possibility of the art. As such, they have their uses, and they constantly turn up new material for the aesthetic philosopher to take account of; but the attempt to erect them into principles applicable to all art can lead to nothing but the most cramping dogmatism or, in reaction against this, the most paralyzing relativism.

Such so-called principles as those of Imitation, Form or Expression theories come closer than legislation of "canons" to serving the purpose with which we are concerned, for each of them can be interpreted as an overemphasis on a structural element that is present in all, or nearly all, instances of the broad aesthetic domain. Thus the Imitation theories, in their wide range, call attention to the fact that the work of art can function as a designative sign—whether a sign of a particular object or of an "idea" designating an abstracted set of properties and relationships approximated elsewhere in reality; and that this potential designativeness, whether it becomes explicit in aesthetic experience proper or not, lends dynamic thrust to the response to the work. The Form theories emphasize the fact that the internal relationships—of graphic design, of tonal linkage, or rhythmic pattern, etc.—within the total aesthetic object or aesthetic sign are susceptible of a higher degree of satisfying organization than in the objects encountered in ordinary experience, and that this organization is a major source of the resultant effect. The Expression theory, at least in those versions which treat expression as capacity to arouse an affectively toned resonance in a qualified beholder (rather than, say, the overflow of an emotion in the artist), comes somewhat closer to the required degree of generality than Imitation and Form theories. For it incorporates the insights of the other two types of theory by treating the representational and formal elements as the carriers of expression, one or the other being more prominent in different artistic styles—e.g., in narrative poetry or in non-objective painting.

The Expression theory itself, however, can be defended as

definitory of the aesthetic only if it relates the expressive element to the formal and representational factors in a total attitude which is distinguishable generically from such attitudes as the cognitive or practical. A definition of the aesthetic attitude by a set of properties A, B, C, . . . would have to be vindicated in a manner analogous, up to a point, with a vindication of a definition of intrinsic goodness, or aesthetic value. It would, that is to say, have to be justified by showing that it corresponded to a basic cleavage in the structure of our attitudes, and would have to enlist and sustain, through a close critical involvement with art, our sense of the importance of such a distinction for our ordering of experience.

Even those recent philosophers who have opposed a sharp separation between the aesthetic and the non-aesthetic nevertheless make a distinction of degree. Thus, for Dewey, the aesthetic experience is more of *"an* experience" than other types of experience (*i.e.,* has more qualitative unity), and it is a richer source of "delightful perception." For Richards, likewise, though the aesthetic experience is composed of the materials and impulses to be found in ordinary experience, it gives them a finer organization, and it does so by keeping the impulses at an "incipient" level.

Just as in recent criticism there is a tendency for the New and the Old Critics to find some common ground by which their two approaches can be combined when the occasion requires, so in recent aesthetic theory some kind of synthesis between the Kantian and the Deweyan approaches seems possible. Although, of course, nothing resembling complete agreement has been reached, it is possible to list certain characteristics of the aesthetic attitude on which there is considerable convergence. The aesthetic attitude is contemplative of the given, together with its charge of immanent meanings, rather than explicitly directed upon objects external to the immediate presentation and signified by them. The aesthetic experience is meaningful, but it consists in an implicit grasp of meanings rather than the kind of explicit exhibition of them that characterizes certain aspects of critical, scientific, and other so-called cognitive activities. The aesthetic experience is highly charged with emotional expression, but tries to keep this charge under control so that it is not placed at the center of attention in such a way as to distract us from the pattern of sounds or visual forms which is at or near the focus of our contemplation. The aesthetic experience is intransitive in the sense that its transitions occur within attention to an aesthetic object rather than pointing us toward something outside this object. The aesthetic attitude is "active" in that it involves an arousal of interpretative attitudes and of incipient strivings toward the object; it is "passive" or contemplative in that it keeps these attitudes and strivings in check, so that we submit ourselves to the guidance of the aesthetic object and do not allow the sign-function of the object to turn us away from it so that we engage in activities prompted by it.

If a more precise and detailed statement of the distinguishing characteristics is offered, this can serve as the defining property of the aesthetic experience presupposed by a definition of the aesthetically valuable. But a statement of such a defining property would have to be somewhat complicated, and much lengthier than we have come to expect a definition to be. If we are to do justice to any type of activity as complicated as the aesthetic, we cannot expect to put its characterization into one small package. The "definition" therefore would in effect amount to an extended summary of an aesthetic theory: the "principle" would turn out to be a rather elaborate network of related principles.

However the aesthetic experience may be defined, such a criterion by itself does not suffice to delimit aesthetic value, for an object may satisfy the criterion for something's being an aesthetic object and yet the criterion may fail for comparative judgments of value, when we ask on what grounds this object is aesthetically better than that. Consequently our definition of aesthetic value must be based on some one of our concepts of value in general, such as intrinsic or inherent value.

Each of the four major theories we have considered would define these—or dub them indefinable—in its own terms. For the intuitionist, of course, there would be a simple, indefinable, unanalyzable, non-natural quality which, when contemplated aesthetically, is the quality of Beauty. Something like an intuitionist theory is presupposed by the more dogmatic literary and art critics of various persuasions. Thus for Clive Bell and the early Roger Fry (who in fact were influenced by G. E. Moore) "significant form" represents such a quality of Beauty. Or, for the more moralistically inclined critics, such as the late neo-humanists, the intuited quality is essentially a moral property rather than a distinctively aesthetic one; thus the ultimate basis of judgment is an ethical one.

For the emotivists, there is no single defining property of intrinsic value, but any property can serve the purpose if, in the particular case, we approve of it without regard to the consequences of the object and try to persuade others to approve of it also. Emotivism in its cruder forms expresses the presuppositions of the impressionistic critic who conducts the soul on an adventure among masterpieces and does not try to analyze the properties which define the beautiful. It also voices the attitude of the solid citizen who says, "I don't know if it's art but I like it."

The Good Reasons approach seems to correspond much more closely than does the emotivist theory to the practice of a good working critic who has no articulated set of principles. The critic is "giving reasons" for an interpretation and judgment of a work of art. These reasons are usually unsystematic: the critic rarely appeals to explicit principles. He proceeds on the assumption that he has a working knowledge of what distinguishes good or relevant reasons from bad or irrelevant ones. In some sense he has confidence that he "knows" what makes a good or bad work when he encounters and observes it, even though this knowledge is not an explicit deduction from principles. And certainly this is all that we can demand of the critic *qua critic:* that is to say, in so far as he can be distinguished from the philosophical aesthetician. But when critics disagree, or when their judgments are challenged, we inevitably call for the reasons behind the reasons, that is to say, for principles, criteria and definitions; and the critic cannot escape undertaking the philosopher's function.

3. An Affective Theory of Aesthetic Value

When the analytical critic, as distinguished from the impressionistic or dogmatic one, does appeal to valuational principles they usually turn out to be of the general type of those proposed by either an affective theory or a conative theory. I. A. Richards, for example, who is almost the only critic in our time who has sought to work out in detail "principles of literary criticism," defined value as the satisfaction of an interest or an appetency. Art gives us a fuller and finer organization of our impulses, even though these remain at an incipient level, than these impulses can achieve in daily life. The experience of art, furthermore, has "carry-over" value: it makes us more vigilant to the complexities of experience, and—to put the matter in Coleridge's language—better able to cope with the "opposite or discordant qualities" that we encounter in daily life, and to bring them into some sort of "balance or reconcilement." The pleasure that we get from art, according to Richards, is a by-product, and too variable and slippery a thing for the critic to take into account in his judgments. The critic, consequently, must base his valuation of the work upon its fitness to produce an organization of impulses, either within the aesthetic experience itself or through its after-effects in the course of our lives. Richards does not make it quite clear which, or what is to be given priority when the two conflict.

The tendency of most working critics who make a distinction in principle between the aesthetic and the non-aesthetic is, however, to favor the affective theory rather than the conative theory. Even the sober Wordsworth, who would not be thought of as a hedonist in his general attitude toward life, writes in the Preface to *Lyrical Ballads:*

The end of poetry is to produce excitement in co-existence with an overbalance of pleasure. . . . The poet writes under one restriction only, namely, the necessity of giving immediate pleasure to a human being possessed of that information which may be expected of him; not as a lawyer, a physician, a mariner, an astronomer or a natural philosopher, but as a man.

This view Wordsworth shared with the idealistic Coleridge. It is noteworthy that one of our leading 20th Century critics, T. S. Eliot, who would repudiate emphatically a hedonistic or utilitarian ethics, nevertheless writes that the aim of poetry is to give a kind of refined intellectual enjoyment. He has commented even on his religious poem, *Ash Wednesday,* that its purpose, quoting Byron's remark on *Don Juan,* is to make the reader "a moment merry." In fact, to give poetry a more exalted function than this is, he holds, to follow Arnold in making it a substitute for religion. Eliot does not, however, deny that art can have other values besides the aesthetic. In *The Use of Poetry and the Use of Criticism,* he quotes Horace's dictum that art is both *dulce* and *utile* to show that historically conceived poetry has served both functions—and many others.

I believe that a carefully stated affective theory can take care of both these functions, and also allow for the carry-over value into daily life that Richards assigns to art. Slippery as enjoyment is, it is more accessible to observation than the neural impulses to which Richards ultimately reduces his appetencies. Commitment to an affective theory does not necessarily imply that the critic talks very much directly about the feelings that the work gives to himself or others. Most of his talk has to do exclusively with the elements in the work which are the *sources* of affect. He is concerned with tracing the statement, repetition and variation of themes or symbols, with the fresh employment of language, with the significance of the ideas that are assumed or adumbrated by the poem or novel, and with the writer's capacity to keep these ideas functioning with due unobtrusiveness, with the shimmer of the aesthetic surface and the achievement of contrast along with the maintenance of unity of tone. But the critic must also keep in mind that none of these things is an absolute or necessarily confers intrinsic value. His concern must be with the individual work, and here anything he may say by way of analysis about its elements or structure can be very wide of the mark unless these are traced back to their consummation in feeling. So "ultimately," as Eliot says, all the critic can do is to point to those features of a work which the critic feels to be good.

William Empson says in effect (*Seven Types of Ambiguity*, revised edition, 1947), that there are two kinds of critical dogs: the appreciative dog, who merely relieves himself against the flower of beauty, and the analytical dog, who likes to scratch around the roots to see what makes the flower grow. Although most of his own work has been in the line of analysis, and he holds that this must constitute the bulk of the attention of any critic who is persistently concerned with literature, nevertheless the complete critic would be both kinds of a dog. He must be aware, so in effect Empson suggests, that the ultimate function of the metabolism of the plant is to produce the flower. And the critic cannot ultimately gain our confidence unless he indicates—even if only by a phrase—the kind of total effect on him that the elements he has analyzed add up to, "so straddling a commotion and so broad a calm."

Criticism becomes a sterile and mechanical exercise without this constant reference to fresh response by way of feeling. All this is not to deny the relevance of a conative theory, provided we assign the impulses and strivings their proper role. The feeling response itself arises only out of a rich interplay of incipient impulses, and these impulses take their thrust from the importance that they have in the more fully executed manifestations that they exhibit outside their aesthetic functioning. There is, consequently, a constant need for concern with the so-called truth of art and with the bearing of its insights on our moral economy. But the aesthetic judgment proper can be delimited through a recognition that there is not a simple equation between the truth or moral importance of an impulse outside the contemplative aesthetic act and its reverberation within it. The work of art is arranged to give us these impulses in such a form that they pay immediate dividends, and often their soundness in the long-run context of life must be sacrificed for this; for the artist does not what he wills but what he can, and whatever his alliances with the philosopher, the moralist and the educator, he cannot aim directly at usurping their functions. Art is what morality or philosophy or religion does in its playtime moods, and it must be granted a margin of license and irresponsibility for the sake of its immediate bounties and glories.

An affective theory, however, is not committed to holding that art must be mindless. In fact, it should recognize that the most inexhaustible sources of enjoyment are those that incorporate the activities of mind; and only those works of art which have profound undercurrents of meaning are capable of giving enjoyment on repeated experiences of them.

But the vindication of aesthetic principles is finally, one should repeat, an enterprise to be carried out not by the aesthetician but by the artist, the critic and the loving consumer, with whatever humble collaboration he may obtain from the philosopher.

13

The Moral Authority

1. The Complexity of the Moral Ought

Even less than aesthetic principles are ethical principles proper capable of being squeezed into one small package of the sort that has usually functioned as a "definition" of the right or the ought. If it had accomplished nothing more, the current tendency toward pluralism, as exemplified by the informalists among others, should have put us on our guard against seeking to deduce a moral judgment from such a concentrated major premise as the greatest happiness of the greatest number, or the Aristotelian definition of the highest good in terms of the development of human capacities, or Perry's harmonization of interests, or the neo-Hegelian doctrine of self-realization, or even a small set of principles such as Kant's three formulations of the Categorical Imperative taken in conjunction.

On the other hand, we need not accept the counsels of despair that the extreme pluralists urge upon us. Order may yet be found, or made, in this domain, if we think hard enough. The multiple factors which enter into our moral decisions exhibit relations to each other which are not wholly fluid. They may yet yield a *structure* if we persist in seeking it, and if we are prepared to take sufficiently diverse elements into this structure.

Earlier in this book we have hit upon two central factors in normative judgments which we must now proceed to complicate. The two factors that are, genetically speaking, basic are the imperative function and the fundamental cognitive or descriptive element, which consists in the constitutive property of goodness or value, or some organization of it. Both factors are present in a normative judgment at whatever level, and derive, as we have seen, from pre-discursive valuation.

The peculiar forms which these two elements take at the level of moral judgments proper are as follows:

(1) The prescription is, in its crucial and distinctive functioning, an unconditional one. The "ought" signifies that the alternatives have been explored as thoroughly as feasible, and expresses a decision. The decision then, assuming that the relevant conditions have been fulfilled, releases or triggers the act.

(2) But the "ought" issues this command only after deliberation—after the pertinent knowledge has been gathered and assessed. The various goods and evils, the assorted ends and means, have been surveyed and the "ought" signifies (as the simple predication of intrinsic goodness or badness, for example, does not) that they have been compounded and weighed. In its cognitive function, then, "I ought to do this" witnesses that the act described is that one which, when its own properties and those of its consequences have been taken into account, will probably effect the greatest good and the least evil. This may be called the optimific principle, or the principle of maximization of value.

Hence, as we indicated earlier, so far as the prescriptive element goes, the "ought" is basic, and the "good" as a conditional prescription is a function of the "ought"; on the other hand, with respect to the descriptive element, the "ought," asserting that the act promotes the maximum organization of goods over evils, is a function of the "good." This is our suggested solution of the much disputed question whether the "good" or the "ought" is primary. Each is primary in one respect, and derivative in the other.

But there is more to the full-fledged "ought" than this two-way dependency. An obscure recognition of the factors omitted by our treatment of the matter so far is perhaps at the root of those theories, like Ross's, which invoke separate intuitions for the various principal meanings of the "good" and the "ought" that make them irreducible to such a relational analysis as we have given.

The meaning of the "ought" includes the prescriptive and descriptive factors just pointed out, but it comprises other factors as well. These other factors are intertwined with each other and with the prescriptive force and the optimific factor. But various facets of them may be indicated under the following topics:

(3) The nature of the moral "authority."

(4) The logical character of the reflective process in ethical judgment, and its weight as preserved in our attitude toward the conclusion.

(5) The apparent conflict of the optimific principle with other principles such as liberty and justice.

(6) The special motivational attitudes presupposed in certain important types of moral approval.

(7) The role that such concepts as those of personality and human dignity play in ethical judgment.

Anything resembling an adequate analysis of the meaning of the moral ought, in its various major uses, would have to include such notions, or those of them that stand the test of criticism, among its "principles" along with (1) and (2). It would be premature to try to systematize or formalize into a postulate set these seven factors—and perhaps anything resembling an adequate statement of the meaning of a moral judgment should add still others—but any reasonably comprehensive analysis of the matter must take them into account as involved somehow in the structure of the ethical situation and the moral judgment. The classical theories, which emphasize one of them, or a few of them, are woefully incomplete and get into apparently hopeless conflicts—for example the long-standing conflict between utilitarianism and Kantianism—as a result.

To consider (3), the nature of the moral "authority": A moral prescription does not come to us out of the blue. It is natural to ask who or what does the prescribing. Neither the answer of the emotivists, that the attitudes of the speaker do the prescribing, nor another answer hitherto considered, that knowledge does the prescribing, will by itself carry us very far. We wish to know by what authority the speaker prescribes, and how knowledge acquires its prescriptive force.

As Margaret Macdonald has pointed out, in the essay cited in Chapter 4, the fact that ethical judgments are usually couched in indicative rather than imperative form suggests that the one who utters an ethical judgment conceives himself to be at most the transmitter of authority and not the authority itself. And even the assumption that he is the legitimate mouthpiece requires to be backed up. The indicative form is better fitted than the imperative to convey the impersonal, public, social and authoritative character of the ultimate source of the judgment. Knowledge itself partly satisfies these criteria. The "reasons" that we give for the judgment include appeal to facts many of which are publicly verifiable; even the recommendation to consult one's own "private" feelings, when it is relevant, assumes that these feelings are of a kind also possessed by other men and bear upon the situation in a common way. When the reasons are of the nature of maxims or principles, it is likewise assumed that these are not idiosyncratic and capriciously chosen, but are sharable and are subject to some kind of process of public testing, as is the inference by which a judgment follows from a maxim or a principle.

But it will not do to conceive this personal, public, etc., character of the ethical judgment naïvely and crudely. It is one to which factors internal to man have made their contribution. The antithesis of "external" and "internal" is too simple to carry us very far, but it will serve as an opposition to be overcome.

The authority invoked for ethical judgments in early societies seems usually to have been conceived as external to the speaker. He was merely the voice of tradition, or the spokesman for the customs of the group, themselves conceived to be as "objective" and "natural" as the forces of nature. When the shift took place to kingship or to an ethical religion, the authority was no longer a "collective representation" but a personal symbol of the collective will, at any rate in those spheres where the king or deity claimed to exercise moral and legal jurisdiction.

The early chronicles show us that in practice there were many rebels against these authorities; and indeed Paul Radin has argued that contemporary aboriginal societies are far from being as custom-ridden as the evolutionary pictures of them assumed—they have about as large a proportion of non-conformists, individualistic mystics, village atheists and cynics as more civilized societies. But it is first in the utterances of the Sophists that we have an explicit and elaborate doctrinal insistence that such authorities were usurpers. In a complex society, particularly one that involved intercourse between peoples, there were many warring authorities, who set up a conflict among the allegiances of the individual, producing a condition which Bastide has called the "interiorization of war." And in the bewilderment produced by this conflict the only authority that spoke clearly for men like Callicles and Thrasymachus was the voice of a man's own impulses. When the external authorities were convicted of imposture and artifice, one's own interests at least presented themselves with the coerciveness of "nature." But these impulses when examined closely were too confused, too conflicting, too flexible, to serve as the authority; and at the level of their brute occurrence they produced more disorder than they remedied.

Consequently it was necessary to return again to seek a social and rational criterion. But, as conceived by such men as Socrates and Plato, it was a social criterion with a difference. The authority was no longer what society in fact commanded but what its welfare demanded. The shift, in brief, was from a social *source* to a social *goal*. This renewed social emphasis, furthermore, was not one that ignored the individual and his own contribution to the authority of the judgment. The voice of authority was at the same time external, in being transcendent of the individual, and internal, as being assimilated and chosen by the rational individual. So we can say that, from the standpoint of the individual, it was neither a purely heteronomous authority nor a purely autonomous authority.

2. External and Internal Factors

In his article, "The Authority of Moral Judgments" (*Philosophy and Phenomenological Research*, vol. 12, 1952), H. D. Aiken has attempted to give both the external and the internal factors their due places. He argues, in defense of the former, that "the full prescriptive force of 'This act ought to be done' cannot be adequately represented in terms of the usual emotivist schema which characterizes it as 'I approve of this; please do so also. . . .' " For, by Stevenson's own theory, the meaning of a term, being a dispositional predicate shared by the users of the language, is an interpersonal rule "which is binding upon the individual only because it is binding upon all." The hearer of a moral judgment is moved by it, Aiken continues, "not simply because it happens to coincide with some half-aroused private emotion which you happen already to feel, but because, as a socially conditioned organism, the rules of society are already written into his nervous system as conditioned patterns of response." Aiken thus agrees with Miss Macdonald that the ceremonial character and the indicative form of the moral judgment express and reinforce this social backing claimed for it.

But he goes on to urge that the internal or the autonomous factor is equally important, and that it has been given insufficient recognition in Macdonald's analogy. The moral judgment has a non-ceremonial as well as a ceremonial content. In effect, he is saying that the judgment is a blend of ceremony and business—the business of living: ". . . No ritual can give significance to an act which is without an independent interest or vital function of its own. . . ." The ritual "does not so much create the value as 'frame' and solemnize it. . . . The ceremonial provides an authoritative social sanction to acts which were in their own right important to both the individual person and the group." The emotive theory thus is not wholly to be discarded; for it recognizes that the moral judgment must enlist the motivation of the individual. Even though he voices the interests of the group, he must have made them his own. And, in individualistic societies, as the authority of the group becomes less and less coercive, the judgment becomes more and more an expression of personal attitudes and decisions. We have a shift, in other words from a "Catholic" to a "Protestant" position. But Protestantism itself, even in its most liberal varieties, retains vestiges of ancient ritual and of appeal to an external source for the internal coercion. Aiken points out that the language of morality even in highly individualistic and emancipated societies resists translation into terms that represent the moral judgment as the naked assertion of the will of the speaker. Our dissatisfaction with the emotivist analysis represents our assumption that some kind of social and impersonal backing, however vaguely conceived, still attaches to the legitimate use of the term "ought."

In Aiken's very suggestive discussion of this point, there is unfortunately a confusion which needs to be cleared up. Sometimes he speaks as though the interpersonal factor consisted merely in "social conditioning" of moral attitudes as distinguished from idiosyncratic personal conditioning; and he seems to suggest that Stevenson's first pattern of analysis of "This is good" could be made adequate if it were taken in the form "*We* (or *they*) approve of this; do so as well." At other times, however, Aiken finds the social element not so much in the conditioning by the coercive factors operating *de facto* in a society as by an appeal to "common focal aims" or to "common interests" in the society, where we are perhaps at liberty to interpret the terms "aims" and "interests" as referring to what would be good for society rather than to what society in fact wants or tries to coerce us to do. Hence it is that Aiken at the end of his essay vacillates inconclusively between a modified emotivism and utilitarianism.

3. *The Social Source and the Social Goal*

My dissatisfaction with Aiken's account lies in the fact that he has failed to deal clearly with the distinction between a social *source* as the moral authority and a functioning social *end* as the authority. Most of the great ethical writers—from Socrates, Plato and Aristotle to Kant and Mill—have agreed in recommending a social goal as determinant of morality, but in rejecting the unconditional authority of a social command. The responsible individual is one who refuses to perform an act merely because his group—or any authority external to himself

—in fact prescribes it. On the other hand, in order to be responsible he must acknowledge the good of others as coercive of the end which he ought to pursue. The social command is obeyed only in so far as it embodies the social demand. Even when, as with Kant, the social well-being is not taken as the whole of the goal, it is an indispensable determinant of it, as he makes clear in his second formulation of the Categorical Imperative prescribing that human beings should always be taken as ends and not merely as means.

On this view, then, the moral individual is one upon whom the social factor exerts a pull rather than a push. He resists the actual claim of society on occasion in order to further its ideal demand—which only a small group, or he himself, may have grasped. He has, of course, been subjected to social conditioning, and this continues to exert an influence. But the element of autonomy comes in between the push and the pull. The responsible moral individual has sifted and discounted the actual claims of society in order to "give the law unto himself." It is, then, a law that he has "freely" chosen; *i.e.*, by submitting it to the test of his reason and his reflectively espoused allegiances. Social conditioning has been screened through the test offered by his reflective self-conditioning.

What we have, then, is something analogous to Tillich's "theonomy" as distinguished from heteronomy or autonomy. According to the heteronomous view, the authority is wholly external to or transcendent of the individual. According to the autonomous view, it is wholly internal or immanent. But on the view we are considering, the individual prescribes the act to himself, but not in his own name. He prescribes it, again to use Kantian language, "out of respect for" the needs of society, even though not in blind obedience to its imperatives. This is what free men, from Socrates to our day, have regarded as the locus of authority in the social ought.

We can, then, answer the question who or what does the

prescribing by saying that in the case of other-regarding conduct it is the social goal springing from our life-involvements that does so, together with our rational processes of criticism.

When we seek to state the total meaning of the distinctively moral ought, we are forced to include such factors as those given by Kant in his three formulations. Kant's mistake consisted in his offering the formulations as supplying an adequate Identifying Property for the moral ought, whereas, as indeed many of his interpreters have recognized, he was stating, in part, the formal conditions for the application of the "ought." In effect, he was seeking to deal with the question of the authority that does the prescribing, and not with the question what properties an act must have in order to be prescribed, except in so far as these formal conditions themselves can be treated, in an indirect and derivative way, as properties of it. At any rate, even an agreement upon those formal properties would still leave open the question as to the choice between the various Identifying Properties offered by different theories.

4. Kant Revised

Kant's three formulations of the Categorical Imperative will, indeed, need a good deal of refurbishing if they are to serve as partial statements of structural presuppositions of the ought, and will have to be divested of much of the methodological and metaphysical trapping in which he clothed them.

The first formulation, for example, would have to be revised to prescribe, not the universalization of the maxim through its capacity to pass the test of freedom from self-contradiction, but the ways in which "reasons" of various types are ascertained to operate in the process of ethical reasoning. And this criterion would have to be rather complex. It would include ideally the requirements: (1) that the judgment should satisfy the principle or criterion of right conduct, when brought under it by the deductive-inductive process indicated earlier; (2) that maxims, or statements of Conferring Properties, where these are involved, should be well-grounded inductive generalizations stating the relation of certain Conferring Properties to the Identifying Property prescribed in the principle, and formulating the conditions under which the Conferring Properties are relevant; and (3) that singular "reasons" should be true and related to the conclusion through the appropriate subsumption under principles and maxims. In other words, the first formulation as so revised would state the logical conditions that an ethical judgment would have to satisfy in order to be deemed a manifestation of a *rational* moral attitude, or in order to be *grounded in knowledge.*

Kant thought he had found, through his test of the universalization of the maxim, a short-cut to a rational justification ·of the moral judgment. But a more empirical—or, perhaps we should say at this stage, simply a logically more adequate— view of the matter could not dispense with a more elaborate scheme for testing, of the sort indicated. This scheme would give ample room, as Kant's rationalistic position did not, to the empirical factors in the process. It would differ from Kant especially in giving maxims a more subordinate position. Maxims, where they could be found, would indeed be "universalized," though not by a simple *a priori* test but by an empirical scrutiny of their soundness as means of implementing the principle under certain conditions. Maxims would also be held more tentatively than in Kant's theory, on the ground that although ideally they would be universal in the sense of being worthy of acceptance if all the conditions could be stated, in fact the conditions can never be fully stated, so that maxims will continue to conflict in practice. And even the principles themselves would be held with greater tentativeness than Kant would have agreed to, since as we have seen, however principles are "justified" this justification is not a process that can ever yield certainty; so that the principles are always open to revision by our developing commitments.

Kant's second formulation of the Categorical Imperative, in prescribing that we regard each individual as an end and not merely as a means, puts in words an assumption of the socially oriented ought that has as much claim as any similar statement can have to be central or essential. It gives us a minimum indication of the Identifying Property of the "right" act, and also prescribes a *sine qua non* of the motivational factor in the morally meritorious act, and thus states one of the conditions of the moral ought. Thereby it expresses a minimum demand of both the Christian and the democratic attitudes.

But, despite the basic importance of this second Categorical Imperative, it unfortunately functions in Kant's own system as an over-simplification. If taken as a complete criterion of the other-regarding or social element in the meaning of right or ought, it appears as a scant substitute for the detailed specification of the social goal that we need, and that is treated much more fully by such philosophers as Plato, Aristotle, the utilitarians and the Hegelian idealists. The second Categorical Imperative, therefore, can be taken as a sound but incomplete attempt to characterize the Identifying Property of the right or the moral ought on the assumption that morality has a social goal. An adequate principle, for one thing, would define the relation of the ought to the good, as Kant does not. This would include, above all, an attempt to show what it is about the human being that gives him intrinsic value, or makes him worthy of being treated as an end in himself; and Kant's doctrine of the "good will" gives us scant enlightenment on this point, setting up a cleavage rather than a connection. The social principle, furthermore, should cope also with such questions as how the social good is compounded, or how the individuals conceived as ends are related to each other. The

Platonic doctrine of a hierarchy of classes based upon function and ability, the more relativistic Aristotelian doctrine of the polity, the utilitarian calculus, Sidgwick's theory of distributive justice, the idealist doctrines of the nature of the self or personality, and of the "organic" character of the state, Lewis' concept of the Gestalt of value in its social aspects and Perry's theory of the highest good as inclusiveness of all interests are attempts to give a fuller treatment of this matter on which Kant tells us only to treat humanity as an end.

These other theories try, as Kant's does not, to deal with the question, among others, what, granting that every individual is to be conceived as potentially of intrinsic worth, should we do in order to take account of the pathetic facts that some individuals are of greater worth than others and that some in practice, *faute de mieux*, must upon occasion actually be sacrificed to the common good and consequently treated as mere means. This cluster of problems is one that we shall treat under the heading of distributive justice.

We cannot, however, equate the Identifying Property of the ought or right with the complete social goal as it operates to determine the concrete decision. For this latter involves also the particular Conferring Properties that assist in identifying the good in a particular society at a particular time, or with respect to the special group of individuals affected by a given measure. Such highly variable Conferring Properties are seized upon, within the governmental sphere, by the practical politician and the political scientist, with such guidance as they can get from the plain man. The Identifying Property, on the other hand, must be restricted to the perennial or structural aspects of the moral situation that are common to all societies. Even so limited, however, there is more to be said about it than Kant gave us.

The moral authority derived from the first Categorical Imperative, then, is that bestowed by the moral judge's or moral agent's having subjected the judgment to the criteria of rational reflection; the moral authority of the second Categorical Imperative derives from subordinating the judgment to a social goal which supplies the network of ends. Both these factors are primarily heteronomous; the third Categorical Imperative, which expresses directly the element of autonomy, subjects them to the responsibility of the individual who adopts and applies the rational and the social criteria. Kant himself says about his third Categorical Imperative: "I will therefore call this the principle of Autonomy of the will, in contrast with every other which I accordingly reckon as Heteronomy."

But here again the principle requires some tinkering in order to be acceptable to our current conceptions of knowledge and of human nature. Kant's most summary statement of the principle is: "That the will would . . . regard itself as giving in its maxims universal laws"; the emphasis is on the words "itself" and "giving": "Thus the will is not simply subject to the law, but so subject that it must be regarded as itself giving the law, and on this ground only, subject to the law (of which it can regard itself as the author)." Kant ultimately accounts for the capacity of the will for self-legislation by referring it back to the noumenal self, which as representative of universal reason gives the moral law by the inexorable operation of its intrinsic nature.

To accord with the revised formulations of the first and second imperatives, Kant's view would have to be reinterpreted on other metaphysical and methodological assumptions than his own; it would have to be restated, for example, to incorporate the qualifications we have made about the logical role of maxims and "laws," so that it would amount to something like the following: that the moral agent should act in accordance with reflective criteria (principles, maxims and facts) which he himself has subjected to a critical test, and in accordance with a social goal he has earned through his reasoned life-involvements. Even in this brief form, however, it suggests that the public, social and universal factors have been brought into harmony with the nature of the individual agent; that they have enlisted his allegiance, not by coercion but through his own choice.

We may summarize the argument of this chapter by saying that the "authority" that prescribes in the case of the fully moral ought derives its public and impersonal character from the public and intersubjective nature of the rational criteria and the social goals to which it has been subjected; that it acquires its authority over the individual agent by gearing these in with his developing commitments and devotions; and that one who utters a moral judgment bases his claim for attention not only upon his ability to convince us that he has invoked the rational and social criteria, but also upon the assumed "sincerity" or "responsibility" which derives from the element of self-legislation.

But the word authority is somewhat misleading as a description of this last element. For, in a society of free individuals, there is always the assumption that the one who is advising others is not asking them to accept the judgment because of his own sincerity, but because the judgment appeals to their sincerity: that is, enlists their own allegiances which are capable of being rationally and socially directed. So it is that, in morals, there are ultimately no authorities in the authoritarian sense; there are only rational and socialized individuals collaborating freely through the exercise of their moral imaginations. This is the assumption of an ideal morality; it appears, of course, to be a visionary parody if taken as a factual description of moral behavior as we find it in the large and the rough. It represents initially our analysis of what most of us would take to be the assumptions of an emancipated moral man at the present stage of moral development and in his best moments. That such a discrepancy should exist between the ideal and the actual state of affairs is the ultimate and not wholly eradicable tragedy of man's moral aspirations. The tragedy enters through the incompleteness of the mode of justification that alone is available to us in our frailty.

14

The Conflict of Ethical Principles

1. Utility, Justice and Liberty

The most serious embarrassment to an attempt to reinstate the cognitive element in ethics has yet to be faced squarely. The issue concerns not so much the question whether there is a cognitive element, nor whether it is, in general, as we have characterized it in relation to the non-cognitive, nor even whether the cognitive factor is subordinated to "principles." Where the trouble looms is over the nature and connection of principles at the level of moral judgment proper, as distinguished from judgments of intrinsic and extrinsic value.

The question can be put as follows: whether in the moral domain we can ultimately find guidance in one coherent set of mutually compatible principles, or must make do with a congeries of them, hazy at the edges, sometimes compatible and sometimes giving rise to conflicts that to the end must resist any effort to unify them.

The view of the cognitive factor as prescribing the maximization of the good has been stressed especially by utilitarianism. But the same major problem arises with regard to any other ethical view that seeks a stable cognitive structure on which to base ethical judgments. It is encountered, *mutatis mutandis*, by an integration theory like Perry's or by Dewey's pluralistic pragmatism; but it constitutes an equally serious problem for intuitionism. Moore and Ewing, for example, proceed on the assumption that a systematic and coherent body of principles is possible for ethics, founded for Moore on the notion of the intrinsically good, and for Ewing on a certain interpretation of "ought" or "morally fitting." Ross, on the other side, is a radical pluralist: there are, he holds, a number of ethical concepts and principles which are to some extent independent of each other, each of which has a *prima facie* claim on our allegiance. The resulting conflicts cannot be settled by appeal to principle but only by an overarching intuition.

The focal issue most commonly appears in a dispute between optimific or "teleological" theories—whether they be empirical or intuitionist—and their pluralistic opponents. An optimific ("greatest-good-making") theory holds that the right, or what we ought to do, is determined by some kind of organization of goodness and badness, aimed at the attainment of the maximum of value, however this is conceived. The right is a comparatively simply function of the good, and in some sense a quantitative function of the good (as that which leads to the "greatest" or "most" good) even though it is conceived as an intensive or non-measurable rather than an extensive or measurable quantity.

Critics of optimific theories hold in effect that there is something more to a moral judgment, even on its cognitive side, than the simple assertion that the right act is the one that will produce the maximum of goodness. The difficulty has arisen within the utilitarian school itself, which has tended to take the optimific principle of greatest happiness as its major premise. Mill proposed a qualitative criterion for comparative goodness, which would not be reducible to quantity, even of the intensive sort. And Sidgwick invoked special intuitions to deal with the problem of distribution of goods, and especially to take care of the impartiality of distribution and its inclusion of as many individuals as possible among those affected.

When we look at the most carefully articulated presentation of utilitarianism that we have had, Sidgwick's in *The Methods of Ethics*,[1] we find the problem conscientiously explored but not solved.

The supreme principle of ethics is stated by Sidgwick as follows: "By utilitarianism is here meant the ethical theory, that the conduct which, under any given circumstances, is objectively right, is that which will produce the greatest happiness on the whole; that is, taking into account all whose happiness is affected by the conduct."

And Sidgwick, in turn, defines greatest happiness as "the greatest possible surplus of pleasure over pain, the pain being conceived as balanced against an equal amount of pleasure, so that the two contrasted amounts annihilate each other for purposes of ethical calculation."

He makes it clear that in rejecting Mill's qualitative treatment of pleasures and pains for a quantitative view he does not wish to return to Bentham's view that pleasures and pains are capable of metric treatment in a hedonic calculus. Sidgwick holds that the quantity in question is "intensive." That is, pleasures and pains can be ranked on a scale of differences of degree, so that A is *more* pleasant than B, and hence *better* intrinsically, although they are not capable of numerical addition and subtraction.

Yet, even as so extended, Sidgwick did not believe that the principle of utility by itself could serve as an adequate criterion or major premise for moral judgments. While he rejects

---

[1] References in this chapter are to the 4th Edition, 1890.

as "sham-axioms" or "tautologies" certain supposed principles that are necessary but empty of content, he finally holds that the principle of utility must be extended by at least the following three genuine "axioms":

Rational Self-Love or Prudence: "That a smaller present good is not to be preferred to a greater future good (allowing for difference of certainty)."

Benevolence: "That one is morally bound to regard the good of any other individual as much as one's own, except in so far as we judge it to be less, when impartially viewed, or less certainly knowable or attainable."

Justice: A principle which Sidgwick never succeeds in stating in a summary way, but which would include "impartiality in the application of general rules" in such a manner as to exclude "arbitrary inequality." Or, in other words, the principle prescribes avoidance of favoritism for individuals and treats them as equals except in so far as the rules themselves embody justifiable "reasons for inequality."

The precise logical relation of these principles to the principle of utility is not clear from Sidgwick's discussion. As he states the problem in general, utilitarianism is called upon to show that the lesser principles "have only a dependent and subordinate validity." By this, Sidgwick evidently cannot be taken to mean that the auxiliary principles can be *deduced* from the supreme principle, or it alone. For they contain notions not clearly contained in this when taken as a premise. Ruling out this alternative, there seem to be two others:

(1) That the auxiliary principles state *means* to the general end of the greatest happiness. If this is the case, however, they would be, on Sidgwick's view as well as our own, ordinary empirical assertions, prescribing what we have called Conferring Properties rather than basic structural properties of the highest good. Sidgwick makes it clear that, in the case of Justice, at any rate, such Conferring Properties are needed in

addition to the principle of justice as stated above; further, that these vary with the particular society, depending on its institutions and potentialities.

(2) That the subordinate principles are further *specifications* of what the general happiness consists in, just as Sidgwick's definition of greatest happiness above is a specification of the notion as formulated in the utility principle which was quoted just preceding it. If this is the case, then these simply make the notion of the general happiness more precise, and "operationally" more applicable.

Sidgwick at times takes both these tacks. Most of the remainder of Part IV of *The Methods of Ethics*, however, is concerned not with the relation of such principles to the principle of utility, but with showing that specific *maxims* of Common Sense morality, such as truth-telling, can, where they are sound, be justified by appeal to their utility without requiring special intuitions.

The matter to the end is far from clear. Sidgwick's main way of dealing with the problem seems to be through the residue of intuitionism that remains in his system. Whatever the precise logical relation of the auxiliary principles to the principle of utility, he rests their acceptance on their self-evidence as independent moral axioms, just as with the principle of utility itself:

Utilitarianism is thus presented as the final form into which intuitionism tends to pass, when the demand for really self-evident first principles is rigorously pressed. . . . The intuitional method rigorously applied yields as its final result the doctrine of pure Universalistic Hedonism.

If the auxiliary principles do rest on intuition, they cannot on Sidgwick's otherwise empirical assumptions be considered as means to the greatest happiness, though it is quite consistent to conceive them as specifications of it.

But this whole question is cast into doubt by the concluding sentences of the book—generally overlooked by those who have commented on it—where Sidgwick apparently leaves open, as an alternative to the intuitionism previously relied upon, another view of the justification of principles which is perhaps consistent with the notion of vindication we have outlined in Chapters 9 and 10:

Those who hold that the edifice of physical science is really constructed of conclusions logically inferred from self-evident premises, may reasonably demand that any practical judgments claiming philosophic certainty should be based on an equally firm foundation. If on the other hand we find that in our supposed knowledge of the world of nature propositions are commonly taken to be universally true, which yet seem to rest on no other grounds than that we have a strong disposition to accept them, and that they are indispensable to the systematic coherence of our beliefs; it would seem difficult to reject a similarly supported assumption in ethics, without opening the door to universal scepticism.

Whatever their method of justification, it seems clear that for Sidgwick the auxiliary principle and the supreme principle are compatible with each other, or that when apparent incompatibilities arise what one should try to do is to restate the principles so that they can be made mutually consistent and supplementary to each other. And on this point, despite their quite different and various assumptions, such theories as those of Perry, Moore and Ewing seem to be in agreement with Sidgwick.

2. Conflict as Irresoluble

As a current representative of the opposing view, which we have called the pluralistic one, let us take Professor Aiken's essay, "Moral Reasoning" (*Ethics*, vol. 54, 1953), which is in general accord with this book on many other central issues. While insisting on the need for a body of cognitive principles in ethics, Aiken holds that it is imperfectly systematic. There is no one supreme principle under which all others can be subsumed; nor are the principles to which we must appeal necessarily compatible with each other. Ultimate and irresoluble conflicts among them can occur, and this is the main source of the tragedy of the moral life. The most general and the most frequently applicable principle for Aiken is that of welfare, or the utilitarian goal of least-suffering-and-greatest-enjoyment, but this does not always take precedence over other principles with which it may come into conflict. It may clash in particular applications with such other ultimate principles as justice and liberty, or even with such still less general rules or maxims as promise-keeping. When this happens, there is no one of these principles, nor any still higher to be hoped for, to which appeal may be made. We have reached the limits of validation, and when the conflict really is ultimate, it has a tragic character: we must sacrifice an ultimate good or accept the choice of an intrinsic evil. In one such case, Aiken argues:

Now it may be supposed that unless the suffering entailed by keeping a promise were substantially greater than that entailed by breaking it, the promise should be kept. The principle of least suffering does not automatically take precedence over the principle of promises. It does so only at a certain point when a great deal of suffering would result from the keeping of a promise. It is only in this sense that the principle of least suffering takes final precedence over the other. But how much suffering is required to make the principle of least suffering take precedence? Here I think that there is no exact prescription, and no clear way of guaranteeing that, granted equal knowledge of the facts of the case, reasonable men may not disagree about the point at which the deleterious effects of keeping a promise absolves one from keeping it.

Nevertheless, I think that most disinterested men in our society would agree that in extreme cases the principle of least suffering does take precedence over that involved in making promises.

Welfare or utility takes precedence over promise-keeping, then, only "in extreme cases"; it does not have even this degree of priority, however, when it comes into conflict with the principles of justice and liberty.

In an analogous conflict between welfare and liberty, the answer seems to be clearer: ". . . Freedom of persons ought categorically to be respected." If liberty is a *categorical* imperative, then, it seems for Aiken to be an absolute which in all cases should take precedence over others. But this would hardly be consistent with his general statement that in the case of all three of these principles "There is no conclusive reason for always giving one claim the right of way over the rest." His meaning seems to be that, although freedom is categorically to be *respected* (that is to say, is always to be given consideration), it is not categorically to be *chosen* in such conflicts.

In any case, it is evident that for Aiken liberty, however categorical its *claims* when it comes in conflict with the other principles, is not a supreme principle in the sense that all the others can be derived from it, nor even that it is always to be followed when it would cause gross violence to the other principles. We have in Aiken's position an irreducible pluralism with respect to principles, isomorphic with that at which Ross arrives on quite different methodological assumptions.

The conflict of principles is adjudicated, for Aiken, in the same way that principles themselves are justified. The moral principles, taken conjointly, supply an analysis of what we mean by "reasonableness" in so far as that is analyzable. But when they conflict, the appeal seems to be, according to Aiken, to the unanalyzed residue of rationality which is not exhaustible by any formulation of it into principles. We have here

something similar to what we have called a global, or operative, sense of rationality consisting in a kind of Gestalt of
directedness, which is partly expressible in principles but in
its totality eludes formulation. Such a sense Aiken refers to as
the "moral consciousness" shared by "most disinterested men"
in our age and society. This sense is also, he says, commonly
called the "conscience of the community" or even the "conscience of mankind." This moral consciousness, however, is
alterable and it does not seem to supply self-evidence to its
deliverances—hence Aiken's divergence from intuitionism.

The moral consciousness, as the ultimate justifying agent in
such conflicts, does not succeed in reconciling principles, or
making them compatible with each other. It chooses among
them non-rationally, and the result, according to Aiken, is
sometimes moral tragedy, of the sort illustrated by the
Antigone and by the *Book of Job:* what we must resign ourselves to is, as Hegel pointed out, "an inescapable conflict of
ethical principles, both of which are 'right' and both 'wrong.'"
We continue to act on one principle—or to refrain from acting because there is no choice between principles—but here
we come up against a final surdity in the moral life.

Such a pluralism as Aiken proposes is no more capable of
refutation that it is of conclusive support, among other reasons
because of the uncertainties in the view of justification we
have been forced to adopt. But the approach we have used
may help to cast some additional light on the matter.

Pre-discursive or sub-discursive judgment, as we have seen
in Chapters 6–8, constitutes the activity out of which finding and giving "reasons" at any level develops. The reasons
always tend to lag behind the perceptions and valuational
habits which generate them. On the other hand, the perceptions and habits themselves are so fallible and mutually bel-
licose that the most reliable way, on the whole, to organize
them and adjudicate among them is to find rules serviceable

for this purpose; and our habits may themselves lag behind the rules adopted to supersede them.

Such a maxim as that enjoining promise-keeping—to start with this example of Aiken's—is formulated explicitly long before any high-level principle for moral judgment is hit upon. When, however, such a principle as that of the maximization of goods is articulated, it is recognized to express such a deep-seated and generally applicable structural presupposition of our nature (whether it be a tendency of our "first nature" or a principle espoused by our "second nature") that a persistent effort is made to validate the more specific rule, as a rough generalization, by means of it.

Aiken holds that the "moral consciousness" dictates that "unless the suffering entailed by keeping a promise were substantially greater than that entailed by breaking it, a promise should be kept." Now precisely this instance has many times been dealt with by utilitarians and other proponents of an optimific theory. When Aiken says that upholders of the principle of welfare have ignored the "hard cases," he overlooks the numerous rejoinders that have been urged against his pluralistic view. Briefly, the rejoinders hold: that promise-keeping is of such widespread and fundamental utility to all societies, as the presupposition of mutual trust and rational collaboration, that it is a rule to be observed unless there are highly conclusive reasons for violating it. And the injunction to observe the rule in most doubtful cases itself rests upon: (a) the difficulty of forecasting the consequences in particular cases so fully that we can be practically sure that the evil resulting from keeping the promise will not outweigh the good done by breaking it; and allied with this argument, (b) the consideration that utility requires not only diagnosing the optimific act in the particular situation but reinforcing precisely such dispositions or habits as promise-keeping—the harm done by undermining the disposition will normally outweight the slight good accomplished by violating it in a particular case.

The argument on both sides can be carried much further, but what has just been said suffices to indicate that in this case both an optimific theory and a pluralistic theory run into the same difficulties in application, and are apt to reach the same conclusion in the particular case. Both would hold that a promise ought to be kept unless there was very strong evidence that the balance of foreseeable goods and evils would be seriously tipped by keeping it, and that when this happens the promise should be broken. A pluralistic theory would justify such a conclusion by appeal to intuition or to some more empirical notion such as Aiken's "moral consciousness"; an optimific theory would justify the apparent exceptions to the optimific principle by an appeal to that principle itself, invoking the partial difficulties of prediction and the usefulness of maintaining social approval of promise-keeping as a general disposition, especially in view of the human tendency to rationalize the breaking of such rules because of self-interest.

Both types of theory, furthermore, run up against the ultimate and not wholly remediable vagueness and indeterminacy of any ethical principle. Ethical theory—and, indeed, all philosophic and much scientific theory—constantly encounters this kind of difficulty; the principle or rule cannot be stated with enough precision, nor quantified to such a point, that the application is decisive as between two alternative theories. When this happens, we ordinarily choose between the theories on the ground that the more general principle, that which is more fertile in application, brings more intellectual order into the subject matter than the less general rule. Sometimes the principle can be reformulated so as to reduce the vagueness. Sometimes we simply have to put up with it and cite Aristotle —though this is often done prematurely—to the effect that in

258

such a field as morals we cannot expect the degree of exactness obtainable in other domains.

What Aiken's pluralism commits him to is the position that promise-keeping has, *per se,* intrinsic value, whereas an optimific theory would find quite sufficient justification for such an act by treating it as an extrinsic value, without denying that, when it becomes a rule of practice, specific acts of keeping promises can and frequently do acquire intrinsic value as an added glory. The only theory of intrinsic goodness that Aiken has given so far (most fully stated in his contribution to *Value: a Co-operative Inquiry,* edited by Lepley), is an affective theory similar to the one we have expounded in Chapter 11. His present pluralism, then, would seem to presuppose the shift to an intuitionist (or crypto-intuitionist) theory of intrinsic goodness, though so far he has shrunk from committing himself to anything like this, and indeed his general position, particularly the doctrine of justification he advocates, is inconsistent with intuitionism except in so far as he admits it through the back door.[2]

---

[2] The notion of promise-keeping is advanced frequently, both by intuitionists and by informalists, as a crucial instance in refutation of optimific theories. The argument has a special plausibility in that when one makes a promise one is *voluntarily* and *explicitly* assuming an obligation. The obligation consequently seems to have a bindingness beyond that conferred by any general obligation to promote the greatest good where there is no such explicit assumption of the obligation. But an optimific theory would account for the additional gravity of the obligation here by pointing to the special utility of upholding the force of any commitment that is voluntarily and explicitly undertaken, as a basis for mutual trust and collaboration; so that such a commitment should be taken as "defeasible" only when there are the most overwhelming arguments against it on grounds of welfare and high predictability of the con-

Such maxims or supposed "principles" as promise-keeping and truth-telling are more restricted in their scope than those of justice and liberty. They respond to the structure of frequently recurring situations that are not as pervasive of human experience as considerations of justice and liberty. Their position near the center of the structure, even though not precisely at it, nor even as close as the larger principles, is accounted for by the fact that effective communication, and hence cooperative action, rests upon our ability to presuppose them as general rules. But these considerations themselves sometimes require that exceptions be made to them, just as they sometimes require that *foreseeable* welfare in some measure be sacrificed for them in order that the habit be maintained. Because of their great social utility, much more careful analysis than has been given is required from those who would treat them shortly as intrinsic values or—what amounts to the same thing—as autonomous principles. They can nevertheless continue to be treated as "prima facie duties" if we interpret this status as referring to their near-universality as stable conditions of welfare. When we call something a condition of a good, however, we are ascribing to it an extrinsic value. Of course intrinsic values may accompany, or immediately spring from, the fulfillment of a condition, but this observation is in no way incompatible with our analysis.

3. *The Claim of "Welfare" to Priority*

When we consider such rules as those expressing conceptions of liberty and justice we must point out, first, that Aiken has

---

sequences. The fact that it is defeasible at all, however, weighs against its being taken as absolute—or even as "intrinsic" in any sense except the unintelligible one which invokes a non-natural quality.

not defined them precisely enough that we can hope to decide from his account whether there is a possibility of a tragic conflict with the principle of welfare or not. It is obvious that many of the rules that we need for the articulation of our conceptions of liberty and justice are at a level of specificity which makes them relative to the structure of a particular society or a particular stage in the development of the moral consciousness of mankind; they are, therefore, what we have called maxims rather than principles, and the resulting conflicts, though often practically irresoluble by any ideal means, and hence fraught with great vexation and even catastrophe, are not such as to affect the point at issue here.

We come upon especially serious conflicts when we go beyond maxims at the level of a bill of rights or a code of distributive justice to such large conceptions of liberty as the individualistic view which conceives it as absence of restraint by the government and other social groups; and, opposing this, a collectivist view which conceives it as inhering in cooperative activity that frees men from the coercions and frustrations of unsatisfied natural wants. Here we get into such titanic clashes as the current one between East and West, or, on a less acute scale, between leftist and rightist alignments within our own society. Such clashes present themselves, in the first instance, not as conflicts between liberty and welfare but as oppositions between alternative conceptions of liberty itself. "Welfare" is not unequivocally on the side of either conception of liberty in the abstract, as Aiken seems to assume in his statement of the issue, when it is presented as one of "making people happy at the expense of depriving them of liberty." In the abstract, it is possible to devise an imaginative experiment, like Plato's *Republic* or Skinner's *Walden Two*— which is the one cited by Aiken—where wants are satisfied, suffering has been minimized and enjoyment maximized, at the same time that most personal and civil liberties are non-existent. But it has not been established that this is a "real possibility" either as a durable social structure in any foreseeable future condition of mankind, or even as a genuine potentiality of the human psyche granted the most hopeful expectations concerning the conquest of nature and the achievement of social controls. Against the first is the need, urged repeatedly by Dewey, for social and political mechanisms conducive to "pooled intelligence" where every man is potentially a contributor; against the second is the consideration that the good life, even at the level of individual happiness, is closely bound up with some measure of rationality, and this in turn is interlocked with the kind of autonomy or rational self-determination we have treated in the preceding chapter under the topic of a reformulation of the third Categorical Imperative.

If we can hope to discern some non-fluctuating "principles" of liberty and justice—as distinguished from the more or less variable codes which are closely bound up with the structure of particular societies—they probably must be very general, and cannot be much more detailed than the statements of freedom as autonomy or rational self-determination, and of justice as impartiality or rejection of arbitrary inequality, that have been given; although there is plenty of room for redefinition and sharpening of these concepts.

Up to a high-level point of indeterminacy, then, liberty and justice as so conceived can be impressively justified both as means to welfare or happiness and as specifications of the perennial structure, actual or potential, of human relationships which supports it. But we are on very shaky ground when we talk about such a perennial structure of human relationships and pretend to have defined it with any accuracy. There are so many imponderables that we cannot be sure that we have disentangled the permanent structure from accidental cultural configurations which we mistake for invariant conditions rooted in ultimate limiting potentialities of human nature. On the other hand, the continuing search for order in the moral domain seems to require persistence in a struggle for it. In the end, what is required is a faith analogous to the faith presupposed by the search for truth in any sphere of knowledge, which is summed up in C. S. Peirce's pragmatic definition of truth as that opinion on which all qualified investigators are fated to agree if they push their investigations far enough. Both faiths can only be vindicated rather than validated; and both are liable to be upset and discarded in the effort at vindication. At present, we do not have sufficient grounds for discarding them; and the pressures toward intellectual and moral order are sufficient to keep the quest alive.

A principle like liberty can be defended empirically as such a basic and near-universal precondition of the good life that it can be impressively justified up to an obscure indeterminacy-point by the principle of utility. But neither the principle of liberty nor the principle of welfare has been—or perhaps can be—stated with enough exactitude that we can be sure there is an ultimately irresoluble conflict between them, whatever hard problems we may get into in practice as a result of taking one concept rather than the other as our immediate criterion in the particular situation. All we can be sure of is that no *formulation* of either principle can be absolute or final and that, as a result, commitments to them run into such uncertainties and confusions in practice that the result often can appropriately be called tragic for society. The point at issue is not the practical one whether tragic conflict can be eliminated from human life—for the answer is clearly negative—but the theoretical one as to its precise locus.

When we come to the principles of prudence and benevolence—and, indeed, this holds to a lesser extent of justice and liberty—a genetic approach can be of assistance up to a certain point. All these principles can be conceived as expressions and ramifications of the urge to maximize values.

This is clearly the case with the principle of prudence. As we saw in an earlier chapter, the tendencies toward integration built into the nervous system of the animal and the child constitute, below the level of discursive and reflective thought, a rough disposition to organize conduct in such a way as to increase goods and diminish evils, and to bring the future into this organization. With the acquisition of the capacity to symbolize and to forecast the consequences of actions, the tendency becomes an explicit rule, if one intermittent in its operations. It is reinforced by the individual's subsequent gratifications and frustrations; and above all by social pressures, which encourage prudence both because it makes him more useful in the roles that society demands from him, and because it keeps him from becoming a nuisance to it. But of course the tendency never becomes wholly a law of his being, partly because of the complexity of his at best dimly understood nature, so that the old Adam is always breaking out, and partly because of the very uncertainties of the future, so that he takes the cash and lets the credit go. Nevertheless, the prudential urge finds such repeated reinforcement that he does not deny the principle—perhaps incorporating into his statement of it, or his working adherence to it, qualifications giving the old Adam his due and assigning a certain scope to the maxim *carpe diem.* But these, in so far as rational, are simply gropings toward a larger and more enlightened prudence.

It is not hard to see how the urge to maximize values also generates principles of benevolence and justice. These grow less directly than does prudence out of the integrating tendencies of the individual organism, but exert their suasion on the individual through the compounding of social demands upon him and the imposition of social types of order. The process could be illustrated by casual personal relations, but it is most sharply exemplified in the *roles* and *functions* that social organization creates and assigns to the individual. He is a parent or a teacher faced with a choice to make for those in his charge, or a judge with an impartial decision to render, or a politician with the survival of his nation hanging upon his action in a crisis.

All these other-regarding jobs are created by specialization of function within the social order. The jobs, by their very nature, are such that successful performance of them requires ignoring the agent's self-interest and tends, up to a point, to make his self-interest coincide with this performance. His assigned job demands inclusion of as many interests as possible, and some kind of impartiality in adjudicating among them. His sense of the *meaning* of the "ought" in the performance of these roles will therefore comprise regard for inclusiveness of persons and "equality before the law" in some one of its interpretations.

The more generalized notions of justice and benevolence are developed and sustained, in part, by extension from these specialized roles. We come to feel that we have similar obligations as citizens and moral beings, in the shifting contexts in which we play these more general roles; though particular duties are less precisely imposed here and evasion of them less readily evokes social censure—hence the comparative weakness or sporadic appearance of the general attitudes. If obligations to justice and benevolence were entirely absorbed into the demands of the special roles, then morality would be wholly institutionalized. We encounter some persons whose other-regarding concern is exhausted by their performance of their jobs, and who, outside them, are timid or heedless as to the welfare of others; but we also see some persons in whom it is chiefly manifested in free-lance moral activities and may even express itself in revolt against the institutionalized channels of altruism, which in any case are always spotty in their incidence and incomplete in their scope.

One engaged by a specific judicial role is placed in a position where his decision is submitted to public scrutiny and will be judged in such a way that any self-regarding consideration, or any favoritism to persons, so far as the particular act is concerned, will normally be censured. From the nature of the social demand which created his job, the adequacy of his decision will hinge upon his wisdom in balancing and allocating among persons the goods and evils which accrue to those whose welfare is entrusted to him. Such a criterion does not, of course, exclude the necessity of setting up, in the social organization which makes such demands, provision for the welfare of the person called upon to make such other self-regarding decisions.

The structure of the situation which creates his social role dictates to his decisions the consideration of impartiality in distribution of goods as well as that of maximum amount. Not only is every individual inevitably a carrier of intrinsic goods and evils, but each is also potentially a contributor to society. Some societies have attained to a partial commitment to this principle; others have not. When such a commitment has been achieved, the roles that accrue to people as social agents will demand that their decisions take account of it.

It is impossible to state a general principle of distribution in such detail and with such precision that it can serve as the sole premise from which an adequate deduction can be made in a particular case; but it must always be supplemented by maxims guiding distribution in the society in question, or by flexible perception—constituting a kind of "empirical intuition"—in the individual case. These adjuncts result from the highly variable character of particular societies and situations, with respect to potentialities, tastes and expectations within them. But it would be chimerical to expect ethical theory to supply premises which would dispense with the work of the legislator, the moralist, the psychiatrist and the educator. The discovery of Conferring Properties may be left in part to such specialists, and in part to the vigilance of the individual moral agent who takes the specialist with a grain of salt. To demand otherwise would be not only to ask that ethics become an exact science, but to distort it into a pseudo-science.

4. Personality and the Greatest Good

Now the notion of a maximization of value, even in the sense of "intensive" quantity, does not by itself imply clauses as to inclusiveness of individual persons or impartiality. It is logically quite possible that, in the particular situation, the greatest total of value can be attained when the interests of some individuals are totally excluded. It is, furthermore, often the case that a preponderance of total happiness over misery can be achieved, so far as the foreseeable consequences are concerned, even when the welfare of all individuals is considered but someone is deliberately sacrificed, as in warfare, for a slight gain to the total. When we are in our altruistic moods we would welcome an intuition which would rule out this kind of conclusion from the optimific principle. What seems to be required is some central principle of the intrinsic worth or dignity of the human personality which takes precedence over the optimific principle itself, and thus makes human personality an absolute. But it is hard to interpret "absolute" here in the way that is usually intended by this assertion. Human personality may be called an absolute in various senses—that every human (or sentient) individual is capable of some measure of intrinsic value, and that only individuals are the carriers of intrinsic value. These are indeed features of the situation that are genuinely structural; it is difficult to conceive of any cataclysmic change in human nature or the human condition which would require them to be altered—except possibly a mutation of the nervous system which would produce androids incapable of having feelings.

It does not follow, however, that personality as such can be attributed *intrinsic* worth without qualification. Personality is capable of all sorts of aberrations and perversions. It can come to the individual to seem a bane, so that he yearns for escape from it into eternal night or an impersonal world-soul.

An alternative view would be that personality is the sole immediate locus and bearer of intrinsic value for human beings, but that upon careful analysis its values are such a tesselated network of goods intrinsic and instrumental, actual and potential, that no clarity or accuracy is achieved by calling personality outright an intrinsic worth. Personality must be the central concept in any normative ethics; it supplies the kind of organization toward which most of our care and our planning must be directed. We cannot judge and forecast in terms of disembodied enjoyments and sufferings; our joys and sufferings themselves are relative to the make-up of the individual personality, as it has been shaped in its social relationships. But the personality is a worker as well as an enjoyer and a sufferer. No derogation to its dignity, and no dissolution of it into a bundle of disjointed interests or feelings, is implied in recognizing its multiple and interlocking functions, but rather the contrary. Even though personality is not without qualification an intrinsic good, it is the *sole locus of potential intrinsic worth,* and therefore the center of moral concern in practice.

Consequently any principle which seeks to maximize values must attribute to individual personality a special "sanctity." It may be possible in the individual decision to predict with some plausibility a greater balance of positive values where some personalities are excluded from participation, just as it is sometimes necessary to sacrifice them in the tough exigencies of life and politics. But our calculations in such matters are at best slippery and hazardous; care for the greatest good cannot justify such omissions either as a matter of an ideal social policy or of persisting individual attitudes. It is too easy to slip from a necessitated harshness in the particular case to callousness as a long-run disposition.

As a practical rule for fostering the greatest good, the human creature being the variable and distractible animal that he is, one might recommend that abstract benevolence and justice be blended with *generosity, compassion* and *charity,* which would temper our concern for the future and the greatest calculable good with a half-skeptical and gay recognition of the ignorance and partial futility within which we move, and to some degree yield to the patent needs of the harried and fragile persons with whom we are thrown fortuitously in the human community.

There is, indeed, as poets and playboys have always recognized, a serious and ever-present danger that ethical theory itself, with its concern for principles, will lead us to strain and ratiocinate to the point where we shall miss the spontaneously attainable bounties of life and commit cruelties in the name of our noblest ideals. But thought is never done: this attitude itself can be absorbed into a principle or a maxim, even though it can operate most effectively not as a rule but as a working habit. Here is another place where the yearning for a return to Eden can neither be wholly downed nor wholeheartedly indulged.

More will be said, though with no pretensions to conclusiveness, on this question in the final chapter on "Naturalism and the Tragic Sense." Here let us sum up the argument of this chapter, fragmentary as it is. Our conclusion is that we are simply not in a position to decide at all assuredly the issue between a pluralism with respect to principles and the possibility of their unification. Both are open possibilities. The latter offers the best hope of satisfying our deep-seated demand for order within the moral domain, yet it cannot be said to have been established as more than a possibility. There is still the alternative, to be taken seriously in morals as in physical science, that affairs are not wholly tidy and cannot be made so by thought, that there is an ultimate residue of chaos or loose play in their structure. But the pluralists have not given us strong arguments for accepting this as an actuality rather than a possibility. Before giving up the struggle, the aspirant to intellectual order will continue making strenuous efforts to find it. When we survey the history and present state of ethical theory, we cannot help being impressed by the lack of sustained and dogged effort to construct a system of principles that has anything resembling the articulation and precision of conceptual frameworks approximated in the recognized sciences. Considering the importance of the subject, this is surprising. On the other side of the question, there is a recognition that the whole domain is in such a state that any strenuous effort to articulate it precisely might be premature or even, in view of its qualitative character, ridiculous; and fortifying this is the realization that in the ethical sphere wide experience of the world, a happy personal constitution and moral tact would still be in most specific situations more important practically than a body of systematic theory, however firm and keen. When all this has been said, there is still the urge to understand. We have not tried to understand hard enough in order to satisfy our theoretical consciences themselves. And it is impossible to evade the conviction that even here theory, if it were good enough, could have a beneficial effect on practice, however unspectacular.

Such questions as we have dealt with in this chapter, in order to be answered more conclusively, would have to be treated in a much richer and more detailed context of empirical materials than could be introduced here. The scope of such principles as justice and liberty cannot be determined by general linguistic and logical principles alone, but only through a study of the conflicts and aspirations of individuals and social groups. This book is simply an effort to propose a general scheme which may help to get ethical theorizing started again from the stalemate in which it has been bogged by the apparently hopeless disagreements of recent schools and, in particular, over the great puzzles about the Naturalistic Fallacy and the cognitive-emotive problem. In the following chapter, let us see what, if anything, has been gained in this modest undertaking.

15

The Naturalistic Fallacy Again

1. Prescriptiveness and Knowledge

In Chapter 5, current formulations of the so-called Naturalistic Fallacy were listed as: (1) That the meaning of a normative term can be analyzed without remainder into non-normative or factual characteristics; (2) That an ethical term can be defined by means of non-normative or descriptive terms alone; (3) That a normative judgment is a descriptive or factual statement rather than some other kind of expression such as an interjection or a command; (4) That a normative statement can be inferred, deductively or inductively, from non-normative premises alone.

The analysis of normative terms and judgments we have given makes it possible to deal with the first three of these together, up to a certain point. We have treated such terms and judgments as having both a descriptive and a prescriptive component, as making at the same time a knowledge claim and an incitement to an action or an attitude. It makes little difference whether we say, in general, that a normative judgment is a cognitive statement with a prescriptive function, or that it is a prescriptive expression whose meaning includes a cognitive assertion resting on empirical evidence. All that matters is to include both elements. If we do so we can avoid the Naturalistic Fallacy in the first and third senses.

A good deal of the pother has been over the scope assigned to the term "meaning." Some writers prefer to restrict it to descriptive reference alone; others, like most of the informalists, assume contrariwise that the meaning is the use, and finding the distinctive uses of normative expressions to be non-cognitive, exclude the descriptive element from the "meaning" to bring it under the "analysis." Both procedures seem to be arbitrary and dogmatic, and a more tolerant use of the term "meaning"—or the substitution for it of some neutral generic term—would eliminate these largely verbal disputes.

As to the issue whether normative terms can be *defined* exclusively by means of factual predicates and relations, the answer must be less forthright. Two questions are pertinent: Can the descriptive element itself be so defined, or defined at all? And is the non-cognitive element so definable?

We have suggested that the descriptive element is definable, or indefinable, to the same extent for normative terms as for non-normative terms. There are simple Identifying Properties having normative force, and complex normative properties, just as there are simple factual qualities and complex factual properties. The simple ones of either sort are in Moore's sense indefinable, because they cannot be broken up into elements. It makes no difference whether the simple quality is an instance of yellow or an instance of hedonic tone. On the other hand, if we consider not particular instances but the universal of yellowness or the universal of pleasantness, we have not simple qualities but continua of such qualities. The yellow area in the color pyramid or the "dimensionlike" range of hedonic tones which makes up intrinsic goodness can be broken down into its component shades. Either continuum as a whole can be defined more or less adequately by reference to its generating conditions, its scope in terms of the included shades, and its boundaries. A definition specifies the limits of the applicability of the term. Often it uses "ostensive" rather than analytic methods to do this; that is to say, it offers ways of exhibiting the range of properties referred to.

Some terms, both normative and non-normative, refer to relational properties including the special class of these called dispositional properties. Relational properties can be defined by stating the kinds of terms related by the relation, the logical properties of the relation, the frame of reference assumed, and the operations used in producing or identifying the relation. There may be an "indefinable" or unanalyzable residue of configurational or Gestalt-quality attaching to the complex but, if so, this holds of non-normative as well as of normative properties: of "circularity" as well as of aesthetic goodness.

In the case of that kind of relational properties called dispositional properties, the definition must include such categorial concepts as that of cause or potentiality. A dispositional property is one that something possesses and would manifest if certain conditions were fulfilled. But these concepts are required also for the definition of non-normative dispositional properties, so that there is no special problem here.

As we have seen, the non-cognitive meaning—consisting in the imperative or emotive or directive component—can be treated as consisting of dispositional properties, and is capable of treatment on naturalistic and empirical assumptions.

Must the non-cognitive function, or the Matrix Meaning, be included in the definition of the normative term? For certain purposes yes, for other purposes no. When we are engaging in ethical theory, we must seek full analyses and, if possible, definitions of the Matrix Meanings of the various normative concepts—e.g., of the "ought" as an unconditional prescription; of the "intrinsically good" as the conditional prescription of an experience in so far as it is considered without regard to its consequences.

The general practice of empirical theories, however, is to mention the Identifying Property alone explicitly in the definition, though the Matrix Meaning may be *assumed*. The "intrinsically good" is thus defined as the enjoyed or the desirable, etc., and the Matrix Meaning stated above is taken as understood.

Whether we define the term by means of its Matrix Meaning alone, or its Identifying Property, or both, depends on the *purpose* the definition is to serve. We encounter a similar situation in logic and the empirical sciences, where the definition is usually stated in terms of the Identifying Property alone, yet non-cognitive functions may be assumed.[1]

------

[1] Let us consider, for example, the definition of "p materially implies q" as "either p is false or q is true." This certainly does not give the full meaning even of material implication. The definition gives the Identifying Property, or an Identifying Property, of implication, and thus supplies the necessary and sufficient condition of the term's use. But material implication also has a Matrix Meaning, embodying the function of the term, or its use in reasoning. This meaning may be expressed as: "Whenever p is true, assert q"; or, if we take the meaning as doubly conditional: "If p is true, the assertion of q is permitted" (*i.e.*, is prescribed provided you are interested in the truth value of q). The use of "implication" in reasoning is not given by the disjunctive relation stated in the definition; the use is that of directing, or permitting, us to infer q from p. Roughly speaking, a Matrix Meaning lies along the pragmatical dimension, and the Identifying Property along the semantical; though the matter may be more complicated than this. The semantical dimension comes to the fore when we are concerned to find the properties that permit us to apply the term; hence the utility of stating the definition as a semantical rule. Likewise, a

2. The Weight of "Unanalyzed Experience"

When all these things have been said, it may still be felt that there is a residue of "non-naturalness" in the properties referred by normative concepts. Such a view cannot be finally refuted, nor does there seem to be any way of establishing it convincingly. As Frankena has pointed out, it remains possible to the end either that the naturalist is suffering from moral blindness in being unable to find such properties, or that the non-naturalist is subject to hallucinations.

But a theory such as this book tries to sketch has still another alternative to propose, unless we are prepared to accept the intuitionist's injunction to freeze the search for understanding at an arbitrary point. The alternative recognizes that the dissatisfaction of non-naturalists with traditioi. ʾl naturalism is in part well founded. This dissatisfaction springs from an uneasy feeling that the usual statement of the naturalist position omits something from the analysis—that in fact it omits a great deal. The naturalist not only has often underemphasized the non-cognitive functions: he frequently has taken a superficial view of the moral "authority"; he has overlooked the complexities both of the cognitive element itself and of the structural context of moral reasoning and moral experience. It is, we may suggest, a sense of the compounded weight of such neglected factors that leads the intuitionists to appeal to mysterious or

---

chemical element is usually defined in terms of such properties as atomic weight or sub-atomic structure, though we also need operational rules, or what Peirce called pragmatic definitions, which prescribe methods of obtaining samples of the thing in question. Such technological rules always prescribe conditionally; since the ethical concern, when present, takes precedence over the technological, only the Matrix Meaning of the moral "ought" is an unconditional prescription.

miraculous non-natural properties to supply the felt want. The moral "ought" has behind it the whole gravamen of our life-involvements—the thought we have put into moral reflection, the rules we have laboriously evolved to express its general characteristics, and the love and respect for personalities, institutions and ideals that have generated these intellectual elements and continue to give them their normative thrust. When such elements are omitted, as they frequently have been by the naturalist, he rejects, in the words of Mill's criticism of Bentham, "the whole unanalyzed experience of the human race."

When we make a moral judgment in its distinctive context, furthermore, we are within the process of choice and action and participating in it, not standing off from it and coolly describing it. We are voicing our deepest commitments and devotions; we feel these as compulsions above and beyond ourselves; we are aware of their present urgency and not of their social and personal causes, whose nature in any case is highly speculative and deeply hidden from phenomenological observation.

Above all, these commitments and devotions are, for the deeply moral man, those on which he would stake his life. If he is also a philosopher, he sees that they cannot be "proved" or justified by ordinary empirical means with the assurance that their felt and earned importance seems to warrant. All the uncertainty that attaches to his basic moral presuppositions through the acknowledged or sensed flaws in the vindication process is transmitted to the specific moral judgments that come under them. At the same time these inherit the fervor that attaches to the presuppositions. "Intuition" whether of judgments or principles is a way of expressing both the fervor and the unprovability, along with the conviction of the principles' objectivity and universality.

Hence the two definite elements in the otherwise obscure

notion of intuition: the element of unprovability and the notion of self-evidence. The intuitionist is correct in holding that
ethical principles cannot be demonstrated; for they can at most
be vindicated. He is mistaken in holding that they are self-
evident; for they cannot stand the logical tests for self-
evidence. Instead of calling them self-evident, we should say
that they have been earned with anguish and generosity. They
may along with that be right, but as disagreements among
intuitionists indicate, they may also be tragically mistaken. In
such a situation the moral agent must persist in acting on the
assumptions, but with humility, being willing to modify their
formulations or even to abandon the principles for others if the
continuing process of vindication forces this.

If this proposal can be expected to carry any conviction to
the intuitionist, all we can hope to do is to ask him to take
these factors, and others like them, into account and to see if
there is still something left over with such a radically compel-
ling tug upon us that we must invoke a special realm of being
to characterize it. And then, if he in turn can hope to bring
any conviction to us, we must ask him to describe that realm
of being more intelligibly than he has done so far.

We come finally to the fourth statement of the Naturalistic
Fallacy: that a normative statement can be inferred, deductively or inductively, from non-normative premises alone.

This question can be dealt with shortly. If any naturalist
actually holds this thesis, it is clearly untenable. It is logically
impossible to get more into a deductive conclusion than is in
the premises, together with the basic postulates of deduction.
It is logically impossible to get more into an inductive conclusion than is required by the inductive leap from the less to the
more general; and what is envisioned here is a jump from one
kind of thing to a radically different kind.

But these objections do not apply to the position we have
outlined, nor do they point to a need for a third or "seduc-

tive" logic. The normative element in the conclusion, deductive or inductive, is derived from the normative element in the assumptions, whether these be explicit premises or working presuppositions. The assumptions include a linkage of the factual or descriptive and the normative or prescriptive elements. This linkage is made neither by empirical verification nor by sheer stipulation, but partly by our congenital structure and partly by our life-involvements, or rather by the two in interaction. These include rational factors, but they do not rest on any *inference* from what is to what ought to be. The linkage is made, not by imitating a logical model, but by the necessities of our developing nature as normative beings. Since we are imperfectly normative beings the links are frail. Hence one source of the moral tragedy.

A similar answer applies to the difficulty caused by the supposedly irreducible pluralism of principles discussed in the preceding chapter. Even if the principles are incompletely systematic, in so far as we use them at all we do so by subsuming the particular case under some one or some set of them, and consequently any logical inference involved is deductive-inductive.

But knowledge of any sort rests on something not itself knowledge: on existents and their properties, on the need for action, on the structure of human physiology and the symbolific character of human consciousness.

3. *The Mountain Range Effect*

There is, finally, the matter of the "open question" or the Mountain Range Effect. We can never entirely evade it in some sense in so far as our whole ethical knowledge is in jeopardy through the lack of finality with which our grasp of principles is infected. No matter what characterization we give of the meaning of an ethical term, we can always turn upon it and ask if it is a good one in the sense of an "adequate" one. But this fallibility is not peculiar to an empirical analysis; it applies also to any intuitionist fixation of the meaning of good or right. Such considerations, in any case, are not vitiating; when we have included a prescriptive or normative element in the meaning of goodness, it is there to stay, and we do not need to ask if the analysis given is "good" in that same sense. The goodness or correctness which can always be asked about is a *meta-normative* or theoretical predicate, a question about the adequacy of language and the finality of knowledge. The doubt raised is not peculiar to ethics but applies to the analysis of basic concepts of any kind. It is, furthermore, the kind of doubt that involves an ultimate lack of total certainty but not an infinite regress. The assumption that there is one correct meaning of goodness or truth which we can approach by approximation is quite compatible with an intellectual humility which keeps us from claiming that we are sure we have attained it. We can never down the possibility that a new peak of knowledge lies ahead; on the other hand, there is nothing in the nature of the cognitive situation which prescribes that ranges must continue to loom without end. There is always the contrary possibility that we have attained the truth and that the higher range is a mirage. This realization can keep us from intellectual despair.

A myth is what one can find in it; and since the story of Eden has been so fecund in interpretations, we may be pardoned for adding one more. The serpent, then, is the craving for certainty which seeks to belie the human condition and emulate the Lord God and his angels. Their role in the story is to hold up before us the ideal of an objective and final truth about first and last things. That there is such a truth is the faith of moral man as of scientific man, and keeps him on his toilsome quest. Enjoyment of this fruit is forbidden to man, who among thorns and thistles must earn his intellectual bread, as his bodily nourishment, in the sweat of his brow. In sorrow shall he eat of it, the sorrow that comes of knowing that one always may be wrong. But the coarseness of the grain of the bread does not keep him from feeding and even, at times, feasting.

16
Naturalism and the Tragic Sense

---

1. "All Things Are Born of Unreason"

In what has preceded, we have tried to reinstate the core of truth in cognitivist theories, and more especially the reference of ethical terms to "natural" properties, rejected by recent analytical schools on insufficient grounds. At the same time, the attempt has been made to incorporate some of the results of the anti-naturalistic and non-cognitivist analyses which have rendered it impossible to proceed within the assumptions of the kind of empiricism that dominated ethical thinking in this century before the challenges offered by these critics.

The larger metaphysical or ontological issues which would be raised by a more complete treatment of the subject cannot be discussed adequately within the compass of this book. These include such questions as whether value is a "category" (see for example E. W. Hall's *What Is Value?*), and other current attempts to ground our ethical commitments in the nature of a larger reality than that human nature which has been treated under the topic of the structural or congenital *a priori*.

Although we have made no assumptions beyond those compatible with a naturalistic theory of reality and an evolutionary account of the origin of life and mind, the term "naturalism" would not in other respects be a happy label for the type of theory that has been suggested. Not only has it been identified, perhaps beyond repair in current discussions, with an impoverished account of personality and human ideals; it has also been too closely associated by some of its adherents with tub-thumping for an arid and unimaginative conception of scientific method, and particularly with the view that normative principles can be inferred from the materials of the factual sciences alone.

There is, further, the question of the relation between naturalism and religion. Most 20th Century naturalists have not shared the hostility to religious tradition exhibited by many naturalists in the 18th and 19th Centuries but, to the contrary, have sought to recover the body of genuine if often dislocated insights into values and into man's relation to the universe embedded in cosmological myth and devotional symbolism. The conception of vindication we have outlined here has, moreover, much in common with contemporary "existential" approaches to religion; but we have stopped short of an effort to sketch a philosophy of religion. If such were undertaken, it would suggest that the ideals and principles which emerge as the claimants to our final allegiance are worthy to be differentiated from other elements, actual and potential, in the natural process, by the name of the Sacred. For they are earned with anguish, imagination, thought, striving and love. An imagery of the sort ordinarily called religious is necessary to hold before us vividly their distinctive status, and to guard us against the heresy of worshipping Nature as a whole, which is too compacted of the good, the evil and the indifferent to enlist our total devotion. A treatment of these questions in the context of religious considerations would be necessary to deal fully with the flaming archetypal myth which expresses man's earliest sustained perturbation over the knowledge of good and evil.

One of the charges most commonly brought in recent years against naturalistic and liberal theories is that they omit the tragic sense of life; that they express a callow optimism about human nature which disregards what, mythically speaking, is called the demonic in man or Original Sin. This criticism has not been made by the "anti-naturalistic" philosophical schools we have considered here, but usually by theologians with polemical intent, or by political writers on behalf of conservative or reactionary movements.

No one should deny that there are interpretations of naturalism which are incompatible with the tragic sense. Historically, two types of naturalism have laid themselves open to the charge. The first is an "evolutionary" version that holds to the inevitability of progress and the perfectibility of man. The second is a "reductive" naturalism that whittles human nature down to a set of biological impulses, or otherwise overlooks the complexity of the human fact as it presents itself to direct inspection. Both these tendencies were widespread in Western thought in the 18th and 19th Centuries, as the result of new scientific doctrines and political and economic expansion. That these happenings should at times have generated enthusiastic expectations about human capacities or, alternatively, that they should have produced crude oversimplifications of the human reality, is not to be wondered at. But neither is prevalent in 20th Century philosophy, and particularly since World War I, though they may have left residues of bias which have not been thoroughly examined; and the critics in question have performed a service by keeping us on our guard against them. Whether the services have been counterbalanced by the remedies they sometimes offer to deal with the situation is yet to be determined.

When both the facts and the implications of evolutionism

284

were better understood than in the first flush of the movement, it was seen that biological and social changes were grim and costly affairs, and could easily take a turn toward deterioration or annihilation. If there were any dissenting voices earlier, they have been stilled since Hiroshima. The prevailing 20th Century versions of naturalism, such as the pragmatic, have in any case been not optimistic but melioristic. They have believed, not that man and society were inevitably getting better and better, or that they could ultimately be perfected, but that they could to an appreciable extent be made better by hard thought and honest effort. An ontological naturalism by itself neither confirms this faith nor destroys it; nor does it tell us to what extent this faith can prevail.

However the tragic sense is defined, we may say that it rests on two presuppositions: that man is potentially, and to some extent actually, possessed of dignity; and that he is liable to folly, useless suffering and disaster. Naturalism in general has not so much denied the second assumption as offered doctrines held to be incompatible with the first. It has even sometimes used the second assumption to undermine the first.

An ancient and popular version of naturalism was given expression by Glycon in the *Greek Anthology:*

> All is laughter, all is dust, all is nothing;
> For all things are born of unreason.[1]

The premise, that all things are born of unreason, is basic to an ontological naturalism, but the conclusion does not follow from it. The origin of things, if we can speak of such, is irrational in the sense that it is still an inexplicable mystery. The cosmogonies of the latest astrophysics come no closer to solving the

---

[1] Πάντα γέλως, καὶ πάντα κόνις, καὶ πάντα τὸ μηδέν·
πάντα γὰρ ἐξ ἀλόγων ἐστὶ τὰ γινόμενα.

mystery than did ancient myth or subsequent metaphysics. Empirical study can discern a *logos* in the development of the natural process, but at some point in the explanation we have to say, we don't know. Yet these cosmological frustrations do not justify our ruling out such dignity as we find in human life, nor such reason—in the sense of goodness and purposeful order —as we can make. Twentieth Century naturalism has not often denied the reality of ideals and of rationality in conduct, but has tended to hold with Santayana that "nature carries its ideal with it" and that the rational life is "the progressive organization of irrational impulses."

2. Aeschylean and Sophoclean Tragedy

Granted both the dignity of life and its precariousness, the possibilities of tragedy are multiple. If we take our clues from the Greek tragedians, we see several sources and versions of it. When conflicts in human life are conceived to be irresoluble by rational effort in such a way as to illustrate the partial moral disorder of the human condition, we have Sophoclean tragedy. When they are regarded as soluble through great anguish and rational striving, to establish a more thoroughgoing moral order, we have Aeschylean tragedy. (Euripidean tragedy is less easy to bring to a moral focus but its most distinctive versions, as in *Medea* and *The Bacchae*, may be taken to be closer to Sophoclean than Aeschylean tragedy in the respects in question, springing out of a disillusioned acknowledgment of the not wholly bridgeable cleavage between man's passional nature and his prudential nature.)

All three versions assume that moral order in the universe at large and in human life is incomplete. In the *Antigone* and the *Oedipus Rex* we have suffering and catastrophe beyond any "flaws" in the characters of the protagonists, or even in their intellectual equipment, but residing rather in the universe

or the human situation. They spring, in the former, from the
two incompatible devotions of Antigone and Creon, both seem-
ingly well earned. In the latter, the disaster arises from an objective situation for which the protagonist is not fully responsible: the hot-tempered Oedipus was at most guilty of man-
slaughter, yet was punished for father-murder and incest. In
the *Electra* and the *Oedipus at Colonus,* on the other hand,
the order of things exhibits an equal disregard for "poetic
justice," yet in the opposite direction. Electra gets away with
murder: she is revealed, in the tremendously ironic central
scene, to be as vengeful and relentless as her mother Clytem-
nestra, yet at the end she goes to a happy marriage triumphant
and exultant, a queen beset by no furies from without or from
within. At the end of Sophocles' last play, Oedipus' sufferings
have not made him less impulsive and stubborn (qualities that
constituted his "flaws") than in his youth, yet he achieves a
queer mystical salvation through his very capacity to endure
—a naturalistic virtue. The two sets of plays exhibit a looseness
in the apportionment of punishment to crime. Sometimes punishment is in excess, and sometimes deficient. And this is an
inescapable element in experience: things can turn out in both
ways. The flaws are not in the protagonists but in a fundamental disparity between the natural order and man's striving to
set up a moral order.[2]

Aeschylus' view, based on a different selection from and
rendering of the ritual pattern, is more melioristic. Without
denying that catastrophe is often for some of its victims blank,

----

[2] In support of this view, see Kitto, *Greek Tragedy* (1950), especially Chapter V, where it is argued that for Sophocles, as for the
earlier Greeks, the *dikē* which constitutes the ultimate order of
things is a non-moral "balance of forces in Nature" and not a
providential moral order.

unmerited and inescapable, he held that this loose play in the nature of things could to a degree be controlled. In the Prometheus trilogy, so the scholars assume, Zeus and Prometheus eventually educated each other, so that natural power could be yoked to the service of benevolence, and humanitarian sympathy to political and scientific realism. In the *Oresteia,* an area of security and order was shaped out of the horror and surrounding chaos by the improvement of social and political institutions. A moral order does not automatically pervade the nature of things, except potentially, but can be partially conquered. The "tragedy," in the popular sense, resides in the costliness of the process.

Aeschylus and Sophocles are compatible, and supplement each other. Human destiny is compounded of necessity, rational moral effort and luck—whether that be good luck or bad luck.[8] There is dignity in making the effort, whatever the outcome, and dignity in accepting the outcome.

Such a view of life can both support our meliorism and temper it. Neither necessity nor luck is within our control: what is, can be controlled only through rational effort. We can't know finally its limits, but must keep on seeking to expand them. At the same time, we must acknowledge that there are limits, and be prepared to accept them: beyond, all that remains is the consolation of final understanding and the poetic vision.

Such a tragic sense is inherent in the notion of justification that we have propounded. The ethical principles which exert a claim upon us can neither be strictly proved by being shown to correspond to a preëxisting natural order that is at the same time a moral order, nor exhibited as self-evident to an infallible intuition. They can only be earned or vindicated by our life-

---

[8] This is also the purport of the Vision of Er, *Republic,* Book X.

involvements, and the process is never final nor the result certain. Therein lies a kind of tragedy which we may call epistemic: arising from frailties in the nature of human knowledge.

This epistemic tragedy may be either Sophoclean or Aeschylean. If ethical principles are ultimately incompatible, the result is recurrent clashes to the death like that of Antigone and Creon. Even if we work on Aeschylean assumptions, that the struggle for a coherent vision of things must be maintained in the hope of an eventual convergence of opposed principles, there is tragedy along the way. For our formulations of alternative principles are never final, and those on which we wager our lives may be hopelessly inadequate.

Justice Holmes came close to the locus of the epistemic tragedy in our moral strivings, and also pointed to such answer as can be found when he wrote: "The highest courage is to stake everything on a premise that you know tomorrow may disprove." If there is a still higher courage, it stems from the realization that the premises are such that tomorrow can neither prove nor disprove them in a way that will fully still our uncertainties. There is no less need for courage, and even more for intellectual humility. But the moral tragedy is not wholly, or perhaps mainly, an epistemic one. Even if we could know the better path, and approve it, we are liable to follow the worse. Demonism and Original Sin are highly charged words for this capacity in man, but the myth-laden expressions are from time to time useful as corrective to a sentimental and superficial optimism, if we are clear what we mean by them.

The operations of Original Sin, however, should not be limited to such great scourges as those of the "Mongol Devils" and the Inquisition in the Middle Ages or totalitarianism in our own day, or the malignant rages to which we are susceptible in our personal intercourse. Attribution of these to a metaphysical principle serves better to alert us against them than

to help us understand and prevent their recurrence so far as
we may. Most of the evil in the workaday world is not the
result of them but of the small, frightened hardening of human
sympathies imposed by the pressure of convention and by
gradual congealment of the spirit through prudential anxieties.
These manifest themselves more through sins of omission than
sins of commission—and demonism itself is most commonly an
Euripidean revolt against them by suppressed natural forces
which have assumed a warped and destructive form.

3. *The Scope of Rational Effort*

The ultimate moral tragedy, perhaps, as the major ethical doctrines philosophic and religious have recognized, comes to a
focus in the recalcitrance of the ego. It consists in the fact that
self-interest and that cluster of other-regarding virtues which
includes benevolence and justice do not wholly coincide, and
cannot be brought fully to do so.

They coincide partially through the personal affections,
which bring with them their own rewards, and partly through
the imperfect sanctions of law, public opinion and religious
commitment. We have also treated at some length, in Chapter
14, the tendency in any social order for roles that emerge
spontaneously, such as those of the parent, teacher and judge,
to generate and maintain attitudes prescribing inclusiveness
and impartiality, where perhaps an awareness of the meaning
and coerciveness of the "social ought" is sharpest. These in
turn can be extended to produce a more generalized if weaker
obligation to benevolence and justice, in spheres outside the
specific role: especially when we reflect upon the arbitrariness
of any stated limits, the same attitudes have some carry-over
value to other people's children and to people in other nations.

There is no reason to expect that adherence to other-
regarding principles will ever reach the point, even if that

were desirable, where the individual will become completely selfless, or even where he will act wholly on the prescription to "count himself as one and only one," making only such concessions to disproportionate self-regard as are dictated by the social utility of having each individual take care of himself as much as possible.

Naturalism has to meet a double test. When we use it as a doctrine of explanation and stand off from the process of moral involvement, we must ask only whether it accounts for as much altruism as is found in the manifestations and aspirations of human nature. Here we must search history and our first-hand observations of human motives in operation. The answer, I think, though this is no place to offer the evidence, is both that altruism is sporadic and that it is in fact just about as prevalent as it could be expected to be in a creature that originated as an evolutionary account represents man to have originated. We may also test naturalism by trying to glimpse ourselves within the process of moral involvement. Here we find other-regarding principles to a certain extent become habitual, but also constantly subject to lapses. When a deviation toward selfishness looms, it is fortunately often prevented by the thought of penalties that law and custom have set up: none of us, as we are now constituted, would be highly altruistic in a condition of anarchy. When such sanctions fail and our principles are placed in final jeopardy, all we can summon to forestall the great refusal is such tenderness for our fellow-creatures, and such concern for self-transcendent goals, as wells up within us, elicited from our moral past and by the present stimulus. Tragically often, this is too little to save us from cruelty, horror and disaster.

Naturalism's failure to supply an iron-clad "justification" of the principle of duty has often been offered as the crucial argument against its adequacy as a basis for ethics. The only reply

is that no ethical system, naturalistic, non-naturalistic or supernaturalistic, can supply such a magic remedy for egoism.

Even though it be urged that the most generally accepted
meaning of the "ought," based on usage derived from roles
demanding impartiality, makes it an analytic proposition that
we ought to regard the welfare of others, we are still moving
within the domain of the linguistic-conceptual *a priori*, and
nobody is going to be persuaded in a concrete life-situation
that he must sacrifice his cherished ego in order to respect the
"self-evident" meanings of words. So that intuitionism, when
carefully analyzed, is seen to be an even shakier basis for altruism than is naturalism, which at least tries in such cases to
evoke the natural affections.

An outright supernaturalism is in no better case. The major
religions, when their tendencies to abet illusion and to generate
institutional self-aggrandisement are kept in check, are precious
repositories of imaginative and symbolic summonses to respect
the lowliest of God's creatures: and through liturgy and good
works they provide rehearsals of other-regarding attitudes
which the colder language of philosophy can never replace.
They will be cherished with increasing respect as these functions come to predominate over institutional militancy. But
even the most thoroughgoing orthodoxy cannot give us the
panacea for selfishness that is sometimes demanded: divine
Grace is offered to all, but admittedly is not accepted by all.
This is the source of moral tragedy in supernaturalism analogous to that inhering in the shortcomings of naturalistic justification. There is, of course, no final tragedy for the saved—
unless they be conceived as gnawed to all eternity by pity for
the damned.

The moral life is thus infected to the end by the imminence
of tragedy. Having recognized the fact, we need not brood on
it. The tragic sense is essential to a complete view, but so are

the comic sense, the lyric sense, the business sense and the political sense. A rational ethics would prepare us to meet the inescapable catastrophe and the unmerited suffering when they come, and to wring from them the residual values offered by the tragic sense. It would not lead us to seek tragedy off the stage nor to make it into an all-inclusive interpretation of life. What our anguished age needs more at the moment than a reminder of the Dionysian abyss is reassurance that life is in some measure amenable to intelligent control, and that the human reason, fallible instrument as it reveals itself to be, is not powerless. Let us, then, make explicit the ambiguity of Sophocles' judgment, but in such order as to preserve the voice of hope: terrors and wonders are many, but nothing is more terrible and wonderful than man.

Index

296

ABOUT THE AUTHOR

Philip Blair Rice holds the Guy Despard Goff chair in philosophy at Kenyon College and is associate editor of *The Kenyon Review.*

A native of Indiana, he was educated at the University of Illinois, Indiana University and Balliol College, Oxford (where he was a Rhodes Scholar in 1925–28). He has taught at the University of Cincinnati and at Columbia and Cornell. In 1953, he conducted a section in humanities at the Harvard International Seminar.

Mr. Rice was president of the American Philosophical Association in 1952–53, and has been chairman of its Committee to Advance Original Work in Philosophy since 1953. He has held a Guggenheim Fellowship, a grant from the Rockefeller Foundation for study in France, and a Bollingen Fellowship.

A frequent contributor to philosophical and literary periodicals, Mr. Rice is the co-author of *Value—A Cooperative Inquiry.* He edited selections from George Santayana in *Classic American Philosophers* and is the editor of a new edition of Santayana's *The Sense of Beauty* (The Modern Library, $1.45). He has also been represented in *Literary Opinion in America, The Stature of Thomas Mann, The Kenyon Critics,* etc.